emotion pictures

Cinematic Journeys into the Indian Self

Narendra Panjwani

emotion pictures: Cinematic Journeys into the Indian Self

First Edition 2006

Rainbow Publishers

19/221 Parishram Apartments
Satellite Road, Ahmedabad 380015

J-33, South Extension, Part-I
New Delhi 110049
email : rainbowp@gmail.com

International Distributors
BIBLIOPHILE SOUTH ASIA
C-127 Sarvodaya Enclave, New Delhi 110 017 INDIA
Tels : 91-11-26864124, 55284748 Fax : 91-11-26961462
Emails : abutani@biblioasia.com / ashokbutani@gmail.com
www.biblioasia.com

ISBN 81-86962-72-7 (Hb)

Designed by Indrani De Parker
Illustrations by Pradipto Ray
Cover Design by Indrani De Parker

Processed & Printed at Frontline Imaging Pvt Ltd.,
B 199, Okhla Industrial Area, Phase-I, New Delhi 110020

Published by Vasanthi Raman for Rainbow Publishers Ltd.

For my parents Devi & Laxman Panjwani,

With love and a huge debt of gratitude.

In memory of Ashok Chandwani,

my Hoshangabad schoolmate, who went away much too early.

CONTENTS

"It is the fashion of the day to ask for true-to-life movies. Note the paradox in our life. On the one hand we often see funny and fantastic movies with romance. In the same breath, to prove the superiority of our taste, we ask for serious, sensible and realistic pictures.

Our real life is rapidly becoming more and more tense, trouble-studded and strenuous. Why should the silver screen reflect the same dark shadow?

We want to forget…true life and enjoy the hidden treasures of life. So we join the characters of the films in making romance with colourful love affairs, laughing absurdly at life and attaining unusual victories, which are absent in day-to-day life. And when we come out of this sensational filmdom, we feel fresh to fight our own battles in life.

Life has made us lifeless. Let us at least keep the screen lively."

Maheshkumar Dholakia, Surendranagar. Letter to the Editor, Picturepost, October, 1971

"Those love films of my school days…are oddly associated in my mind, not so much with famous pairs like Dilip Kumar-Madhubala, or Raj Kapoor-Nargis, but with the villains - played by Ajit, and especially Pran. My mother, I remember, would gnash her teeth each time Pran entered the screen for the first time – 'O God, no!' she would curse. 'Now everything will go wrong, all the problems will start - the bastard. Why can't he keep away for once, so that these sweet young people can get on with their lives?!"

Asha Rai, school teacher, Hoshangabad, 1997

Chapter Three

“Letter to the Editor

Deepal Raj, Gauhati: If I become an actor, can I kiss the heroine?

Editor's Answer: If kissing is your only object in joining films and acting, it is better you do all the kissing at home and not on the screen.”

Picturepost, Bombay, December 1966

Chapter Four

“In my fifteenth year I saw Mughal-e-Azam. I remember it well… It was a rare film in that it did not have the stock-in-trade of all Indian films: a comedian. No one laughed during its screening; indeed no one… even moved, though everyone cried. We did not so much watch Mughal-e-Azam as immerse ourselves in it…

Mughal-e-Azam was one of the five main texts of my youth, and its star, Dilip Kumar, was my guide and pathfinder. He was not just my 'hero'… He was my guide through the complex world of human emotions; he opened certain paths and invited me to journey through them, to examine and cross-examine what I discovered en route…”

Ziauddin Sardar, in his article, "Dilip Kumar made me do it" [*]

*Source: Nandy, Ashis, (ed.): The Secret Politics of Our Desires OUP, Delhi 1998.

"Good movies are stimulating. For me in my twenties, in a strange way, they were recipes for self-confidence - in getting ready for the dreaded job interview, my first court appearance, my first dance with a girl at a party (when you hardly know her!), or conquering real-life villains who are like Obstacle Hills you must cross...

I knew then...I know even today that whatever happens, Raj my hero will somehow get along, sometimes sad, but always hopeful. In movies I mean, like Anari, like Sanjeev Kumar in Gulzar's Aandhi, or even Shahrukh in films like Raju Ban Gaya Gentleman. He will win, even if he loses. Aandhi is a classic example of that.

There is a nasha, a basic optimism in the best of our films, which rubs off on to you – if you let it..."

P. K Verma, Lawyer, Jabalpur, 1998

"We all want to escape from this consumerist 'real' world around us; what differs is where we escape to. A friend of mine 'goes' into books about life in the days of the British Raj, 150 years ago; I 'go' to the films and songs of the 1950s & 60s - each of us seeking a simpler, nobler time and place you can identify with, sort of live in...for a few hours.

This tripping may or may not be therapeutic... but it is fun! I feel young, and carefree again! Especially when I watch Dev Anand's Paying Guest, or Shammi Kapoor in Laat Saheb, or Professor!! You should try it; some of these films are like tonic. With many side effects, all of them good!"

Mansoor Alam, Journalist, Lucknow, 2001

"Going to the movies was a big event in those carefree high school years, always with my two best friends…Films like Pyaasa, Chaudvin Ka Chand, Daag, Aawara, Hum Dono, Mere Mehboob, Mughal-e-Azam, Baiju Baawra. Talk of cinema, and these films come up, spontaneously - they are my cinema. …What else can I say?

The three of us looked forward to the latest releases of directors like Bimal Roy, Mehboob, K Asif, Guru Dutt, Raj Kapoor, Vijay Anand, etc. We knew what to expect when we went to see their films, and we were not disappointed. It was a thrilling way to pass time…And some of their songs, oh don't get me started on them, for I will lose my business for the whole day, today!!"

Firoze Khan, shopkeeper, Bhopal, 1999

"Our world was quite small – there was the family, there was school, that's it. So film was our only window to the world beyond. There we met people, went to places, entered situations we would otherwise never have done. It was a mental, musical adventure!

People went to see films for a purpose, not just time-pass. They opened our mind's eyes and ears, especially Guru Dutt, Raj Kapoor and Vijay Anand's films…"

Sunita Mhatre, Insurance agent, on life and cinema in 1950s-'60s Bombay

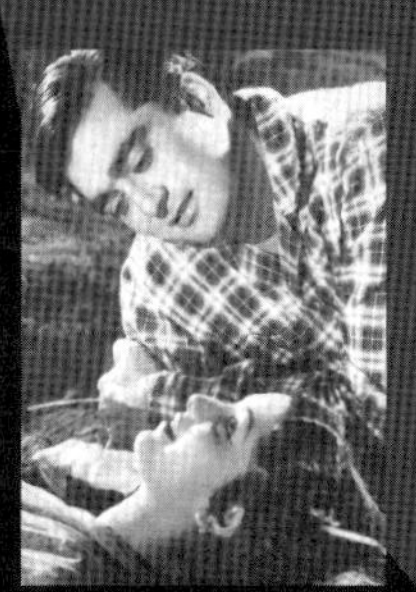

PREFACE

Book writing is often an act of carving out a small individual space within the peer group of which one is a part. This individual space is one's personal identity, which has the habit, occasionally, of going into a crisis. That was the frame of mind in which Emotion Pictures... began, while I sat facing a blank computer screen far away from my home in Bombay way back in May 1995. I was determined that morning not to get up until some words came out, from inside, from 'the depths of the soul' as they say. After two hours or so, they began coming, slowly, in garbled form. By sunset, the verbal chaos on my computer screen had begun to take the shape of some questions, which boiled down five days later to one big question - about adolescence, movies, and the person one had become.

But books evolve, as do their writers. This book has now become much more than a personal statement. While discussing our underground relationship with Hindi films with a wide range of friends in Hoshangabad, the small town where I grew up, and later with students and fans of Hindi cinema in Bombay, Bhopal, Indore, Delhi, Pune, North Carolina, Berkeley, etc., it became clear that I was on to a widely shared passion - for those 'trashy' films and all that they had meant to us, especially their songs. Nostalgia was a part of it; but was by no means the whole story. These films have also been a formative, lasting influence on our personalities and values, in strange little ways which people are now beginning to discover - each in their different ways.

Emotion Pictures... is a product of such discoveries. It is also a sociological exploration of the experience of popular Hindi cinema - for the generation who grew up watching films in the period 1951-81, before Television arrived on a mass scale in India.

This book has been eight years in the making, mainly because it had to be written outside work hours, which have grown longer with each passing year. It is time now to acknowledge the institutions and people who have made the writing of this book a pleasure by providing a special environment in which the author got a chance to grow - as a student of cinema. The first of these enablers are the staff of the National Humanities Center, North Carolina, USA, who invited and hosted me for a 9-month period in 1997-98, thanks to a post-doctoral fellowship grant from the Andrew W Mellon Foundation. The grant meant that I had 9 months in which to read, write and discuss the first draft of this book in a series of seminars with other fellows at the Center. For a journalist working with the Times of India newspaper in Bombay, that was a lot of time, and a really special opportunity.

I am grateful also to the Times of India's management, who were generous enough to give me this 9-month leave of absence, and accept me back into the fold on my return. I wish also to thank professors Lydia Liu, Anton Kaes, and Robert Goldman for inviting me to teach a full course on Indian Cinema in the Fall 1999-2000 semester at the University of California, Berkeley. Teaching this course provided me a 'captive' and very bright young audience on which to test my book's hypotheses. I learnt a lot from them.

The high point of my stay in Berkeley was the home of professors Larry & Cornelia Levine. As historian extraordinaire of American popular culture, Larry was really hard to please when it came to his subject area. The few times I managed to get his nod of approval, were especially gratifying.

The staff of the South Asia Center at UC Berkeley was very helpful, as were the faculty at the university's department of South Asian Studies. Among them I especially benefited from discussions with professors Vasudha Dalmia and Bob Goldman. To all of them my sincere thanks. The Center is a great 'home' for visiting scholars.

Returning home, special thanks are due to my colleagues Jerry Pinto and Hutokshi Doctor at the Sunday Times magazine, in the years when the book was just an idea buzzing in my head. They encouraged me as only fellow journalists can. Hutokshi went on, subsequently, to be this book's editor, and improved the manuscript in dozens of little ways.

I also owe a special debt to Professor Sriram Tamrakar, film columnist with the *Nai Duniya* newspaper in Indore, who encouraged this book's writing in many ways, including providing rare photographs and for stimulating discussions on the history and experience of Hindi cinema – in the world of little India, the India of small towns like Indore, Hoshangabad, Itarsi, etc.

Talking of close friends who adopted this book as their own project, almost, it is a pleasure to thank Laurie Patton & Shalom Goldman in Emory, Atlanta, Veronica Magar in Chapel Hill, Bina Agarwal, Medha & Vijay Lele in Pune, for some valuable, searching inputs on the various drafts this book has gone through, as well as Indra Munshi, Zarine & Darryl D'Monte in Bombay. A heart-felt thank you Dithhi Bhattacharya and Sanjeevini Badigar, who compiled the index. Thanks are also due to the book's designer, Indrani De Parker for the imaginative way in which she married picture and text on each page thereby making the book attractively readable. A very special word of thanks is also due to Vasanthi Raman and Smitu Kothari, members of the board of directors of Rainbow Publishers, who have taken a really keen, personal interest in the book and helped improve its form and content in dozens of ways... My sisters Renu, Shobha, and my brother Sanjay have contributed to improving this book in more ways than they realize.

Finally, Mariam my wife and our daughter Tara, have lived with this book and kept me focused through its numerous ups and downs. Without them, and without the stimulation, love and the hard questions thrown at its drafts over the years by Mariam, this book would not have been half as good as it is. So if it stands up to some intellectual scrutiny, I have to thank her, my soul mate for it.

Its limitations and mistakes, however, are my own responsibility.

Narendra Panjwani

Mumbai, January 2006

INTRODUCTION

Indian Cinema is at once a nightclub and a temple; a circus and a concert; a pizza and a poetic symposium…

(Mohan Segal, well-known Bombay filmmaker)

This book is an invitation to explore the experience of popular Hindi cinema from the viewpoint of the movie-goer. It looks at our relationship with 'the pictures' (which is what films are popularly called in much of India), in a somewhat autobiographical way. I do not believe that the pictures (and the 'mass media' more generally) are some external 'thing', which impacts us with 'effects'. Real people, I believe, are a little more complicated than such theories give them credit for.

For me, and for dozens of people (including taxi drivers, doctors, housewives, engineers, account clerks, college students, school teachers, and self-confessed 'film nuts') I interviewed over hours and months in the course of writing this book, there is an ongoing affair with Hindi cinema, which has many levels, the first of which is personal. And that is where this book starts.

The pictures — some songs, scenes, and characters within them — have been part of our growing up from adolescence to adulthood. And yet, nothing in life is linear: this growing up business is not a simple move from A to B; we keep zigzagging, in puzzling, yet creative ways. These pictures of ours — especially 'the classics' from the 1950s to the most recent — often work on adults by taking you back to adolescence, sometimes, while taking you forward. Our affair with the movies, in short, is pleasingly complicated.

This book starts from the author's school days in a small town in central India called Hoshangabad in the 1960s, and travels with him to Mumbai where he currently lives. The aim: to explore our personal and collective relationship with the pictures, by combining the author's narrative with that of many others. These others have 'spoken' both directly through interviews, and through newspaper reports, film magazines, novels, and film biographies.

The book's eight essays map this relationship between Hindi cinema and Indian society by travelling around Hindustan — exploring its cities and villages, its lovers, its brand of masculinity and femininity, its morality and its music. Hindustan is an imaginary country, a utopia created by the movies in which we 'live', along with passing time in a hard, unmanageable 'fact' called India. The latter comprises reality-bytes like clocks, office hours, traffic jams, stable marriages, losing jobs, homelessness, failing to get a distinction in your school exams, and so on. The former, our personal utopia, is a place where time stands still when you want it to, where even homelessness is romantic (as in *Paying Guest*, 1957, *Shri 420*, 1955), where losing your job sometimes gets you the girl of your dreams (*Anari*, 1960), and you don't have to marry her until the very end.

Take for instance this little scene from S.U. Sunny's 1955 film, *Udankhatola* (Flying Car), featuring the 1950s superstar Dilip Kumar, playing a pilot whose plane crash lands in a remote tribal kingdom that is a world unto itself. Its ruler happens to be a single woman, and the handsome young stranger is duly arrested and produced before her:

Tribal Queen — "Where are you from, stranger?"

Dilip Kumar — "From Hindustan, O queen."

The Queen — "Hmm…so what is your Hindustan famous for?"

Dilip Kumar — "Music and Romance, O queen."

Queen — "All right then, I hereby set you free, and we'll see how well you sing very soon."

[This exchange of words helps save our hero from being imprisoned or even possibly executed. The prematurely widowed queen happens to be looking for a young lover. She does not exactly fit his idea of a beauty queen, but then whoever said life was all roses in Hindustan?]

The cinematic 'nation' of Hindi cinema is, in other words, a Kingdom of Opportunity where every viewer-citizen gets a second chance to live his life all over again. What sort of 'life' does one live here, you will ask? Well, for the duration of your three-hour visit, you can be a *shaayar* (or better still a *badnaam shaayar* [poet of ill-repute]), you can be an *aawara*, a *musafir* (a vagabond, a traveler), a professor, a prince. But whichever guise you choose to wear, the one constant here is that every young man in Hindustan is an *Aashiq* (lover-at-large), and every young woman a heart-stopping, self-confident beauty whose persona is built around the Big Search — for Mr. Right, whom she will shortly meet. That she will meet Mr. Right is certain; it is foreordained.

All visitors can therefore discard their baggage of anxieties and self-doubts on this count when they enter this fabled land, and live the certainty of falling in love. What happens after they meet and fall in love, however, is another story. It varies just enough each time to lure you back to this friendly neighbourhood utopia, every other week or so.

It's not all fun and games, however; there is cruelty and violence aplenty in Hindustan, but there is punishment too — in the here and now, not in the uncertain future as in reality-ridden India. Hindustan is a powerfully moral universe where God personally resides, ensuring that bad boys and girls get their just desserts soon after they have caused havoc, and where Love is the main game in town, with which everyone is somehow connected.

Vengeance is the other game, but villains in the movies of the 1950s & 1960s usually played that one, until Amitabh Bachchan came along in the mid-1970s and complicated that neat division of labour in films like *Deewar*, *Sholay*, etc. In almost every film before this big change, there was a moment when the hero, the heroine, or his/her mother looked up and made a personal call to God, and sure enough He was there.

Our Movies, Our Selves

> Imagining, perhaps, is one way we think. Through imagination we can make connections, draw parallels, see resemblances — and draw distinctions, separating like from unlike, shades of difference. And imagining, being a human activity tends to move towards order, toward a larger synthesis, envisioning a general pattern. We aspire to understanding, and we rise toward it through successive images. (Lahr & Price 1989: 137).

Their steadily increasing popularity in the period 1935–75 made Hindi films and their protagonists metaphors for self-making which help one cope, at the level of one's imagination at least, with the highs and lows of everyday life in 'India'. Metaphors like the *Aawara* as played by Raj Kapoor in the 1951 film of that name, like *Mother India* as played by Nargis in the 1957 film of that name. Even in films that were not so self-consciously metaphorical, the protagonists were exemplars who showed us how best to respond to new social facts like industrialisation and rural-urban migration. Recall Shankar the gutsy tonga-driver played by Dilip Kumar who refuses to grovel at the brash young village boss's feet in *Naya Daur* (1957), or the sensitive and humane taxi driver played by Dev Anand in the film *Taxi Driver* (1955). He has to deal with a young woman who has run away from her village to the big city — to give herself a new life.

On screen moreover, this self-making is part of a larger project — that of situating the self within a paradigm of Indianness, which in film rhetoric, is synonymous with *Insaaniyat* (Humanism), and Cultural Pluralism. Values and hybrid identities — pieced together from the subcontinent's diverse lifestyle mosaic, and from the West — came together in attractive star characters brought to life onscreen in the 1950s with such power and new-look credibility as to have made them memorable for a whole generation, and for the one following it. Memorable for having given Indianness a new face, a style, which went into making a very contemporary, progressive pantheon of male and female personalities — for an audience, a nation-in-process which was looking for just that, without knowing it.

The enduring appeal of Hindi cinema's attempt to relate individual selves-in-process to a larger imagined community makes its landmark films (which were also box office hits of the 1950s and 1960s) very important — as windows into post-colonial Indian culture, into who we think we are, and ought to be. The years 1951–81 are richest in this regard: Hindi cinema's much-loved Hindustan came into full bloom in this period.

An Album of Emotion Pictures

The pivot on which Hindustan stands is the individual moviegoer, for it is he/she who confers reality on this landscape of the mind by dropping in for a visit every now and then. This visit is not as casual as people like to make out; it is an emotional transaction whose significance dawns on you, as you grow older, grayer. These transactions take place in a 'country' whose population consists entirely of a few fictional characters and their bewitched visitors. The number of visitors varies from as much as 20-25 million on some days to as little as 10 million or less on other days. Manmohan Desai's *Amar Akbar Anthony* (1977), which ran for over 25 weeks in 11 cinemas simultaneously in Bombay alone, is one recent film that caused a temporary population explosion in Hindustan. An even bigger explosion was elicited by Ramesh Sippy's *Sholay* (1975). The big draws of the earlier decades included Mehboob Khan's *Mother India* (1957), *Baiju Baawra* (1952), and S Mukherjee's *Kismet* (1943), which 'occupied' Calcutta for three years without a break, even while the Second World War raged outside. In contrast, Guru Dutt's *Kaagaz Ke Phool* (1958) was a failure at the box office despite its high-minded story and good songs. This variation has to do with something called 'audience taste', which makes one film hugely popular, and another an equally big flop.

A successful feature film, goes the film industry's unspoken rule, has to be an Emotion Picture — a moving, dramatic story (usually a coming-of-age fable thanks to the influence of Hollywood, and European literature on Hindi cinema) that touches viewers at a gut level. Touching viewers is not enough, however. It must be art that is powerfully engaging and universally accessible; it must connect actively ('Electrify!' in the language of film ads) and agreeably, with one's deepest personal hopes, wishes, and fears.

By fulfilling these conditions, Hindi films of the 1950s and 1960s (as well as those of the 1970s) came to stand for the collectivity of film viewers; they created the images in which a culture consented to see itself. This book's essays map out these images.

References

Kabir, N.M. 2001. *Bollywood, The Indian Cinema Story*. London, Channel 4 Books. and many others.

Lahr, J. & J. Price. 1989. *Life-Show*. NY, Limelight Editions.

Nandy, Ashis (ed.). 1998. *The Secret Politics of Our Desires*. Delhi, Oxford University Press.

Segal, Mohan. 1985. "Dance in Indian Cinema" in *70 Years of Indian Cinema*, edited by T.N. Ramachandran. Bombay, Cinema India-International Publication.

Film alone reveals the extent to which reality yearns for another world that is not itself...

George Linden

A small town goes to the movies

Come with me to Hoshangabad, a small town with a population of roughly 30,000 people in central India in the mid-1960s. Hoshangabad had only two schools — one for boys and the other for girls — and one cinema hall. The schools faced each other: the only thing between them was the town's main street, barely 30 feet wide. Our classes began and ended at the same time, and the main mode of transport for most students was the bicycle. So at 9 a.m. each morning, hundreds of bicycles would converge at the two school-gates (which faced each other), and the same scene would be repeated at 4 p.m. in the afternoon. Ninety per cent of the bicycles would turn towards the older part of town, where most people lived. Less than 10 per cent would turn in the opposite direction, towards the new town, which was also further away. I was one of those housed in the new town, along with my friend and classmate, Vikram. Both of us then were 14 going on 15.

As was bound to happen — those were the *Mere Mehboob* and *Love in Simla* 1960s, after all — we began to fancy two of the girls who lived on our side of town. We encountered them every day on the way to school. One day there was a girls'hockey match on our school ground, because they didn't have one. Many of us were there, and Kavita, one of the two we had set our sights on, was the team captain. She wore a short skirt; most other girls were in trousers. She looked stupendous! And on that day both Vikram and I flipped for her — head over heels.

My problem, however, was that Vikram was clearly taller and better-looking than me; he was a better sportsman too. So it seemed natural that I would have to yield to the inevitable and let the best-looking couple in Hoshangabad get together.

Well, it didn't happen. It could not happen.

Why? Because both Vikram and I were tongue-tied, comprehensively tongue-tied in front of those girls, and the girls even more so. For two-and-a-half years we gazed at each other, we cycled in and out of school together. Sometimes we even exchanged a ghost, a teeny-weeny hint, of a smile, but for all Vikram's smart looks, he couldn't bring himself to say a word to Kavita; nor I to Priya, the other girl. All we could do was yearn, fantasise, and watch films

where the hero was in much the same situation, adopting different strategies to overcome precisely such odds and of course, finally breaking through. But on emerging from the cinema hall, courage would mysteriously fail us. So much for the alleged influence of cinema on young, impressionable minds. Here we were, dying to be influenced, dying to begin speaking and expressing our feelings like the hero on-screen; but no, the hero remained up there, and we remained down here — unable to connect.

Thus, perhaps, was born the sense that Reality is more unmanageable, and certainly less fun than cinema. This unbridgeable distance between reel life and real life did, however, have an important effect on us: it took us beyond Hoshangabad into a larger reality. Films such as *Love in Simla* (1960), *Kashmir Ki Kali* (1964) and *An Evening in Paris* (1967) opened up a half-conscious distance in our minds from Hoshangabad's reality. These films gave us a sense that our small-town world was not all there was to life. This idea, that life could transcend reality, had the effect of gradually lifting the burden of reality from our imaginations.

If scenes from the streets of Simla and Paris broadened my small-town imagination, glimpses of village life onscreen seem to have had a similar effect on Bombay-born and bred theatre personality, Sabira Merchant:

> How can I forget *Do Bigha Zameen?* I was very young and impressionable when I saw this film. The plight of the landless farmer, depicted by the legendary Balraj Sahni, and that of his wife by actress Nirupa Roy, completely devastated me. I was leading a very sheltered and comfortable life in the city and when I came face-to-face with reality, it shook me emotionally. I couldn't sleep for nights. I think director Bimal Roy brought out the dark side of the zamindari system in all its nakedness. Scenes of Balraj Sahni leaving his village to become a rickshaw-puller in Calcutta, the wife and child in abject poverty, are something that haven't been erased from my mind...(Merchant 2000: 4)

The experience of cinema is unlike our experience of any other art form — there is something exhilarating about the drama, the fast-paced action, and in the midst of it all, the poetry of the camera. The camera's poetry lies in its emotion pictures, in the way it opens your eyes (and heart) to feelings that reside under the skin of your private 'reality' — rather like someone taking you aside, just you, no one else, to whisper a secret into your ears. Feelings like your secret relationship with say, a bicycle or a doll — objects which for some reason were more important than anything else in the world at one stage in your growing-up years. As the French film scholar, Andre Bazin puts it:

> The aesthetic qualities of photography are to be sought in its power to lay bare the realities. It is not for me to separate off...here a reflection on a damp sidewalk, there the gesture of a child. Only the impassive lens, stripping its object of all those ways of seeing it, those piled-up preconceptions, that spiritual dust and grime with which my eyes have covered it, is able to present it in all its virginal purity to my attention and consequently to my love. (Bazin 1945: 18)

This young lady, played by Naaz, has just committed the biggest sexual indiscretion of her life, in First Love *(1961). The camera has caught the state of her mind at this moment.*

The French psychologist, Lucien Seve, makes the point slightly differently:

> 'The cinema asks of the spectator a new form of activity: his penetrating eye moving from the physical to the spiritual...' (Seve 1947: 46)

Cinema, and not just art films like those of Satyajit Ray or Fellini, but also the popular stuff like *Mera Naam Joke*r and *Sujata*, is a peculiarly powerful kind of art because it shakes up so many of our given assumptions about art. Neither wholly realistic nor wholly fantastic, cinema draws us into a new, imaginative world which is simultaneously real and fantastic. What films gave us small-town teenagers in the 1960s, in sum, was a breathtakingly vivid counter-reality[1] against which to measure and compare our social world which now had shrunk to one micro-reality among many — the micro-reality of Hoshangabad, as distinct from that of Jhumritalaiya, Bombay, Madras, and so on.

Meanwhile, back to the teenagers of Hoshangabad and their little problems, which of course seemed gigantic back then.

Scene: Basant Talkies, the town's only cinema hall, perched on a hillock at the town's southern edge (as though to keep cinema's 'pernicious influence' at some distance). Hoshangabad being a small town, the films we got to see were often not in any chronological order; a recently released film being followed by one released in Bombay months or years ago.

A visit to Basant once every two weeks or so was our gang's practice. Sometimes we were even in the same cinema hall with those two girls. Smiles would be exchanged, clearly but furtively. At show's end we would be out in the prison of reality. And there the matter ended. There was no question of chatting with them. Kavita and Priya were never alone; they were always part of a larger group of family or friends.

Why was it so difficult? The four of us were in an *avant-garde* of sorts, the tongue-tied *avant-garde*. That, at least, is how we felt when reflecting upon our failure to do what we wanted so much to do. But we were by no means alone in this plight: Hoshangabad's other youngsters on both sides of the gender fence were worse off — if that was at all possible. In other words, this problem of communication across the gender line was a general one for 1960s India, even in the big cities like Bombay and Calcutta. Consider, for instance, this real-life anecdote recalled by Bombay-based Shashi Kapoor, who was a major new film hero in the '60s:

> Shall I tell you about my first date? I was 13, I borrowed some money from Shammi (his elder brother), probably his bush shirt too and asked Caty for a movie date. She lived at King's Circle. I phoned her and said, 'There is a good film at Metro, would you like to see it? I will pay for your ticket.' She agreed, but said, 'I can afford my ticket.'
>
> We went by bus, exchanging not a word with each other. Shammi had told me to discuss interesting subjects with her. By the time I could think of one, we were already in the auditorium; the picture had started and then the great problem of hand adjustment while sitting. Finally, I kept my hand to myself. There was a kissing scene and I felt awfully mean. What would Caty think of me, bringing her to a vulgar film like this? When the picture was over I was busy thinking how to fix another date, and I was still thinking when we reached her house. We did not say a word to each other on the way. 'Won't you meet me again?' I blurted out. She looked blank, and I left her. This is the sad story of my first date. (Kapoor 1966: 15)

'It's okay,come down now. I won't bite you,' Shubha Khote tells Mehmood who is petrified at this, his first encounter with the woman he has wanted to talk to for weeks now. Scene from film Dil Tera Deewana *(*1962*)*.

Or take this excerpt from a short story in Hindi by Vijay Chauhan, set in a college in Benares:

> An opportunity for speaking to Miss Bannerji arose one day all of a sudden. After classes were over he observed Miss Bannerji walking to the library. Her usual girl-friends were not with her. Vachaspati promptly fell behind her. On the pretext of looking for books he kept spying on her from behind the bookshelves. When Miss Bannerji had sat herself down at a desk with her book he made so bold as to go and sit opposite her at the same desk. Miss B read her book with total absorption and Vachaspati wondered furiously what to say to start a conversation. Just then he happened to look up at a wall with a sign saying 'Silence Please'. This dampened such courage as he had been able to muster. After a few moments Miss B rummaged in her bag, looked up at Vachaspati and said, 'Excuse me, I forgot to bring my pen today. You wouldn't have one I could borrow, would you?'
>
> One could have knocked Vachaspati down with a feather. He nearly broke out in a sweat. What he wanted to say

was that he wished to lay down his life for her, to say nothing of a pen, but no words escaped him. He mumbled something and began to search each of his pockets in turn for a pen. He too had forgotten to bring a pen. He got up all in a fluster saying, 'Just a moment.'

Tearing out in a rush he never heard Miss B say after him that it was all right, she had now found her pen. When he returned with a pen a little while later Miss Banerjee had already left…(Chauhan 1994:109-110)

So, what was the problem?

We Indians like our pleasure in small doses. Forty-five minutes of love and fun must be followed by suffering…

To put it simply — none of the four of us had any experience of talking across the gender divide to teenagers outside the family. Oh, we knew how to chat with brothers and sisters of the same age; we also knew how to deal with cousins, young aunts/uncles. But Kavita and Priya were not even remotely related to us. How in that situation, that no-man's-land, do you start a friendship? The problem was never that of starting a stray conversation; no, for that many ruses could have been used. The problem was how we would sustain the conversation. What would we say, if thrown together for an hour or two? Shashi Kapoor, as we saw above, had the same problem on his date with Caty.

This non-family space which we inhabited with respect to each other was a confined space. Confined by so many problems and questions: 'Why do you want to spend one hour, one whole hour, with Priya, hmmm? And where will you spend this hour? She can't come to your school; you can't go to hers. She can't come to your home; you certainly can't go to hers. If you meet in the bazaar, everyone will know. If you meet at the only restaurant in town, at least half-a-dozen people will know; and will she agree to meet you, alone, in a restaurant? Are you two getting married, are you engaged at least? If not, then what's up? Why do you want to meet Priya, and not any of the 200 other girls?' and so on.

All these questions didn't even begin to address your real problem — that you wanted to spend an hour with Kavita, not Priya; that you'd had to 'give up' Kavita for Vikram's sake in the tradition of the good film hero. Sacrifice was a key term, a mark of character, for us at the time. Sacrificing present well-being for future career, sacrificing this picnic for that exam, sacrificing this girl for that friend…

Now take this character, 15-year-old Mr Sacrifice, to the local movie hall, and watch him go to a 1961 film called *Aas Ka Panchhi* (Bird of Desire). Pause with him for a moment at the very sound of the film's title, and see his expectations soar while he turns the words over in his mind. The film opens with the hero, a handsome young Rajendra Kumar, in his last year at college, freeing a bird, a pigeon accidentally stuck in his bicycle seat. He finds the bird on returning from an hour of rigorous military training, plus some very encouraging words from the NCC camp's commanding officer. These words have put him in good humour despite his accountant father's fierce disapproval of his dream to be an airforce pilot.

Buoyed by the officer's encouragement, he finds symbolic significance in freeing the trapped bird, and goes singing homewards. He sings about how his heart today feels like a bird of desire, how this world belongs to the young, who will solve all its problems. '*Dil mera ek aas ka panchchi, / Udta hai oonche gagan par, / Pahunchega ik din kabhi to, chand si ujli zameen par*...' As you watch and listen, your soul too takes wing with the bird of desire, and there you are rolling along beside the hero on his bicycle, the wind caressing your faces.

'Dil mera ek aas ka panchchi, Udta hai oonche gagan par, Pahunchega ik din kabhi to, chand si ujli zameen par...'

And then, naturally, his eye on the free bird in the big, open sky, the hero must collide with a beautiful young woman on a scooter. Enter the heroine, played by Vyjayanthimala.

She gives him a talking-to — for being a poor driver. But he barely hears what she says. He is aware only of the storm she has triggered in his heart. She roars off on her scooter; he stands dazed, recovering from this awesome experience of 'love at first sight'. Over the next hour or so of the film, our hero woos the heroine, and they duly fall in love. That was the fun part — watching the tricks he and his pal devised to engineer meetings with her, to charm her, and so on.

But we Indians like our pleasure in small doses. Forty-five minutes of love and fun must be followed by suffering. It is now time for Sacrifice: his ailing father, on his death-bed, extracts the promise that he will abandon all ideas of becoming a pilot, and take up the job already fixed for him in his father's company, as a junior accountant. Thus emotionally blackmailed, our hero must sacrifice his dream career, and almost ends up losing his girl. In the end, of course, everything works out, and they live happily ever after.

For us at 15, the happily-ever-after conclusion was of marginal interest — marriage was the last thing on our minds. What was of much greater interest was the confirmation that sacrifice is not just your destiny but that of others as well. And that sacrifice brings rewards; that it is heroic to sacrifice.

Self-recognition via the hero's persona, and reinforcement and confirmation of one's beliefs — these were crucial parts of the 'entertainment' that cinema provided.

Inspired by the film's hero and his sidekick who plays at being a far-

Rajendra Kumar plays the anxious son looking on at his ailing father played by Nazir Husain in Aas Ka Panchhi. (1961). *Moments after the doctor leaves, comes the father's demand that the son give up his dream of becoming a pilot...*

seeing sadhu at a clinching moment in the hero's courtship, the big question for us later that evening was how to engineer the meeting and first tentative conversation with the two girls we had set our sights on. Should we try the cave-and-sadhu trick that had worked for the hero in *Aas Ka Panchchi?* We didn't exactly have a cave outside Hoshangabad, but there was a stone quarry, with some dark nooks and crannies; all that remained now was to decide who would be the sadhu, Vikram or I?

But by lunch-break the next day at school, the whole scheme had to be abandoned — on learning (from our sources) that Kavita and Priya had seen the same film, a day before us! So this sadhu trick just wouldn't work, not on them at any rate. Thwarted again.

That was one problem with films: they were widely shared, too widely shared. On the other hand, you could quote a line from a popular film song, or a dialogue, and the listener would immediately know all that it implied. So cinema had its uses, but only within the social constraints of your little corner of India.

These social constraints can be understood by turning back to the family as the primary social theatre in which our lives as teenagers were acted out. The family in India is not one household in Bombay or Hoshangabad; it is society itself, it is the city, the village, even the cosmos — our gods and goddesses are all related. The family is everything.

We imagine and label our private as well as public affairs primarily in terms of the family metaphor: Mahatma Gandhi, the leader of the anti-colonial nationalist movement, was called the 'father' of the new nation; the man who became the first prime minister was dubbed Chacha (uncle) Nehru.

A few years after Jawaharlal Nehru's passing — which was mourned like a death in the family by millions of Indians — his daughter Indira, who was by then a widow, became Indiramma (Indira, the mother). More recently, there is the case of her daughter-in-law Sonia Gandhi scoring as the nation's *babu*, a metaphor which has reduced her Italian origins to insignificance.

But let us return once more to the teenagers of Hoshangabad, undone by the first emergence of carnal desire in their, 'behave-yourself, don't-do-this, don't-do-that' lives.Every film we saw revolved around the romance of young love.The fact that this romance had no basis in everyday reality only served to make the films more compelling, more desirable than 'reality'.The endings of these films, moreover, unlike those tragic old legends of Laila-Majnu and Shirin-Farhad, much-loved by our parents' generation, were startlingly positive, with love triumphing against all odds to live happily ever after — again, and scandalously again.These happy endings are just stories, just fantasy, the elders would caution us. Isn't the tragic ending of Laila-Majnu also only a story, we wanted to ask, but never dared.

The pursuit of personal happiness, these films seemed to tell us, was okay; it did not always have to be a ticket to tragedy a la *Devdas* (1935 and 1956).We were undone, however, by the fact that what was so gloriously possible on the cinema screen seemed unthinkable in our small-town world. Reality and the Pictures were related, just as desire was related to our puritanical upbringing.The very distance between the two created an interesting tension.This was especially so because the romancing characters on screen were recognisable — they were college students, taxi-drivers, garage mechanics, unemployed poets, office clerks, schoolteachers.They were people like us; we could identify with them.

The very distance between Reality & the Pictures creates an interesting tension, which appeals to our inner self...

These people like us tantalised us by opening up a world of possibilities. Our imagination widened to a reality beyond our immediate surroundings.There were new stories buzzing around in the heads of regular movie-goers.The cinema of those years altered the hopes, expectations and desires of its viewers, and altered in turn their actions and their lives. But you can't usually see this effect with an interviewer's eyes, or even with a powerful, hi-tech TV camera. It isn't out there.The change in expectations and desires has taken place inside your head, silently, over years, in ways that vary from one individual moviegoer to another.Your life history, the state of mind in which you saw an especially appealing movie, all this goes into your emotional transactions with the film onscreen. You therefore have a better chance of seeing the effects of cinema with your mind's eye, rather than with hi-tech equipment.

Am I exaggerating the point by calling simple movie-watching an 'emotional transaction'? Aren't popcorn, potato chips and ice cream cones the only 'transaction' (i.e. business) that happens besides relaxing and watching a film in the cinema hall? Yes, and no.

Consider this account of the Hollywood film *Gilda* by American novelist Leonard Michaels. It takes you inside one viewer's head:

Threr is a new story buzzing around in Helen's head as she sits musing about her feelings for the man she has fallen in love with – in Cha Cha-Cha (1964).

> Rita Hayworth stars in *Gilda*, but she isn't seen for the first 15 minutes, while the friendship of two men, played by George Macready and Glenn Ford, is established. Macready saves Ford from being robbed on the docks of Buenos Aires, then hires Ford to manage a gambling casino owned by Macready...Rita Hayworth, with her amazing blond light in this dark movie (where almost everything happens in rooms, and even the outdoors seem indoors), suggests that ...dark is evil, light is good. Gray represents confusion of good and evil
>
> I certainly didn't think this when I saw the movie (as a teenager)...I didn't think anything. I felt the meaning of things, especially the morally murky weight of the gray...bedroom scene where Rita asks Macready to unzip her dress as she lies on the bed. She says more than once that she has trouble with zippers, a helpless girl imprisoned in the dress of a grown-up. Zippers, a major erotic trope of '40s movies, represented a man's access to a woman's body...
>
> I didn't want Macready to unzipper Rita Hayworth's dress. I didn't want Macready to touch her, though she is married to him, and she herself invites physical intimacy. Macready had told Ford he is 'crazy about her', so his heart is in the right place. Nevertheless, I didn't want him to touch Rita...*I knew he didn't love her*; didn't even feel desire or lust, only a sickening idea of possession...
>
> She had so much beauty and vitality that I assumed she would recover from what Macready did after unzippering her dress. Whatever it was, it wasn't good, but I supposed it happened a lot in Hollywood, where men go about touching women without feeling love, and — utterly unbearable — there are women who want to be Macreadied. Zip. She is

sacrificed and apotheosised. I had to remind myself that Gilda is a movie, not real life, and George Macready is a fine actor, also probably a nice guy.

No use.

The creep touched her.

I understood that real life is this way.

Nothing would be the same for me again. I wanted to forget the scene, but it had happened as if to me, and was now fixed in my personal history, more indelibly than World War II...(Michaels 1991: 79-83)

And now let us flip the coin and look at how two of Hindi cinema's biggest film stars of the 1950s experienced us, their fans, in this excerpt from a travel diary kept by one of them, Nargis.

Ootacamund

We went outdoor shooting for *Shri 420*. On our way back from Ooty we stopped at a small village for the night. We went to a Travellers' Bungalow. Since we were all tired motoring the whole day, we retired for a good night's sleep, expecting to leave early the next morning. I looked out of the window, and what did I see? The bungalow was surrounded by a horde of villagers — hundreds of them — old and young, women and children.

Nargis symbolises the Modern Woman of 1950s India, glamourous and desirable without being threatening.

I went cold thinking that they had come to drive us away. So we went out to see what they wanted.

One of the men talked to us in Hindi, explaining that they had come from the neighbouring villages to have 'darshan' of Raj Kapoor and Nargis! Some of them went to the extent of trying to touch our feet. We were surprised — how did they know us! We were also told that there were many touring cinemas catering to the villages — my *Jogan* and Raj's *Papi* were the latest pictures they had seen...

Moscow

We attended the premiere of *Aawara*. After the show an old man came up to us and spoke to us in broken English.

He said, 'I am 75 years old. I was in the army of the czar. Then I took part in the Revolution. I lost my entire family during the war. I was left alone, but I have never shed a tear. But today, as I was seeing your picture, my eyes filled with tears.' He blessed us – we called him Grandpa, which he liked very much.

A couple met us; it was obvious that the girl was expecting a baby. She told me it was their first. She said that they had decided that if it was a boy they'd name him Raj. If it was a girl, they'd call her Rita. I am known in the Soviet Union as Rita. It was the name of the part I played in *Aawara*. (Nargis 1956: 34-35)

Cinema and its effects

Perhaps 'effect' is not the best term with which to map the relationship between viewers and movies. Perhaps much more happens inside us in the cinema hall's darkness than can be captured by the term 'effect'. Especially when we get involved in a film, as happens sometimes. Let us instead start by positing and then exploring the sheer novelty of film as an art form in the Indian context.

Before cinema, art in the popular Indian imagination, as embodied in folk theatre, pictorial representation, storytelling and song, was populated by kings, queens, *avatars*, ghosts and bandits. But now, thanks to cinema, we suddenly have among us the vagabond, the student, the college professor, the office clerk, the jobless cartoonist, the dancing girl, the police detective, the engineer, the doctor, the truck driver, women as lawyers, as schoolteachers, and so on. These 'common' characters have been given admission to the world of Indian art for the first time — by cinema.

Not only have they been given admission, by the 1950s they had all but displaced kings, queens, *avatars* and ghosts. The only ones who survived this new cultural churning were bandits — now reborn as towering *daakoos* of the Chambal complete with handlebar moustaches and big black *teekas* on the forehead. This trend began with Sunil Dutt's *Mujhe Jeene Do* (1963).

Sunil Dutt plays the dacoit in this scene as he tries to persuade Waheeda Rehman to put up a dance show, in Mujhe Jeene Do (1963).

The experience of watching films in the cinema hall was a very intense one in the pre-TV era of small-town India in the 1960s. There were only two media that were connected to our hearts — the radio, which broadcast film songs, and cinema, where the songs came from. Paraphrasing Saddam Hussein, you could call cinema in the quarter-century after independence 'the mother of all entertainments'. You sat in near-darkness, in rows of seats facing the big screen, separated from one another, but sharing an experience with the rest of the audience. You saw large images — which allowed an astonishing closeness to the figures on screen, a closeness not afforded in everyday life. In the chemistry between cinema and its audience, the close-up works deeply and surreptitiously to bring the character home to the viewer.

In the words of sociologist Herbert Blumer who was part of a nation-wide research project to document the impact of movie-watching on American teenagers in the 1940s :

> Much of the peculiar effectiveness of motion pictures comes from the use of the 'close-up'....In motion pictures, as contrasted with the theatre, the physical distances between spectators and the actors is not fixed. This distance may be varied at will.
>
> Through the close-up the audience may be ushered into the very midst of the scene of action. This increases their sense of participation, but the experience I wish to stress is that it establishes feelings of rapport and intimacy. Here I think we find a genuine case wherein a decrease of physical distance is marked by a decrease in social distance. The close-up brings the spectator into touch contact with the characters. It permits him to observe at intimate range the play of facial and bodily gesture. My belief is that the close-up inevitably induces a sense of intimacy and privileged familiarity.
>
> Thornton Wilder informs me that the fanmail of movie stars appears to be much more intimate in tone than that received by theatrical or opera stars. In the latter the adoration is distant, seemingly conforming to the physical separation set by the theatre...(Blumer 1971: 131-2)

In the film *Barsaat Ki Raat* (1960), for instance, you see the Indian screen's Marilyn Monroe, Madhubala, after her brief and accidental encounter with Amaan Saheb (played by Bharat Bhushan), a poet she loves without ever having met, snuggling up very close to the radio in her bedroom, just listening to him singing. His voice gets to her, deep inside. He recalls this brief encounter with her in song, without knowing that she is tuned in at the very moment. You see her caressing the radio with her cheek, playing with her *dupatta*, enjoying every word of his song, and discovering gradually that it is about her! At song's end, she knows that it was him she encountered, but not what he looks like. He, poor fellow, knows what she looks like but not that she is a fan of his, nor her name or anything else.

Salma Agha in Oonche Log (1985), *gives us a feel of the intimacy of a closeup.*

The close-up brings us into 'touch' contact with the characters. You observe at intimate range the play of facial and bodily gesture. Even this imagined Meena Kumari from Daaera *(1953) will do for this purpose.*

You, the viewer, are thus in a privileged position: you know who met whom, before even Madhubala does; you also know how sensuously she drank in his song, and her innermost thoughts, which she utters as she lies down on the bed thinking of him. But — and this is the power of the close-up — you the viewer knew, felt, her emotions about the song and the singer, even before she uttered them. Even if she had never expressed her feelings, the close-up ensured that you knew — by seeing her face, her lips, her eyes, from a distance of barely an inch or two. You had made 'touch contact' with the character, as Blumer puts it above. Though this virtual touch contact ends when the film ends and you are out on the street, the experience will not have left you untouched.

This suggestion, that the movie travels with you from the dark cinema hall into the glare of reality, may be doubted by those who believe that films are 'just entertainment, just fantasies which have nothing to do with our lives'. In all humility, I disagree. This book is a result of that disagreement.

My disagreement is echoed, in a way, by Dr Seth, a lady doctor in Santa Cruz, a Bombay suburb, reminiscing about Hindi movies of the 1960s:

> Mere Mehboob aroused my interest in the Urdu language and culture for the first time. I even tried to learn it. What a tongue, how good and grand those characters sounded! ...Yes, maybe some of us even dreamed of bumping into a guy as Sadhana does in the film, with her books all scattered...But the problem was we didn't wear a burqa, not being Muslims...
>
> Another high point in my life was seeing Madhubala sing that song in Akbar's Sheesh Mahal — *'Pyaar kiya to darna kya'* — with her image attacking him from every glass piece on the Mahal's walls. She hit him and freed herself with poetry, and then with her dancing body image. Wow!

Her reference is to K. Asif's film *Mughal-e-Azam* (1960).

What we are entertained by reveals more about us than perhaps any other aspect of our lives — the subject we study, the work we do..... Maybe our fantasies and our entertainments are the most revealing mirror of our souls. Now that word 'just' before entertainment: is it not overly defensive? Especially since these very films at other times are attributed great power by the same people who dismiss them as 'just entertainment'. If films really have no after-life outside the theatre, why do we find ourselves periodically bemoaning cinema's allegedly evil influence on our 'great 5,000-year-old culture', which has been around so much longer than cinema, which is barely 100 years old?

In fact, however, the 'evil influence of cinema' has now become such a popular dogma that the Mumbai police often attributes every other bank robbery and 'mindless' murder in the city to 'the pictures'. What we have here is a situation where we sense that these films do have a powerful effect on our lives; we're just not sure what that effect is.

Meanwhile, a simplistic impact theory, which believes that violent film scenes cause young viewers to behave violently in real life, rules the day, despite sociological evidence to the contrary. What studies of movie-going have found time and again is that this search for 'effects' suffers from an over-simple stimulus-response model of human behaviour which was popular in the West until the 1930s, but has been given up long since. Surveys done with this model are premised on viewing films and their mass popularity (especially among the young) as a 'social problem' needing to be 'arrested before it is too late'. This gives the survey a moral agenda, not scientific authority. As Andrew Tudor sums up:

> There is no doubt that most research is little help in understanding the general effects of film. Because they (the effects researchers) deal with an atomised and socially isolated situation, there is rarely any safe route for generalisation. They do demonstrate that the images on the screen have some effects, especially on the emotions. But that needs little demonstration; if they had no such effects the cinema could hardly have survived this long. In other respects they waver. Although some influence on beliefs and conduct can hardly be denied, its depth and pattern remains undiscovered.
>
> The best one can say is that the experimental studies are inconclusive. They serve only to demonstrate that there is no simple one-to-one relation between the movie and any effect it may have, that there is no simple pattern to media effects... (Tudor 1975: 99)

What we are entertained by reflects more about us than perhaps any other aspect of our lives... Maybe our fantasies are the mirror of our souls.

Quite apart from the issue of evidence, the very people who believe screen violence causes real-life violence are sceptical when asked about the positive influence of screen love and screen goodness on real life! Tell them, however, that all those love scenes are encouraging the young to be licentious, and they will heartily agree. In short, popular cinema is believed to have a deep and strong influence — but for some reason that influence is deemed to be negative only. The logical inconsistency here points to the widespread confusion about our relationship with cinema, which this book attempts to clear to some extent.

Know thyself

Let us leave aside this talk of effects and look into our own psyches for a moment. Here is an American psychotherapist, D.S. Bond, offering some basic principles about what we routinely do as viewers in the darkness of the cinema hall:

> ...(The) film in the theatre is not the picture you watch on the screen, despite your perception. The film is in the projection booth, inside the projector where no one sees it. What you watch and respond to, laugh and cry with, is only the projected image of the film on the screen. Much of the drama of our outer lives is but an image of our projected inner film — perhaps more so than we care to know. (Bond 1993: 8)

Frank McConnell adds an interesting insight into this process in talking of cinema's special brand of realism, for that is surely one source of its power over us:

> It is seductively real, the world that film gives us; and, as with most seductions, part of the pleasure of our yielding to it is the suspicion that the yielding is somehow — we don't quite see how, and that too is a pleasure — dangerous. It is no accident that the guardians of our public morality like Time and Newsweek worry more about sex and violence in the film than any other medium...(Film) is an art that seems absolutely artificial and absolutely realistic...The living, breathing reality films record is...(however)...a sham: it is an elaborately encoded transcription of light that deceives us because it so intimately resembles the decoding process through which we normally perceive the world...The film is projected onto the screen, but it takes place somewhere in the brain cage of each spectator..." (McConnell 1975: 14-18)

The very people who believe screen violence causes real-life violence are sceptical when asked about the positive influence of screen love and screen goodness on real life!

Cinema only acquires meaning when you give it one. Its heroes and heroines become your personal role models, so much so that you begin to talk and dress like them; its songs and scenes become high points in your personal biography. It is common to hear friends talking about their favourite song, and why this or that film meant so much to them that they saw it several times. Actors become 'stars' because fans make them so.

This star-making process affects both the star, in boosting his career, and us, the makers of stars. As scriptwriter Javed Akhtar put it in a recent extended interview on the public and its stars,

> If you admire somebody from a distance, you make an image of him or her and you fall in love with that image and soon you are no longer in love with that person, you are in love with the image you've created. And that image is the extension of your fantasies, so that image is finally you. It's a kind of self-love... (Kabir 1999: 7)

Viewing a film is a form of mental activity, discounting which has prevented us from understanding the multi-faceted power of popular

Sudhir Kakar goes so far as to say that 'the Indian cinema audience (is) not only the reader but also the real author of the text of Hindi films...the role of the filmmakers, the ostensible creators, is purely instrumental and akin to that of a publisher who edits...the audience's manuscript.

cinema, a power of which we are the unconscious authors. Psychoanalyst Sudhir Kakar goes so far as to say that

> the Indian cinema audience (is) not only the reader but also the real author of the text of Hindi films...the role of the filmmakers, the ostensible creators, is purely instrumental and akin to that of a publisher who edits...the audience's manuscript. (Kakar 1995: 28)

It is our manuscript in at least two senses: one, that the makers of popular cinema depend on us buying tickets in millions, day after day, and we oblige — but not without causing at least four flops for every one film which is allowed to succeed at the box-office. Consequently the filmmakers, especially the distributors behind them who finance film production, are so afraid of antagonising the public's sensitivities that they err on the side of caution — by flattering us, and providing us images of ourselves which we would like to see. Is it any wonder then that we love the movies?

The second sense in which popular films are our manuscripts is that they articulate our latent aspirations, they give form and shape to our half-conscious fears, wishes and desires. The successful filmmaker is usually one who has a hotline to our aspirations, who knows them better than we do ourselves. Their films give us characters, images, responses to situations which give us the double surprise (and thrill) of self-recognition and discovery — often otherwise expressed as 'Yes, that's right: you've taken the words out of my mouth!'. Popular movies, similarly, take the images out of our hearts — images embodying aspirations which we didn't even know existed.

This intimate relationship between the movies and us also makes film study a way of studying ourselves. So intimate and active is this relationship that it does not even leave the stars unaffected. Here is what acting for us in the movies did to the late Meena Kumari, in her own words:

> I have lived so long with the Meenas of other people's imaginations — the fans, the publicists, the newspaper columnists, the scenario-writers, the directors, the public — that I now wonder whether there ever will emerge from the innermost regions of my own being, a single integrated personality instead of a mosaic of so many fragments...I wonder whether I will ever be able to recognise my true self and pointing, say — 'There! There's the person who really is Meena Kumari!' (Kumari 1966: 5)

Imagination as subversion

Take now a scene in *Dil Deke Dekho* (1960), when the young Neeta (played by Asha Parekh) who has just returned after getting her college degree in London, rebels against the condition attached to her rich

aunt's generosity in financing her studies. The price she must now pay is to marry the aunt's nephew. We see her face clouded with suppressed anger as she takes leave of her father to return to her friends sitting elsewhere in the house. To them she confides that she hates the nephew, 'because he has robbed my right to dream about whom I will marry. He has taken the romance out of my life. I hate him for that!'

This hating made sense, it echoed deeply among us teenagers, boy as much as girl. Something which takes the romance out of your life has to be bad. A dangerous little seed had been planted, dramatically, in impressionable young minds. For the next few weeks, 'the right to dream' became a new phrase we threw at each other as a joke. In private, reflective moments it buzzed in our imaginations as an interesting new idea. We took special pleasure in the fact that those of our teachers and parents who had also seen the film, had all somehow managed to miss the phrase altogether. 'Naturally, what else do you expect of them,' we would tell each other in tones of new-found superiority.

The scandal of cinema in a puritanical culture

Quite coincidentally, it so happens that *Dil Deke Dekho* figures prominently in Kiran Nagarkar's novel, *Ravan & Eddie*, about two boys growing up in a Bombay chawl in the 1950s-60s. Here's how Nagarkar describes the impact of the film on Ravan:

> Vivekanand met Ramakrishna Paramhansa, Mephistopheles found Faust, the Buddha sat under a pipal tree and gained enlightenment, the Virgin Mary woke from a deep sleep with an immaculate conception, Ravan saw *Dil Deke Dekho*...Most Hindi commercial films in those days were love

> stories but they were sad and woebegone. And even if they weren't tragic, their heroes and heroines were mature adults. *Dil Deke Dekho* was revolutionary. It was about youngsters, teenagers...
>
> When the lights went out, Ravan saw a houri, an apsara, a celestial creature in black and white of incredible beauty and vivacity. He was hard put to understand how such a rarefied and refined aesthetic experience could induce such painful tightness and tension in his groin. He would have been horrified if anyone had opined that her thick lips gave the impression that they were just a trace out of sync with the words she spoke or that the slacks she wore only helped to emphasise the magnificence of her hips. How could anybody be so gross about a creature so ethereal? His dilemma was altogether different: would Neeta, the heroine of the movie who was so mischievous, carefree, adorable, fall in love with the hero or would the villain get her? But if Neeta rocked the earth under Ravan's feet, the hero Raju swept him off his feet at gale winds of 700 mph... (Nagarkar 1995: 182-89)

Hum tum, ik kamre mein bund hon, aur chaabi kho jaaye,/ Socho kabhi aisa ho to kya ho!?/ Hum tum- mmm... (What if the two of us are locked in a room and the key gets lost. Just think what would happen then!?) [Opening line of a popular song from the film about teenage love called* Bobby *(1973)].

These films gave us teenagers in small-town India our first exposure to images of interior reality — the interior reality of adult feelings and passions. They took us inside the protagonists' most private, most intimate moments, and that blew our minds. Out in reality's homes and streets, you were lucky if you even heard anything intimate about the lives of your neighbours/friends. A fleeting smile from a girl to a boy while passing each other on the road shared by our two schools was enough to set tongues wagging for a whole week; a quarrel overheard between two newlyweds, or their choosing to spend more than just the nights together in your neighbourhood, tended to shake the local earth. There was also a mystique around the alleged sexual goings-on, the general debauchery, in the low-caste fisherfolks' hutment on the other side of the local river, barely a mile across. No one we knew had actually been there — 'It's too dangerous, yaar' — but that only added spice to our imagination.

Meanwhile on the cinema screen, we actually saw Dilip Kumar (as Prince Salim) draw very close to (Anarkali) Madhubala in *Mughal-e-Azam* for instance, and proceed to lovingly stroke her cheeks, the nape of her neck, her whole face, with a beautiful white feather. And we saw how it turned her on, moment by moment. Her face glowed, her eyes closed in animal pleasure. We could hear the sensuous effect of that feather's touch — not only onscreen, but down there among us as the hall filled with 'mmms' and 'ooohs' from every corner.

The sheer thrill of getting to see such events — without being punished for this voyeurism by any parent or elder — made movie-going an extra-special experience.

Calling this kind of experience 'just entertainment' — as people do when asked what movies mean to them — somehow seems too banal, too flat. 'Entertainment' here sounds more like a euphemism, helping to hide what really goes on between those movies and us. Perhaps part of the answer, which certainly seems closer to cinema's secret appeal to the young (but not only to the young) in a puritanical, middle class culture, lies in this remark of French psychoanalyst Christian Metz: 'Film viewing is legalised voyeurism, it is desire within the limits of the law.'

Metz here is indirectly hinting at our role in films, which remains unacknowledged in much of the conversation about cinema, even among the educated. The repression that seeks release in voyeurism is ours; the desire, and the wish to remain within limits — while letting the beast loose — is also ours. The decision to ban the kiss from the Indian screen (from 1932 onwards) was not taken by filmmakers; it was taken by us, by our government, by self-appointed guardians of our morality.

A storied world

Voyeurism, however, is only part of the answer. Cinema also gave meaning to our inner lives. These images, these peeks into the secrets of other people's hearts and lives, came at us framed in a coherent

Madhubala, enjoying Dilip Kumar's feather touch in 'Mughal-E-Azam' (1960).

narrative context, as drama and story, thereby making them doubly satisfying. Unlike random real-life glimpses, which you catch while passing by, say, your neighbours' rear windows, these were whole scenes from an unfolding, realistic story — a story which, like new wine pouring out of old, familiar bottles, was both comforting, and intoxicating. (The realism in these film stories is admittedly of a rather special, Hindustani kind: it is wishful thinking rendered in a photo-realistic garb, somewhat like the representation of Hindu gods and goddesses in calendar art.)

What is comforting for the viewer is the way in which popular cinema dramatises and reiterates an acceptable account of social order, peopled by families like our own, and by good guys and bad guys. This dramatisation, done in a familiar idiom, relies on the language of family, of honour, of good and bad. It is, in short, a storied world which we consent to inhabit whenever we 'get into' a film. Comfort, familiarity and identification are all very well, but what made it intoxicating for us young viewers was the rebellion, the brand-new individualism of the heroine as much as the hero — these characters did not bend before the status quo, typically embodied by the world of their parents and the Family.

We liked that; they did what we barely dreamed of.

In fact the whole drama animating each hit film's narrative in the 1950s and 1960s derived from the protagonists' courage to rebel, to openly say, as the character Neeta does in *Dil Deke Dekho*: 'I hate him!' To openly be a Junglee, and scream-sing 'Yaa-hooo!' as Shammi Kapoor does halfway through the film *Junglee* (1961), thereby signalling his total rejection of the image of the good conformist, which is what his grandmother would have him be. That the rebels won each time, that their rebellion led to a richer, more exciting life was, of course, the icing

Don't you ever go out with him again! — says father (Jeevan) to his love-stricken daughter (Ameeta) in Pyase Panchchi *(1961).*

on our cinematic cake. This rebelliousness was not just for the heck of it. It was the rebelliousness of individuals, of young sons and daughters who were setting out to author their own lives for a change.

Shammi and Saira Banu in Junglee (1961) *just after he has announced his love for her with a Yaahoo!*

Put this rebellion in the context of the quasi-feudal and patriarchal culture of Indian society, and its full significance begins to emerge. This sense of its significance is accessible now, long after the event of your teenage years — when you look back, and ask why these love stories appealed so much and why a few basic plots are repeated in film after film, with minor variations. The family as both home and prison, it was suggested earlier, is a key matrix within which we lived, and through which we perceived the characters of popular Hindi cinema.

Interestingly, popular cinema confirms this fact in its own way by offering us lead characters who have a love-hate relationship with the family, which always needs a big, melodramatic climax for its final resolution. In the by-now clichéd rhetoric of Hindi cinema, the family is *duniya* (the world), it is also *ghar* (home), it is *hamara khandaan* (family tradition), *log kya kahenge* (what will people say), and much more.

Yeh ishq nahin aasaan! [2]

Within this *duniya* in which we were growing up, romance had no place. It existed, of course, but strictly on the sly, and was a scandal each time. (For that very reason perhaps, romance was central to the plot of almost all the films we saw.) Marriage in the real *duniya* was a pragmatic coupling of families, a traditional alliance of clans, a way to maintain the domestic economy (the money which went out as the daughter's dowry came back as the dowry received at the son's marriage) and safeguard the rearing of children. Within this patriarchal world, the separation of the sexes is the norm, secured through the institution of gender-assigned tasks and spatial divisions consonant with them. Housework is women's work; the men work and engage with the world outside.

So pervasive was this division of space and labour along gender lines that men and women sat in separate sections in most of north India's cinema halls until the end of the 1960s. Cinemas in metropolitan centres like Bombay, Calcutta, Delhi, were perhaps the only exception: there it was possible to take your girlfriend for a 'date' to the cinema hall.

In Hoshangabad it was not even conceivable: 'dating' was not part of our emotional vocabulary. It may not be far-fetched to suspect that the Hindi language, which was our medium of education and general communication in Hoshangabad, has no word for dating.

And why should it, in a *duniya* where marriages (which are better described as 'marital alliances') have had nothing to do with love for as long as anyone can remember? On the contrary, marital alliances in traditional India are settled early in the child's life cycle and lead soon after to the assumption of adult gender-specific duties. Hoshangabad's small-town *duniya* had, of course, moved a few steps beyond this rustic culture, but the difference was essentially one of degree. For this moving away was still so tentative in the small towns of the 1950s and 1960 as to be a minority pursuit, restricted to the children of the professional middle class. But even they, as our lives and inhibitions vis-à-vis Kavita and Priya reveal, barely knew how to entertain the idea of love. The attempted passage from imagination to expression found us tongue-tied.

Love, on second thoughts, is too strong a term for what we wanted then to express; 'infatuation' as in 'being foolishly in love' may well have been more like it. Infatuation in this dictionary sense dismisses the sentiment of 'love at first sight' by viewing it as an illusion, a mistaken identification of love with the fleeting feeling of sexual arousal. And this carries a double ideological message: intense and immediate emotions are deceptive and unreliable, and sexual attraction is an insufficient and dangerous reason to choose a mate. If this makes infatuation sound terrible, don't worry — at 15 years of age, we had the advantage of being blissfully unaware of the difference between infatuation and love. All we knew was that there was a little storm in our breasts, and Hindi films were the only media with which to interpret that adolescent experience. Just beyond our small middle class enclave, however, was the spectre of old, feudal India where romantic love was both scandalous and open to severe punishment. Unfortunately, even today, occasional news reports surface about young couples being murdered by villagers because they were carrying on 'an inter-caste affair', or 'had eloped'. In Hoshangabad, thankfully, scandal was all that love provoked.

Jabeen being told in no uncertain terms by her father that she cannot go out with her boyfriend ever again, in the film Ragini (1958).

Entertainment versus a culture of concealment

To sum up the argument so far, these films were like a counterpoise to family life, its dark underground. The filmmakers' commercial compulsion to keep expanding the limits of permissible thrills and intimacy had the effect of providing us more and more glimpses of lives behind the curtain of privacy, while the rules of middle class social etiquette in small-town India — perhaps in India as a whole — centred around concealment. Both schoolteachers and parents strove to teach us restraint, whereas what the movie hall gave us — clothed in acceptable, realistic 'family' dramas — were forbidden glimpses of people crossing the boundaries of good conduct in blown-up spectacle.

A culture of concealment and gender-based segregation in real life gave rise, in short, to an art form whose popularity depended on the fact that it provided revelation as compensation. The good hero gets drunk at a shady little bar, and then comes the skimpily-clad vamp to seduce him. Of course she doesn't succeed — heavens, no! — but you get to see a full three-four minutes of her 'shamelessness' in various close-up angles on the screen. Teenage hero and heroine are caught in a storm one evening, and there's no way to get home. What then do they do with this night of privacy? They make love, and the camera shows you suggestive little scenes of their love-making, as in *Dhool Ka Phool* (1959), a cautionary fable about hot-blooded youngsters driven astray by sexual impulses. This night of indiscretion will, of course, be followed by months of suffering (especially for the young woman), but being hero and heroine it will all end happily. In the light of that denouement, the night of indiscretion loses some of its negative aura; you come away thinking it can happen to the best of us. To err is human, and all that.

Where have all the bow-lifters gone?

Consider in this context of cinematic transgression the great paradigmatic marriage — that of Sita with Ram in the Ramayana. She is offered the chance to choose her spouse from a wide range of eligible men in and around the kingdom. The method of choosing from among them is, however, chosen by her father: he who first lifts a giant bow and fires an arrow from it, will be her husband. The bow is so heavy and unwieldy that only an *avatar* like Lord Ram is able to lift it, and thereby 'win Sita's hand'. So much for Sita's choice — she was 'won' by the bow-lifter, whether she liked him or not.

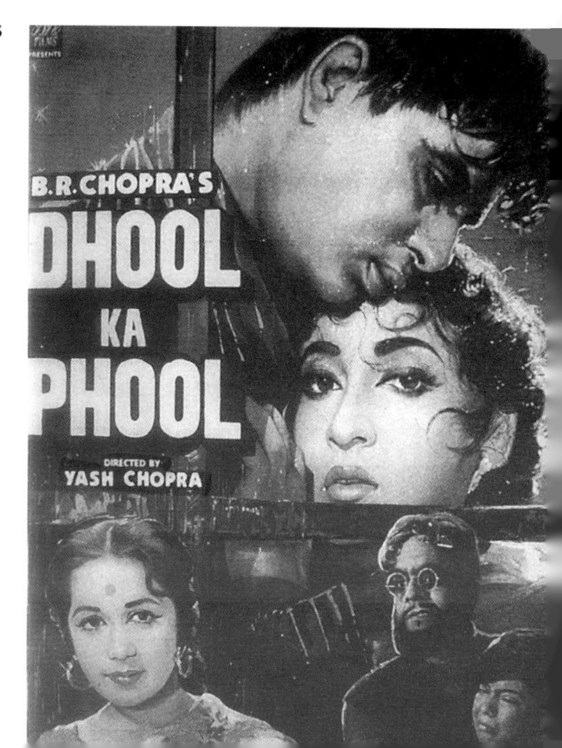

How would a film director describe Sita's role in this story of her marriage? Here is a likely script: 'Enter stage left, sit in the balcony, keep your *ghunghat* (veil) fully over your face. Watch the bow-lifting contest. No one has seen your face yet — just a hint of your lovely profile is all they can see through the *ghunghat*. Keep your face covered, keep the mystery intact. Cut.

'Next scene: The contest begins — all eyes on the suitors who come up one by one, and fail to lift the bow.

'When your father, sitting on the throne below, finally rises to applaud the first man to successfully lift the bow, you move. Rise and exit stage right, down to the hall. Pause behind the curtain, check your make-up — this is your big moment! The curtain parts, you walk slowly, demurely, like a good Indian bride. And now as you finally lift the *ghunghat* just enough to reveal your face — the audience gasps at your beauty! Shot in left profile — six-second close-up. A second later you step forward and garland your husband-to-be. Full frontal shot, standing next to Ram. Cut. End of role.'

What would her father's reaction have been, you wonder, had Sita ventured to say that she is not interested in a he-man at all, but rather in a poet, a painter, someone who may not be the kingdom's greatest bow-lifter, but can lift a common word or an image and make it Art? The father, like most Indian men, would have been flabbergasted, recovered a moment later and thundered in true filmi style — 'Seeetaaa! Have you lost your senses, child!?...'

The point of recalling the above fable is that it brings us to the scandalous news that the Sitas of post-independence Hindi cinema have ignored their fathers' warnings and actively chosen to 'lose their senses' in film after film — and lived happily ever after. In *Aawara*, Nargis, our 1951 Sita, loses her senses to a handsome young thief with green eyes who can also sing and bring back the purse which was stolen. In 1952, Gauri (played by Meena Kumari) in *Baiju Baawra* loses her senses to Baiju, who is a singing

Nutan and Sunil Dutt – in Sujata (1959).

prodigy. Oh, he can lift a sitar, but a bow? What bow? He hasn't played with one since he was a child. Besides he's a peace-loving romantic. One of the big hits of 1954 was *Aar Paar*, in which the heroine loses her senses to Birju (Guru Dutt), a taxi-driver who's also a car mechanic. He can also sing and whistle beautifully while repairing cars. Can Birju lift a bow? Hmmm yes, maybe, but what for? What her father really wants is that Birju should have a decent middle class job and a place to stay.

Guru Dutt and Shyama in Aar Paar (1954).

In the process of thus losing their senses to all kinds of strange fellows — Vidya, the schoolteacher heroine of *Shri 420* (1955) loses her senses to a laundry worker only because he's honest and a graduate, and the list goes on getting stranger and stranger — our 20th-century Sitas have also changed the whole methodology of mate-selection, often giving pride of place to the prospective mate's singing skills, and occasionally his ability to rescue her in distress. But a rescuer who can't sing doesn't stand a chance. Bow-lifting, as a result, is not *de rigueur* anymore.

Another reason for the obsolescence of bow-lifting in these modern times is that marriage between hero and heroine on screen has to be a love marriage. No one is quite sure why, but that increasingly became the rule from the 1951 *Aawara* onwards; it certainly makes for much more watchable cinema than marriage by parental consent. That being so, courtship has become a new and necessary prelude to marriage onscreen. As the male suitor, you cannot anymore appeal to the girl's parents; it is she you must appeal to. Her parents come into the picture much later — usually after the interval.

These films, our films as Sudhir Kakar insists — which are mostly courtship fables — have glamorised and legitimised the idea of love, in a society which has yet to fully come to terms with its individualistic,

A son goes to war against his father, in the name of love! Prithviraj Kapoor, Dilip Kumar and Madhubala in Mughal-e-Azam *(1960).*

democratic implications. Meanwhile, on screen, love is the knife that cuts through the whole web of established society — *duniya* and its *duniyadaari* in filmi shorthand. It pits sons against fathers, daughters against fathers, breaks up big, happy, joint families, pits employees against the boss, occasionally even the individual criminal or dacoit against his own gang. Perhaps the starkest generational conflict ever depicted in Hindi cinema occurs in *Mughal-e-Azam*, set in 16th-century Delhi, where it actually leads to war between the father, Emperor Akbar, and his son, Prince Salim. The cause — Salim is in love with a servant girl, Anarkali, whom he wants to marry, thereby raising the scandalous prospect of her becoming the empress of Hindustan when he ascends the throne after Akbar.

Or take Raj Kapoor's *Aawara*, which presents the vagabond hero's love for his heroine - a lawyer — as part of a larger quest. He struggles, soon after falling in love with her, to stop being a petty thief and slowly disentangles himself from the gang's boss. At the film's climax, in prison for the next two years, he resolves to educate himself so that one day he can be a lawyer, 'or maybe even a judge'. Love, in short, has given him the motivation to change his whole life and redeem himself.

The big box-office hit of 1952 was *Baiju Baawra*, where we see love and the pain of separation from his beloved helping the young singer Baiju to accomplish his fondest dream — to defeat the great singer Tansen in a public contest in Akbar's court. The film dwells in some detail on Baiju's transformation from raw talent to mature genius, via love, and some serious soul-searching with the help of his guru.

In a much lighter vein are films like *Dil Deke Dekho, Junglee, Bluff Master, Mr & Mrs 55, Solvan Saal* and *Mere Mehboob*. In each of these, however, love is only part of the story, the other part is an identity story, a quest story. Take *Mere Mehboob* (1963) from this lot, for instance. Its hero, a poet making ends meet by combining tuitions with editorial work in a small magazine, must come to terms with his unmarried sister's long-standing affair with an older man who does not marry her, and with the fact that she is a *mujra* dancer by profession, which means that the two cannot be seen together in public, lest he become tainted like her. In the film's second half, he must 'sell' himself in marriage to a rich young woman he hardly knows, in order to earn a large sum of money to save his beloved's family from ruin. Well, he does put his head on the marriage block, so to speak, but since the rich young woman is good and generous, it all ends happily: she returns him to his beloved.

Generosity and self-sacrifice are the two principal aspects of good character in Hindi cinema, and this woman has both in full measure. (This sacrifice by the young Muslim woman is reminiscent, when you pause to think of it, of the character of Prince Bharat in the Ramayana, as well as other legendary characters from India's folk epics. But it is a subconscious, silent echo of the epics, leaving you with a warm glow

Today's Sita looks different, a look created by Nargis, in the 1950s. Here she plays Vidya, the school teacher in Shri 420 (1955). *The man she has lost her senses to is Raj, a laundry worker played by Raj Kapoor.*

inside…)

What we see again and again in the landmark films of the 1950s and 1960s are young people at the brink of adulthood, inspired by their love for each other — growing into exemplary men and women. On the way to accomplishing their union they must overcome a whole range of obstacles which test their love for each other, and the strength of their character. The villain, the family, socio-economic inequalities, caste prejudices — the whole of Indian culture and society is pitted against the 'blindness of young love'. The very existence of such love is a challenge to the established social order of 'appropriate' marital alliances, women's subordination and parental control over the young. This culture-decreed appropriateness is an idea against which every Hindi film's protagonist rebels.

It is not all noble rebellion, however. This is mass-market cinema, after all, whose audience consists of youngsters as much as their parents. Both sides must be catered to, if the large viewership is to grow and be sustained. So you find that these films glamorise rebellion only to end up with a general reconciliation — of the young with their parents, and the establishment more generally. The rebels, barring a handful of exceptions like *Pyaasa, Mughal-e-Azam, Baiju Baawra*, end up living happily ever after as homemakers. As the public emerges from the cinema hall, there are smiles on the faces of the young and the old; both have got their money's worth…

Endnotes

1. I owe the phrase 'counter-reality' to McConnell 1975.

2. Love is a difficult business.

References

Bazin, Andre. 1945. *The Ontology of the Photographic Image, 'Qu'est que le Cinema?'* Volume 1, Les Editions du Cerf, Paris, 1958.

Blumer, Herbert. 1971. "Moulding of Mass Behaviour Through the Motion Picture" in *The Social Fabric of the Metropolis*, (ed.) James Short, University of Chicago Press.

Bond, D.S. 1993. *Living Myth*, Shambhala Publications, Boston.

Chauhan, Vijay. 1994. "The Whirligig of Time" in *The Penguin New Writing in India*, (eds.) A Behl & D Nicholls, Penguin Books, New Delhi.

Dickinson, Emily. 1964. *Selected Poems,* Harper & Row, New York.

Kabir, Nasreen Munni. 1999. *Talking Films*, Oxford University Press, Delhi.

Kakar, Sudhir. 1995. *Intimate Relations*, Penguin Books, Delhi.

Kapoor, Shashi. 1966. *Star & Style*, 1 August, Vol XV, Bombay.

Kumari, Meena. 1966. *Star & Style*, 15 October, Vol XV, Interview Profile by Bunny Reuben.

McConnell, Frank, D. 1975. *The Spoken Seen*, Johns Hopkins University Press, Baltimore.

Metz, Christian. 1985 "Story/Discourse: Notes on Two Types of Voyeurism" in

(ed.) Nichols, B., *Movies and Methods,* Vol.2, Berkeley, University of California Press.

Merchant, Sabira. 2000. "Chalo Cinema", *Bombay Times*, 18 October, Bombay.

Michaels, Leonard. 1991. "Gilda - The Zipper" in *The Movie That Changed My Life,* (ed.) Rosenberg, D., Viking Penguin, New York.

Nargis. 1956. "Jottings from the Scrap-book of", *Filmfare*, 17 August.

Nagarkar, Kiran. 1995. *Ravan & Eddie*, Viking, Delhi.

Seve, Lucien. 1947. "Cinema et methode", *Revue Internationale de Filmologie*, Juillet-Aout, Vol I, No 1.

Tudor, Andrew. 1975. *Image and Influence - Studies in the Sociology of Film*, St Martin's Press, New York.

The real is not only what one sees
but also a result of how one sees it...
John Ashbery in 'Reported Sightings'

Yeh Ishq Nahin Asaan
Cinema & the Language of Love

No one can define 'romance', but we all think we know what it is. In a way, the movies have given us this strange confidence — of knowing romance without necessarily being able to define it. They have given us images, a personal handful of songs, and memorable lines of dialogue, all of which have contributed to our conception of romance. Particularly moving scenes or songs have stayed with us for years and years, marking a personal milestone in the making of our identities and our sense of romance.

Romance in Indian cinema is unfulfilled love; it is love not fully recognised; it is understatement; it is taking a risk that could be fatal. The conquest of anxiety by desire is romance.

Romance is a song like '*Pyaar kiya to darna kya*! (Why should I be afraid to have fallen in love!)' sung by Anarkali before a menacing Akbar, emperor and father of Prince Salim, her lover, in the film *Mughal-e-Azam*. Anarkali sings and dances with attitude — in front of her doubting lover, the emperor and his whole court. She knows that it will lead to almost certain death, and yet she sings. Romance is the energy of that suicidal defiance by a lowly young woman; it is the defiance of a soul empowered by love.

As Anarkali puts it by way of justifying her scandalous confession: '*Pyaar kiya koi chori nahin ki,/ Phir ghut-ghut kar aanhein bharna kya* (I'm guilty of love, not theft,/Then why should I suffocate myself with guilt)'.

Fifteen years after *Mughal-e-Azam*, we saw Ramesh Sippy's *Sholay* (1975), in which once again we see a woman — Basanti, played by Hema Malini — defying death as she dances barefoot for love on uneven, rocky ground littered with shards of glass. Sholay was a mega-hit, as we Indians put it, which broke all previous box-office records. Basanti's dance was one of several reasons for its success.

Romance is the song '*Tu hi ray* (You, only you)'... in the film *Bombay* (1995), or '*Na jaane mere dil ko yeh kya ho gaya,/ Abhi to yahin tha, ab kho gaya...* (I don't know what's happened to my heart,/ It was here a moment ago, but now it's gone....)' the one Simran (Kajol) and Raj (Shah Rukh Khan) sing post-separation at the end of their summer holiday on their way home from the railway station in *Dilwale Dulhaniyan Le Jayenge* (1995).

It is, especially, the dazed look on Simran's face as she stands — forlorn and completely still — at the London railway station platform just after Raj has left her. It is the cold wind in Sadhana's coat collar after Joy Mukherji has left her in *Ek Musafir Ek Hasina* (1962).

A school teacher who is an incurable romantic— Shubha Khote in Didi (1959).

Or take this song from the film *Didi* (1959) which presents us with a female character, a schoolteacher who is an incurable romantic. In trying to cope with the loneliness of life without her lover who has been incommunicado for several weeks now, she sings: '*Tum mujhe bhool bhi jao, to yeh haq hai tumko/ Meri baat aur hai, maine to mohabbat kee hai.../Mere dil ki, mere jasbaat ki, queemat kya hai, tum jo yeh bhi na batao to yeh haq hai tumko.../ Tumko duniya ke gham-o-dard se fursat na sahi...* (You have the right to forget me,/ But I can't, because I love you./...My heart, my feelings for you — what price would you put on them? It's okay, you don't have to tell me their worth. / For you're an important man preoccupied with the sufferings of society at large. / But not me, for I can only love you.)'.

This song is sung for Madhav (Sunil Dutt) by Shobha (Shubha Khote), in *Didi*. He is a crusading journalist, a social worker and a schoolteacher; she is only a teacher. Her resignation to the loss, her acceptance of pain and rejection, is what draws you to her and to the situation. For this is not simple resignation; it is resignation poeticised. The song, the way it is rendered, introduces you to a character who rises above her pain. By the end of the song her love seems as noble, if not more so, than the social work he is so busy with.

Pyaar jhukta nahin[1]

If poetry and self-sacrifice are one side of love onscreen, the other side is acting on forbidden impulse. Romance in *Satyam, Shivam, Sundaram* (1978) is Zeenat Aman, the conservatively brought-up, deeply anxious village girl, daring to touch Shashi Kapoor's naked, wet back, because of a sudden, uncontrollable rush of desire for this stranger from the city. The impulse is strong, stronger than anything she has ever felt before. She gives in.

It is allowing him, just a few minutes later, to kiss her — despite the fear that he, Shashi Kapoor, would be shattered if he even glimpsed the burnt, scarred side of her face. She takes a huge risk in letting herself go at that moment, while hiding part of her face, but she does so nonetheless. That is romance. That flirtation with disaster is romance.

'Tu hi ray', the song from *Bombay*, is the cry of two young people in a small coastal town beset by enormous difficulties in establishing contact, in getting to be with each other for just a few moments. So when they finally have their first rendezvous, it is at an abandoned fort far out of town. He has been waiting for an hour or more, hoping she will come, and yet half-afraid that she won't because there are a dozen family restrictions on her movements around town. Defying Culture and Family, she finally does come. Late, and running to reach him, she throws off her black veil, which is swept by the wind to the giant anchor of an abandoned ship, and there it flutters, caught.

This conservatively brought-up Muslim girl's impulsive decision to leave the veil and all it symbolises behind, rather than spend time disentangling it — is romance. No further explanation of romance is needed here — this picture, this action, this anchor with all its symbolism, speaks a thousand words. You can spin them any which way you like…

Trouble in paradise: Raj Kapoor telling his wife Nargis in Anhonee (1952) *that she is testing the limits of his patience.*

Vidya (Nargis) on the verge of accepting Raj's (Raj Kapoor) marriage proposal in this close-up of the iconic love scene in Shri 420 *(1955).*

Take now a singing-in-the-rain scene from the 1955 film *Shri 420*, which is an icon in the Indian cine-book of romance.

Raj has taken Vidya (played by Raj Kapoor and Nargis respectively) out for tea to celebrate his first job — as a laundry worker. But he has yet to get his first month's wages. Vidya, who is only a little less impoverished, pays for the tea at a roadside stall on this their first date, much to Raj's embarrassment. Barely have they finished their tea when it starts raining. Vidya has an umbrella, Raj does not.

Further embarrassed at the lack of an umbrella, Raj turns the tables on her by declaring his love for her and proposing marriage the very next moment — all this in a song which begins: '*Pyaar huaa, ikraar hua hai,/ Pyaar se phir kyon darta hai dil*? (We both know we've fallen for each other/ Why then is your heart afraid to admit to love?)'. Vidya is taken aback, hesitates, and worries about the precariousness of their future given their meagre income. She sings: '*Kahta hai dil, rasta mushkil,/ Maloom nahin hai kahaan manzil*...? (The road ahead is difficult, fears my heart. / Our future's so uncertain....)'

Jawaani diwani[2]

Raj ignores her question, preferring instead to continue dreaming. There is a certain madness here — which he transmits to her, in brushing aside her anxiety. Call it the madness of youth, the madness of desire, plus the desperation of two young people who are on the brink of a big decision involving each other for the rest of their lives. Believe for just a moment, Raj says, that love will help us overcome, believe in Us! Vidya is so taken in by the power of his feelings (and her own as they now slowly surface), that she agrees to stop worrying and start celebrating this moment as the beginning of a new life for them as a couple. That is romance — to be able to rise above material constraints, purely on the strength of feeling and desire. Anxiety has been conquered by desire.

What gives the conquest a special emotional edge, paradoxically, is its temporary nature. As the story of *Shri 420* develops, it turns out that the conquest is also fragile. Raj's sudden success at work, shortly after this intense moment, leads to alienation between him and Vidya, which lasts almost until the film's end.

There is a ring of familiarity in these ups and downs in the plots of our favourite films. We have been brought up to believe that unadulterated happiness, the union of two souls in love's first flush, are temporary things which must be cherished, if and when they happen. Storms and stresses follow these special moments, almost inevitably. Once those are overcome, the story ends: and then they lived happily ever after. Such is the power of cinema that questions like 'Did they, really?' do not arise until the effect of the film has worn off minutes, maybe hours, later.

The calm after the storm: Kuldip Kaur and Karan Dewan in Rakhi (1949).

It is as if, in acknowledging the evanescence of intense happiness, and the hunger for it, we allow our real-life anxieties about love a brief airing, and then quickly seal them up in a box labelled 'Happily Ever After'.

Real-life anxieties about the fragility of the relationships we construct, about self-worth and identity, do occasionally find space in the depiction of romance on screen. Indian cinema's love stories are not only about sons and daughters rebelling against parental orthodoxy. There are a few films that show the young lovers getting married halfway through the story. What happens in each such marriage, however, is that it soon begins to sour, then encounters major turbulence like a ship at sea, before finally reaching calmer waters and coming to rest at a port called 'domestic bliss'. Lest you begin, like a good sceptic, to wonder whether this bliss is again the calm before the storm, the film ends!

Waheeda Rehman as Hirabai the Nautanki dancer who falls in love with a rustic simpleton, Hiraman, In Teesri Kasam (1966).

Popular cinema is about entertainment, remember. It plays with and touches on our anxieties ever so lightly. If you want more reality, there is always real life to turn to — with its psychologists, cure-all gurus, alcoholism, drug abuse, divorce courts and mental institutions. Examples of films which 'play' with our post-romance, marriage-related anxieties in this sense are Subodh Mukerji's *Love Marriage* (1959), B R Chopra's *Gumrah* (1963), *Hamraaz* (1967), *Ek Phool Do Maali* (1969), *Abhinetri* (1970), Anil Ganguly's *Kora Kagaz* (1974), Gulzar's *Aandhi* (1975), Gulzar and Meraj's *Sitara* (1980), Gulzar's *Ijaazat* (1988), Govind Nihalani's *Drishti* (1991), and of course the popular B R Chopra comedy *Pati, Patni Aur Woh* (1978). Consider in this connection a most unlikely candidate, *Teesri Kasam*, the late poet Shailendra's only film, made in 1966. It is a love story with a sad ending.

In *Teesri Kasam* (The Third Vow), Waheeda Rehman as the female protagonist plays Hirabai, a dancer with a travelling *nautanki* (a folk song-and-dance troupe). At the film's climax she chooses, much against her will, to opt out of a possible marriage with a rustic bullock-cart driver whom she has met and fallen in love with. Raj Kapoor plays Hiraman the driver. He is presented as a 30-year-old child of nature who is both wise beyond his years and innocent of life and occupations outside his small, idyllic agricultural universe. He does not know that she must occasionally double as a prostitute; he does not even know what a prostitute is.

Hiraman just loves her, and wants to make her his bride.

While Hirabai is utterly charmed by his simple-minded devotion (who wouldn't be?), she is worldly enough to realise that her urbane cynicism and his rustic innocence will not be able to co-exist for long. The film ends with her leaving town, with broken heart firmly concealed — for good. Our rustic's innocence — for what it is worth — is thereby preserved.

So near, yet so far

Such films are few and far between, however. The basic formula which Hindi cinema resorts to in dealing with the anxieties of romance has been well (even if unintentionally) caught by K Valicha in this excerpt from his recent biography of the late actor-singer Kishore Kumar:

> The highlight of the film *(Jhumroo)* is the song *'Koi humdum na raha/ Koi sahara na raha/ Hum kisi ke na rahe/ Koi hamara na raha...* (I've no friend left/ Nor anyone to lean on/ I am nobody for anyone/ Nor is there anyone who needs me...)'. It is one of the finest songs in Kishore's career. Balancing precariously an ambience... (of) deep longing and a sense of loss, Kishore uses some exquisitely elongated *taans* to add strength...to the mood of tender yearning...The rendering, as it rounds off the ascents and descents, does a subtle interpretation...The impact it produces is coloured by a delicate nearness to, as well as a poignant distance from, fulfilment. (Valicha 1998: 150)

The key phrase here is 'a nearness and a distance' — simultaneously — from romantic fulfilment. This duality — so near and yet so far — defines romance in Hindi cinema; thus my suggestion that romance is unfulfilled love.

A nearness and a distance—from love as fulfilment. Dharmendra stung by his beloved Tanuja's 'No', on the left. On the other side, Tanuja can't stop her tears following the 'No' which was forced upon her. Nirupa Roy, her sister, tries to console her, with little success in Chand Aur Suraj (1965).

The duality can be found in all the examples cited above: it is there in the *Bombay* song '*Tu hi ray....*' It is there in the *Dilwale Dulhaniyan Le Jayenge* scene where the film's heroine Simran (Kajol) is shocked to discover — just after they have parted at the railway station, perhaps forever — that she has fallen deeply in love with Raj (Shah Rukh Khan).

Amaan Sahib (Bharat Bhushan) the radio singer-cum-poet sings 'Zindagi Bhar Nahi Bhoolegi... (I'll never forget that night...)' in the film Barsaat Ki Raat *(1960), to Madhubala's remembered image.*

Rewind to some of Hindi cinema's most famous love scenes from the 1950s and 1960s, and the duality is there again. Take, for instance, the hero and heroine's first encounter in *Barsaat Ki Raat* (1960), where the all-too-brief scene is re-presented to us a few minutes later through the song that goes '*Zindagi bhar nahin bhoolegi woh barsaat ki raat* (Never will I forget that rainy night, when a clap of thunder drove you into my arms, and how you recoiled a moment later...)'. What makes the hero fall for her most of all is the fact that she *recoils* after jumping into his arms, so to speak. Or consider one of the most popular love songs of the early-1960s from the film *Mere Mehboob* (1963) which is also about would-be lovers losing contact with each other after a moment of accidental but intense intimacy. So near (she's a student in the same campus), and yet so far (they haven't met since that first time). The film's title song goes thus: '*Mere mehboob tujhe, meri mohabbat ki kasam.../ Phir mujhe nargisi aankhon ka sahara de-de*'. To put its chaste Urdu in American slang (in sheer perversity), what hero is saying to heroine is: 'Dearest love, just gimme that mind-blowing nearness again, pleeez, it's now or never!'

Notwithstanding this plea, he does not get her (until much later in the film).

Strangers in the night/ Exchanging glances...

It is interesting how love often happens in the midst of, or just after, accidental encounters in most of these films. Two strangers thrown together on a rainy night in *Barsaat Ki Raat*, an upper-class young lady compelled to reach out to a garage mechanic for help when her car breaks down on a rainy night in *Chalti Ka Naam Gaadi* (1958); two students who collide with each other while distractedly crossing paths in a university campus in *Mere Mehboob*; two students again in *Dilwale Dulhaniyan Le Jayenge*, who get to know each other by sheer chance on a tour organised by some friends of theirs, and so on. Such stories point, perhaps, to the 'real' fact that men and women do not usually interact in Indian society, outside the family context. This gender segregation was of course truer of India in the 1950s-60s, than it is today.

And yet, love stories then as now have to be outside safe familial settings if they are to be interesting. They have to be the total opposite of arranged marriages to appeal to our secret yearnings. For the modern idea of love — which is very urban in origin — has something to do with total strangers coming together to build a new bond, a new nest. As a very popular love song from *Baat Ek Raat Ki* (1962) has it: '*Na tum hame jaano,/ Na hum tumhe jaane./ Magar lagta hai kuch aisa,/ Mera humdum mil gaya-aa*...(You don't know me,/ Nor I you./ But somehow now that we've met,/ It seems we were meant for each other...)'

Strangers in the night, exchanging glances. A moment after the exchange, Waheeda Rehman wants to think it over, but the man, Dev Anand, seems much surer that she is the one. Scene from Baat Ek Raat Ki (1962).

A girl soaking wet, comes to my garage late at night... sings Kishore Kumar in his first encounter with Madhubala in Chalti Ka Naam Gaadi (1958).

Another hit song, this one from the film *Chalti Ka Naam Gaadi*, comes to mind at this point: '*Ek ladki bhigi bhagi si,/ Soti raaton mein jaagi si,/ Mili ik ajnabi se,/ Koi aage na peechhe, tum hi kaho yeh koi baat hai!* (A girl soaking wet, awake at night when the world sleeps,/ Met a complete stranger, with no one else around for miles./ Anything could happen then, you'll agree...)'

Imagining and then depicting such accidental meetings gives popular cinema's love stories at least some credibility in our otherwise love-less culture[3]. Credibility is actually only the first step. Aspiration enters the picture next, and with that your fantasies of how you, the real you, would like to encounter and then fall in love with, a complete stranger. Having grown up with such stories, I find myself looking forward (with well-concealed anticipation) each time to meetings with strangers of the opposite sex. You never know what might happen, says the movie-nut inside me. Unlike in the movies, most often nothing much comes of these real-life encounters. But occasionally it does; yes, occasionally life does imitate art. Cinema has thus added a shot of romance to one's humdrum life, and fostered an openness of mind towards all kinds of strangers.

Why only love stories

Given the impossibly difficult course that love must traverse in real life in India, is it any wonder that nine out of ten Hindi films are love stories? Another reason for the dominance of love stories could be that other kinds of stories — historical and political ones, for instance — were commercially dangerous minefields in the first two decades following independence. They still are. In a new, deeply multi-ethnic nation still trying to define its post-colonial identity, historical and political themes are fraught with the danger of provoking a public controversy. Indian culture, moreover, is full of sacred cows: there is always the possibility of the political/historical film being banned or censored by the government's censor board.[4]

Love stories, by contrast, do not plunge the information and broadcasting ministry (and its censor board) into a crisis; they are viewed as harmless and inconsequential from the point of view of government and its guardianship of the national image.

Outside of the love story, what we are left with is the mythological, the thriller, the war film, the dacoit fable, and the *tawaif* (prostitute-with-a-heart-of-gold) fable. That's it. While these genres have been exploited by Bombay's filmmakers from time to time, the box-office returns on them have been fitful and unpredictable at best. The public seems to tire of everything except the love story.

So the canvas of popular cinema has been limited by the viewers and the censor board over the last five decades. Within this limited canvas, the romance has lent itself to maximum variations. The love story in Hindi cinema is never just about two young people in love. It is also a *quest* fable, a story of the broad direction the protagonists' lives are to take, a story of what kind of persons they wish to become — revealed indirectly in the way they respond to major crises in their lives.

Shri 420, for instance, is the story of a young small-town graduate, Raj, who migrates to Bombay not just to find a job, but also his identity and his lady love. The manner in which he conducts himself after reaching the city shows that this is a journey into his soul, into adulthood, as much as into the labour market. And that really is what makes Raj's journey interesting enough for us to watch over three hours in the cinema hall.

Not surprisingly, the most dramatic part of this film is the moral dilemma created by the sudden riches that come his way, and the manner in which he resolves the dilemma. The love affair with Vidya is a small part of this quest fable.

Shri 420 is just one example of this type. Take any filmi love story

Raj and Rita (Raj Kapoor & Nargis) treating both life and identity as projects—open to change—in Aawara *(1951).*

which comes to mind from the treasure-chest of Hindi cinema post-1947 — *Aawara, Baiju Baawra, Shikast, Barsaat, Barsaat Ki Raat, Paying Guest, Mere Mehboob, Ujaala, Love Marriage, Mughal-e-Azam, Guide, Rajkumar, Hum Dono, Kashmir Ki Kali, Madhumati, Ek Musafir Ek Hasina, Love in Simla, Sujata, Anupama, Anubhav, Sahib, Bibi Aur Ghulam, Bobby, Ek Duje Ke Liye, Muqaddar Ka Sikander, Aandhi, Dilwale Dulhaniyan Le Jayenge, Kuch Kuch Hota Hai*.... the list is endless — and you find that each of them is also a quest fable. In each film the would-be couple is required by 'circumstances' and/or 'society' to prove themselves worthy not just of each other, but also of our regard as viewers.

And this regard doesn't come cheap — it is not enough for the lovers to be good-looking and desire each other. Good looks are but the starting point from which the story takes off — a sort of 'minimum guarantee'. Thereafter, she as much as he, must also be seen to be admirable, eloquent and heroic characters on screen.

There is a flip side to this, however: the stars of popular cinema must be both larger-than-life heroic and small like us in order to be credible characters. For credibility is a basic issue in the making of persuasive fictions — especially with cinema as your medium. The characters onscreen must be seen to be real[5], thereby facilitating one's involvement in their life stories. As the viewer's surrogate eye, the camera thrives on the close-up, on catching its subjects in their most unguarded, vulnerable moments. Look no further than your family photo album — you will find that the snapshots of family members, which today are most appealing, are the ones that caught them at their most vulnerable moments.

Personal vulnerability, ever since Charlie Chaplin, has quietly become an essential component in making heroes and heroines credible in popular cinema worldwide, and Indian cinema is no exception. Once that nerve

Raj Kapoor celebrated the common man by adopting Charlie Chaplin's tramp persona in films like Shri 420 (1955). *The result, after a series of such films, was to redefine male heroism in Hindi cinema.*

is touched, we are ready to go with our heroes anywhere. These are emotion pictures after all. And cinema, as Bombay's filmmakers know only too well, is about giving the public captivating scenes and characters soaked in basic, primitive (and credible) feelings.

There is also a historical dimension to this credibility factor, which highlights Hollywood's deep influence on Hindi cinema. From the mid-1930s onwards, following the worldwide popularity of Charlie Chaplin's tramp character, the classic Frank Capra movies (*It Happened One Night, Mr Smith Goes to Washington, Meet John Doe* etc), and many left-liberal Hollywood films of the 1940s (*Casablanca* etc), heroism came to be redefined in Hindi cinema.

There was a new democracy at work in Hindi cinema's portrayal of great heroes and great lovers. The 1930s and '40s were also a time in Indian society when the common man/woman (especially the rural poor) was being celebrated and gradually brought to centrestage by Mahatma Gandhi, and by left-wing nationalists — especially the Indian People's Theatre Association (IPTA). The common person, thanks to Mahatma Gandhi's adopted *fakir* persona, was dramatically placed at the head of our nationalist identity-building project by the end of the 1930s.

Vidya's conscience has rejected the new Raj, but her heart cannot bear losing him. Nargis enacts her character Vidya's dilemma in this scene from Shri 420 (1955).

As a result, the protagonists of Hindi cinema were given scripts that required them to earn their hero status by starting from where we are, and then going beyond. A scene from *Shri420* which comes to mind here depicts Vidya's (Nargis) dilemma over Raj's new-found prosperity, which is based on fraud and gambling. Her conscience rejects the new Raj, and yet her heart cannot bear losing him. The scene dramatizes this dilemma by showing us a Vidya split in two. This trend could be glimpsed in the 1940s in films like *Kismet* (1943), *Humraahi* (1945), *Do Dil* (1947), *Andaaz and Barsaat* (1949), before it became dominant in the 1950s, beginning with Raj Kapoor's 1951 hit, *Aawara* (The Vagabond), Bimal Roy's *Do Bigha Zameen*, and culminating in Mehboob's *Mother India* (1957). The hero must fail before he succeeds in his plans; the heroine must lose the man she loves because she was tongue-tied (like us) at the very moment when she needed to speak.

In *Sahib, Bibi Aur Ghulam* (1962), Jaba (Waheeda Rehman) complains of just this after Bhootnath, the man she loves, has left, perhaps never to return. The song she sings at this moment, '*Meri baat rahi mere man mein, kuch kah na saki uljhan mein*...(My feelings remained in my heart, I just couldn't say a word in all the confusion of the moment...)', found a permanent place in thousands of young hearts across the nation, for it expressed so completely their own emotions.

In *Pyaasa* (1957) too, the heroine goes up to the terrace to hold her lover, the poet Vijay (Guru Dutt), and tell him finally how much she loves him, his unemployment notwithstanding. Vijay is unaware of her presence. He stands with his back to her, gazing at the black sky. But she can't do it. She doesn't even manage to touch him, though she goes up very close behind him. Something inside holds her back. Those brakes have been slammed on again. And we viewers loved her for that inability to do and say what she most wanted to.

Women are not the only ones defeated by these inner brakes in Hindi cinema. Male characters are equally undone, albeit not as often as their female counterparts. Bhootnath in *Sahib, Bibi Aur Ghulam* is the epitome of the tongue-tied man, the rustic who cannot voice his conflicting desires, and yet must learn to deal with the storm they are causing in his breast — for he is carrying on with two beautiful women simultaneously, and one of them happens to be married. So clumsily has he bottled up his feelings that one of the two women, Jaba, mocks him for being a fool who cannot see the interest he has aroused in her, the woman he meets every day at work: '*Bhanwra bada naadaan hai, jaane na, jaane na — kaliyan ki muskaan hai*...(This bee is so ignorant, it does not even notice the flowers sending it a welcoming smile...)' Hindi cinema's love stories are, in short, coming-of-age stories.

This dual quality — of quest fables dressed up as love stories — characterises the romance genre in Hindi cinema at its best. Sometimes, though not often enough, there are other levels too, as in *Sahib, Bibi Aur Ghulam* (1962), *Sujata* (1959), *Guide* (1965) and *Mughal-e-Azam*, to name only a few.

Each of these four films contains more than just a hero and a villain, supposedly the two stock characters of 'formula-ridden box-office cinema'. *Sahib, Bibi Aur Ghulam* has the key third character of Chhoti Bahu, played brilliantly by Meena Kumari as the 'other woman' in the hero's life; *Sujata* has the foster mother as a key character on whom the fate of the relationship between the hero and heroine depends; *Guide's* third key protagonist is the discarded husband of Rosie, who is in love with Raju Guide. The husband's return influences the entire course of the second half of the film, which has no traditional villain. And *Mughal-e-Azam* has the great Prithviraj Kapoor playing Akbar the father, who must rescue his rebellious son Salim from the emotional clutches of that *kaneez*, that servant girl, Anarkali. The film's villain is another *kaneez* who is Anarkali's rival for Salim's affections. The father's opposition cannot, however, be reduced to simple villainy.

The romance which rocked a whole kingdom-Anarkali (Madhubala) and Salim (Dilip Kumar) share a moment of sensuous bliss. Salim is already dreaming of their future. But all this is before his father, Akbar, learns of it—in K Asif's Mughal-e-Azam (1960).

He is determined that Salim recognise reasons of state as more compelling than reasons of the heart. He understands that his son is in love with Anarkali, but the marital alliances of princes and kings are matters of state — above and beyond personal desire and heartbreak. Salim begs to differ, and father goes to war with son.

The result, in each of the above films, is to make you look at the story not only from the viewpoint of the protagonist in conflict with society, but also from a third angle. Perhaps it is these other levels which the romance also touches that makes it India's most popular cinematic genre.

Love then and now

Even before cinema came to dominate the narrative universe of the Indian imagination, however, love stories had been our favourite stories — the stuff of popular legend and folk mythology. In her study of the *quissa* (fable) tradition as embodied in Urdu/Hindi folktales that were very popular in north India until the 1930s, when the Hindi movie put them in the shade, American historian Frances Pritchett says:

> Quests may have various goals: the answer to some mysterious question, the possession of some magic object, the destruction of some deadly monster (like Mogambo in the film *Mr India*, or Gabbar Singh in *Sholay*, you might add, just to take passing notice of the continuities between oral folk tales and contemporary Hindi cinema)...
>
> But the most commonplace kind of quest is the search for union with some beloved. Stories like *Laila Majnun* and *Shirin Farhad*, in which passionate love appears as the central obsession of the lovers' whole lives, have been a minor, though persistent, part of the quissa tradition. (Pritchett 1985: 8)

The big change from India before cinema, to India today may be that passionate love stories have now graduated from being a minor to a major part of our narrative universe. But this passion, this love story, these lovers of today, are a little different from Laila and Majnu. Lovers' options in the face of parental opposition are *not* now limited to sacrificing love or death, as was the case with our legendary couples.

Today's lovers can elope; there is another world out there. The train leaving town (or village) travels much faster than the horses on which our legendary lovers tried to escape — often in vain. Lovers today — both on- and off-screen — have the option of migrating to the big city and getting lost in its anonymity, as happens in Mani Ratnam's *Bombay* (1994); or of wearing down the opposing parent through a series of chess-like moves, as the hero does in *Dilwale Dulhaniyan Le Jayenge* (1995).

These are two of a dozen new options offered us by the love fables of Hindi cinema over the last 50 years. The message at the end of each film is — love is blind, maybe, but it is the most sacred, most life-enhancing state of being you can hope for during your residence on earth.

This availability of choices for lovers is part of a new, post-colonial and post-war urban-industrial culture of self-authorship, in which identifying and pursuing your career has become one of modern life's most significant acts. Careers in this modern sense fill life with meaning — onscreen as well as off. Aspirations, dreams, success and failure all come into play in this new pursuit — making your life an adventure, a romance. Fiction, to be relevant and appealing — 'popular' in one word — explores and depicts these issues at the level of the imagination.

Thus we have a whole series of films like *Aawara, Shri 420, Bambai Ka Babu, Barsaat Ki Raat, Madhumati, Anari, Mr & Mrs 55, Pyaasa, Satyakam,* and Sai Paranjpye's delightfully light-hearted *Chashme Baddoor* (1981), followed by her *Katha* (1983) — which are all about careers and individual lives. Falling in love, identifying and winning over a complete stranger who will be your lifemate, is part and parcel of this new project (called modernity).

I love you, but I also love the fact that you have a career, Madhubala seems to say to Bharat Bhushan in this scene from Barsaat Ki Raat (1960).

From *karma* to career

In a society like Old India, steeped as it used to be in the oral tradition until the 1920s with a literacy rate well below 10 per cent, says sociologist David Riesman,

> 'individuals have life-cycles — they live through childhood; they are initiated; they become adult; they grow old; they die. But they do not have careers in our modern sense of the term...'(Riesman, 1955 : 6)

(This is not to run down the oral tradition, which has many plus points; it is merely to note that careers and identity crises are not part of that culture.)

To find a career is to treat life as a project, a malleable entity — open to change. Not just life, your identity is also a project in this sense. Aspiring to a career means individuals pursuing personal agendas through education and training geared to particular job-tracks in the industrial economy. This whole identity/career thing became a popular aspiration in urbanising India after mass schooling and the availability of industrial/administrative jobs for degree-holders began to change the landscape of our collective imagination.

In this changed landscape, the movie viewer looks at stories of characters pursuing their individual quests/careers onscreen (as well as

Student lovers in a changing landscape. Rajesh Khanna & Sharmila Tagore in Safar (1970).

in 'bestseller' novels), and finds them deeply engaging because they offer a psychic mobility. You come away with a vivid even if imaginary sense of what it is like to travel down one career path as against another.

Riesman continues, suggesting another parallel:

> 'The novel of the 19th century, as its critics contended, doubtless disoriented many chambermaids and a few duchesses, but on many more occasions it helped prepare individuals for their careers in a disorienting world of rapid industrialisation and urbanisation, where, indeed, fictional moves and actual ones were not so unlike, and life and art could almost imitate each other.' (Riesman 1974 : 35)

The dramatic structure of the Hindi movie has done in a largely illiterate India what the novel did in 19th century Europe. The European novel, especially the *Bildungsroman* or quest fable, with its focus on the protagonist's motives, demanded of the reader that she/he project herself into the experiences portrayed. So, in a way, has the Hindi film at its best. One thinks of films like *Sujata, Aawara, Andaaz, Taraana, Amar, Pyaasa, Mughal-e-Azam, Sahib, Bibi Aur Ghulam, Anupama, Guide, Benazir*, to name a few from the 1950s-60s.

The Hindi film at its best invites the viewer to project himself into the experiences portrayed on screen.

Consider this remark of a Bombay housewife, P Bhargavi, interviewed recently in a special feature by a city newspaper:

> Mughal-e-Azam! Wah, what a great film. I was very young when I saw it, and I still remember the Sheesh Mahal (glass palace) set erected specially for the film. Beautiful Madhubala dancing to 'Mohe panghat pe nandlal...' Ever since, I have dreamt of becoming a dancer. Every time Prithviraj Kapoor would deliver his dialogues, I would tremble in my seat. I still hate the vile looks of Nigar Sultana as the vamp. I wonder why a commoner cannot love a prince? (Bhargavi 2000: 4)

Some other things have also changed in the way we fashion our love stories today: love does not usually end tragically, as did the romances of Laila-Majnu, Devdas, etc. On the contrary, it often ends happily. So imperative has the happy ending now become that film director K. Asif had to modify the climax of the great Anarkali-Salim love story in which, history records, Anarkali was buried alive. In Asif's *Mughal-e-Azam*, Anarkali is allowed (by the emperor himself) to escape from her grave through an underground tunnel on condition that she never returns to Agra and that the world—including Salim—continues to believe that she was indeed killed. She accepts, and leaves town to start another life, a loveless life.

A small window of possibility, the possibility of another chance at life for both Anarkali and Salim, was thus opened up, amending a medieval legend that had for generations been known as a tragedy ending in Anarkali's death. Asif's amendment may not be a happy ending, but it is not completely tragic either.

By the 1960s, dying for love had become passé, as Sunil Dutt & Waheeda Rehman show us in this happy ending scene from Ek Phool Chaar Kaante (1960).

Our Anarkali (the Anarkali of 1960s India), could not die for love. Dying had become passé, without anyone consciously saying so. That sort of ending had somehow become unacceptable for love stories in Nehruvian India, perhaps because more and more people now found themselves able to accept the idea of love.

Bunny Reuben, Bombay-based film journalist and novelist, in his collection of movie memories, *Follywood Flashback*, makes a perceptive observation on the depiction of love in Hindi cinema:

> Somebody once quipped that it was Raj Kapoor who invented love on the Indian screen...What Raj Kapoor actually achieved when he first stormed the gates of *Follywood* in the late-forties was this: he kicked open the doors of prudery and let in a great gust of fresh air which vitalised the art and technique of film-making in general and the art of filming the love scene in particular, both of which had suffered from an overdose of dialogue.
>
> When Raj Kapoor made *Aag* (1948-49), he introduced for the first time...a new and intense romanticism which consisted of stylistic and highly visual love scenes...so that even without actual kissing, these love scenes had a bold and startling impact. (The) love scenes of *Aag* and later of *Barsaat* fired the imagination of the young generation...(Reuben 1993: 249)

Raakhee & Rajesh Khanna in Shehzada *(1972) show us how to love intensely while maintaining a two-and-a-half milimetre distance between their lips.*

A popular song expressing this change, from *Gora Aur Kaala* (1972), comes to mind at this point. It has a point-counterpoint form, and begins with the heroine urging her lover to be a little less open about announcing his love for her: '*Dheere-dheere bol koi sun na le, sun na le koi sun na le*...(Speak softly please, someone might hear what you are saying!)'

He: '*Hum ko kisi ka dar nahin, koi zor jawaani par nahin*! (I'm not afraid of anyone, for youth cannot be punished for just being romantic.)'

She again urges: '*Dheere-dheere bol koi sun na le, koi sun na le*. (Speak softly...)'

He: '*Hum ko kisi ka dar nahin, koi zor jawaani par nahin.../ Kuch kah le, kuch kar le yeh sansaar, hum premee hain, hum to karenge pyaar*...(Be not afraid of being young, let the world say or do what it will, nothing can stop me from loving you...)'

She: '*Koi dekh le, koi jaan le*...(What if someone sees us, what if someone finds out about us...?)'

He: '*O jaan le, koi dosh hamare sir nahin, koi dosh jawaani par nahin*! (Let them find out! We haven't done anything wrong, we are just young, and youngsters cannot be blamed for falling in love!)'

What made this song a big hit with audiences may well have been the fact that in real life too, falling in love and marrying someone of your choice was not by the 1970s as much of a scandal as it was in the 1870s, or the 1920s. Romance, even in real life, was not inconceivable anymore. Oh sure, it shook the local earth, but only for a while, and then many such couples got married in increasing numbers of cases, and lived pretty much the way couples who had had arranged marriages did.

To get a fuller sense of this slow acceptance of the idea of the 'love marriage' over the last 50 years, an event of major cultural significance on the nation's social and imaginative landscape, will be the aim of what follows.

Women in love

... a moment later the camera pulls away and shows you how her whole frame looks, and feels... Just after her loved one has left. Rose in Hamari Betiyan (1936).

Let us begin by switching lenses and looking at love in cinema from the female point of view. Consider firstly, this summary of a popular piece of folk theatre, the *Laila-Majnu* legend, as regularly presented on stage in the villages and towns of north India. The following passage explains what happens after Laila's family discovers and disapproves her love for Majnu:

> The family's preoccupation with *izzat* (reputation, honour) necessitates 'protecting' Laila, preserving her in a chaste and chastened state until a suitable marriage is contracted. The family's fear of losing *izzat* causes them to withdraw her from school to prevent the lovers from meeting...At every turn her movements are controlled by physical force...The play is full of parents' and elders' preachings about female virtue...The restraints imposed on Laila as a woman...are not present for Majnun as a male...(Hansen 1992: 148)

The female protagonist of popular love legends from *Heer-Ranjha, Laila-Majnu, Sohni-Mahiwal*, right up to the film *Devdas* (1935), was someone who had little or no control over her own life — especially after her love affair is discovered. She lived in a safe, tightly-insulated family space; all

This is the world in which love starts as scandal and ends as a tragedy. Nanda's tears, in Mohabbat Isko Kahte Hain *(1965, bespeak her anxiety about whether her truckdriver lover will ever return...*

her movements were marked. For a person so confined, falling in love was a *scandal*: a woman could not act as an adult, as an individual with a mind of her own. An unmarried young woman in the male-dominated 'Indian tradition' had the freedom only to be a child. If she dared to cross the clearly-defined boundaries, her brothers, parents and village elders quickly brought her to book.

Romantic love, in the sense of persons making individual, personal, idiosyncratic choices about who they will love and marry, has no legitimate place in Indian culture. This is the world, the 'tradition' we are coming from. This is a world in which love starts as a scandal and ends as a tragedy.

Within such a male-dominated culture centred on *izzat* (family honour), the love story coming to dominate Bombay filmdom's output year after year was itself a scandal. What made things worse was that these scandals had happy endings! And titles like *Pyar Jhukta Nahin, Pyar Ki Jeet, Love Marriage, Dil Tera Diwana, Dil Deke Dekho, Honeymoon, Love in Tokyo, Love in Simla*, and *Cha-cha Cha*!

But one can't get very far with this term 'scandal'. It is best used as a pointer to something beyond itself — to the social processes that were already in motion before becoming movie material.

Social processes like the westernisation of urban India under British colonialism (especially in cities like Bombay and Calcutta), like mass schooling that was age-graded, open to both boys and girls, secular and independent of the caste system. By the 1930s the youngsters coming out of this European-style mass education system were so many that they constituted a 'new generation', which was already pro-change, and nationalistic. By the 1940s, this social current had intensified further, and films like *Khandaan* (1942), *Kismet* (1943), *Humraahi* (1945), *Andaz* and *Barsaat* (both 1949) reflected this change, which had already been initiatated by 1930s films like *Achchut Kanya* (1935), *Graduate* (1936), and *Jawaani Ki Hawa* (1935).

In the background but equally significant were industrialisation and the growth of cities that employed thousands of anonymous, faceless people in factories and offices. This anonymity could also be a boon, however. It enabled you to pursue your individual dreams without the whole world getting to know about it. And even when some part of the world got to know of your pursuits, there were those who silently supported you. Consider in this context the case of Shweta Shetty, a young Bombay-born pop singer who made waves in the music world in the 1990s:

A beauty with brains: Sadhna embodies the 'new generation' in this reflective close-up from Asli-Naqli (1962).

> Shweta Shetty, born to a conservative South Indian family, invited the wrath of her father and six years of his silence, by straying from the path of early marriage and child-bearing. Her father was further enraged by the fact that her mother used to sell gold and ornaments gifted by him to provide Shweta pocket-money. Even as her three sisters were duly married, Shweta entered the Mumbai stage as part of Shiamak Davar's Best of Broadway troupe, which is where she was spotted and singled out for a host of live gigs and a deal with Magnasound (a music company)...(Mehta 1999: 7)

Many similar real-life stories can be found in the biographies of Bombay filmdom's female stars, and even more so among young women who didn't make it in filmdom but went on to blossom elsewhere. This was such a trend in 1950s India that one of the big hits of 1954, *Taxi Driver*, focused on just this theme.

Colleges, cycles and courtship: Youth on wheels

Since the 1930s, factors such as urbanisation, higher and postgraduate education in universities for increasing numbers of young middle class men and women, the motor car, the scooter, the motorbike and the bicycle, together contributed to the birth of a youth culture that was different from the culture of the traditional family. The young in their teens and 20s had places (like colleges, libraries, sports grounds, restaurants, cinemas, and out-of-town picnic spots) to go to and escape the family for the better part of each day. In these new spaces, a vibrant youth subculture had begun, gropingly, to take form. The bicycle — with its combination of personal mobility, affordability and privacy — was one expression of it. You could go off on your own, or together with friends on out-of-town picnics, which became increasingly popular as a 'youth' thing in 1950s India — both onscreen and off. Two bicycle films that immediately come to mind are *Anari* (1959) and *Chhalia* (1960); they both feature the female protagonist (Nutan in both cases) out picnicking with her friends. The sight of young women having fun singing and cycling was quite revolutionary for audiences in the 1950s.

Love on the bicycle and Love in trees: Shyama & Johnny Walker in Duniya Rang Rangili (1957).

The movies, especially the Hindi movies of post-1947 India, logged on to this nascent youth culture and gave it form, style, content — at a time when no other institution was doing so. Hollywood and West European cinema, it must be acknowledged here, had set the ball rolling in this respect all over the world, including in cities like Bombay, Karachi, Lahore and Calcutta. Bombay's film industry picked up the trend and Indianised it with great success, especially in the first two decades after Independence. In those two remarkable decades alone, the movies became an integral part of India's public and personal culture.

The opening lines of another bicycle song from the film *Shararat* (1959) summed up this new mood: '*Hum matwaale naujawaan,/ Manzilon ke ujaale,/ Log karein badnaami,/ Kaise yeh duniyanwale*? (We the spirited young, who are society's future,/ Are often maligned for being so full of life,/ What sort of society is this?)'

Enter, the unmarried young woman

Look a little closer now at popular love stories on the Hindi screen from 1951's landmark film *Aawara* onwards. It is not just that they have happy endings; the whole narrative, including the way the hero and heroine enter into a relationship, bespeaks social change from the moment they first meet.

The first difference is that the female protagonist in these films is not just a picture of girlish innocence, frailty and beauty; she is also a thinking adult with substantial reserves of courage and inner strength. Almost every movie comes to a point where the heroine's strengths are severely tested, and she comes through with flying colours each time.

Vidya in *Shri 420*, Anarkali in *Mughal-e-Azam*, Sujata in the film of that name, are just three of a thousand such films that come to mind. Here is just a brief listing of films on the unmarried young woman in Hindi cinema: *Miss 1933* (1933), *Actress* (1948), *Ajeeb Ladki* (1952), *Akeli Mat Jaiyo* (1963), *College Girl* (1960), *Dr Vidya* (1962), *Gumraah* (1963), *Policewali* (1949), *Shama* (1961), *Main Abla Nahin Hoon* (1949), *Miss Chalbaaz* (1961), *Modern Girl* (1961), *Miss Coca Cola* (1955), *Miss Goodnight* (1960), *Miss Mala* (1954), *Miss Mary* (1957), *Miss Bombay* (1957), *Miss India* (1957), *Gypsy Girl* (1961), *Rocket Girl* (1962), *Madam Zapatta* (1962), *Madam Zoro* (1962), *Shrimati 420* (1956), *Vidya* (1948)

What we get in these films is a Sita-like strength from someone who is not yet married, as Sita was.

Miss college girl on a bicycle: Meena Kumari on wheels in Miss Mary *(1957).*

Cinema broke completely from folk theatre and the older mythology of which it was part, in its portrayal of the strength and moral courage of the unmarried woman. Hitherto, only married women in our mythology, our 'tradition' both high and low, could possess such qualities. Vidya, Anarkali and Sujata are all unmarried, as are most other major female leads on screen — like Rekha (Shakila) in *Reshmi Roomaal* (1961), and Rita in *Aawara*.

In the two big Indian archetypes of the woman as wife (modelled on Sita, the pure sati-savitri), and the woman as mother (as embodied in the goddesses Durga and Kali), there is no place for the unmarried woman. Folk culture, especially folk theatre between 1870 and 1930, did create room for an additional archetype of woman as suffering widow and/or young, betrayed mother with illegitimate child. But nowhere in all these popular representations is there any room for the single, young, unmarried woman.

Girls just wanna have fun! Mala Sinha in Gumraah (1963).

How do you deal with a woman in her 20s, who plans to study until graduation, and maybe work after that? Rajesh Khanna worries over this question, while Hema Malini the young, unmarried woman dances on his head (almost) in Prem Nagar (1974).

How do you deal, culturally and symbolically, with the woman who is just entering her 20s, who plans to study until graduation and beyond before getting married, or one who has just finished her degree and plans to work — as a lawyer, a teacher, a doctor, a business person, a hotel manager, sometimes even a police officer? In filling that gap in the vocabulary of femininity, popular Hindi cinema has created a whole new mythology of the unmarried woman as 20th century India's Heroine No. 1.

This new figure was not created *ex nihilo* by our filmmakers; mythical figures never are. They tend instead to be a blend of old and new figures. So the new post-colonial woman the 1950s movies gave us was part-Sita, and part-educated, modern person growing up in a democratic culture.

What happens in *Aawara*, in *Taxi Driver*, *Shri 420*, *Nau Do Gyarah*, *Mr & Mrs 55*, *Sujata*, *Barsaat Ki Raat*, *Anari*, *Mere Mehboob* and other films is that the heroine, like the hero, is also shown as a person with a mind of her own, and with the resources to choose her own mate. In *Aawara*, Nargis plays Rita, a lawyer who summons the courage to take up Raju the vagabond's case against her own father, the court's judge; in *Taxi Driver* (1954), Mala, the poor, homeless migrant (Kalpana Kartik) declines a career as a singer in films so as not to jeopardise her relationship with the taxi driver she loves. He, in turn, goes out of his way to support her dream of a singing career. In the end, of course, they get each other, and nothing else seems to matter thereafter. Such noble souls both of them — one competing with the other to be nobler than thou. Where will you find such nobility these days?

Not in real life perhaps. But in that flattering mirror called cinema, you will. It feels good to know that way back in 1954 our heroes and heroines were so sensitive to each other's needs as individuals. While there is no easy measure of the social effects of such positive feelings and ideas in dozens of popular films, their cumulative impact has surely been a civilising one in a post-colonial nation still grappling with its identity. (This, at any rate, is the impression you get every time you chance upon 40- and 50-year-olds chatting and reminiscing, over a drink or two after sunset, about films from the black-and-white years. The confessional anecdotes come tumbling out, as do lines from this or that 'unforgettable' song. Unforgettable, it often turns out, for its role in giving one's adolescence a sense of direction.)

In *Nau Do Gyarah* (1957), the heroine Raksha (Kalpana Kartik) runs from the marriage hall minutes before the ceremony is to begin. And this is not because her lover is waiting to help her escape; no, she leaves by smuggling herself into the boot of a stranger's car parked nearby, and she does this all alone. Reason: she will find her own mate, maybe even a career, and risk the possibility of failure in this quest, but she will not accept an arranged marriage. 'I'd rather die than live like this,' she seems to say. And the viewer applauds her sentiment...

Reflections in the camera's eye

The movie camera has a lot to do with this change in our imaginative landscape. The camera encourages filmmakers to change the image of woman as Victim and *Abla* ('the powerless one': a synonym for 'woman' in colloquial Hindi) to the woman with the self-confidence to rewrite her life! Cinema as a medium demands that its characters be engaging in a particularly intense and forceful way; if they are not, our attention wanders. The camera derives its power from the large amount of information it can encompass in one shot. At its best, the movie camera has a richness that exceeds the human eye.

It takes you within a touching inch of the character's skin, then gives you a sensuous close-up of her lips, and the half-smile in her eyes. A moment later it pulls away from her face and shows you how her whole frame looks, and feels, standing against a blank wall, or in a doorway just after her loved one has left. In addition, there are the simultaneously operating elements of light and shade, of background sound/music. And don't forget the set — what the French call the *mise-en-scene* — that the camera directs our meaning-seeking eyes to.

Placed in the midst of such a multi-faceted medium, you the viewer, identifying completely with *Mother India*'s Radha or *Mughal-e-Azam*'s Anarkali, must magnify yourself, just to be worthy of the power of the movie camera. The 'real you' is perhaps too small and vague for the actor facing a movie camera; perhaps it is best left at home. What the camera revels in is you the actor — the unreal, larger-than-life you.

Little wonder then that on the Hindi screen, if nowhere else, men and women are equals. This is not to deny that almost all our films are man-centred. But despite this male bias in the narration of story and development of character, the heroine is perceived as an equal — by the hero.

The heroine — as presented to us by Nargis the spoilt, rich daughter who throws out a big, burly bearer who brings her food on her father's orders in the film *Chori Chori* (1956), or as Meena Kumari who dismounts from her horse with practised ease after her daily exercise in *Azaad* (1955), or as Mala Sinha marching into class with a brief contemptuous glance thrown at the male students whistling at her in *Pyaasa* (1957) — has an equal right to the pursuit of happiness, and is usually more than the hero's equal in strength of feeling and character. It is because she is perceived as an equal that the hero must woo and win her. Parental and social obstacles come later, but the first and most important step is winning her heart. The story cannot move unless he takes on this primary task.

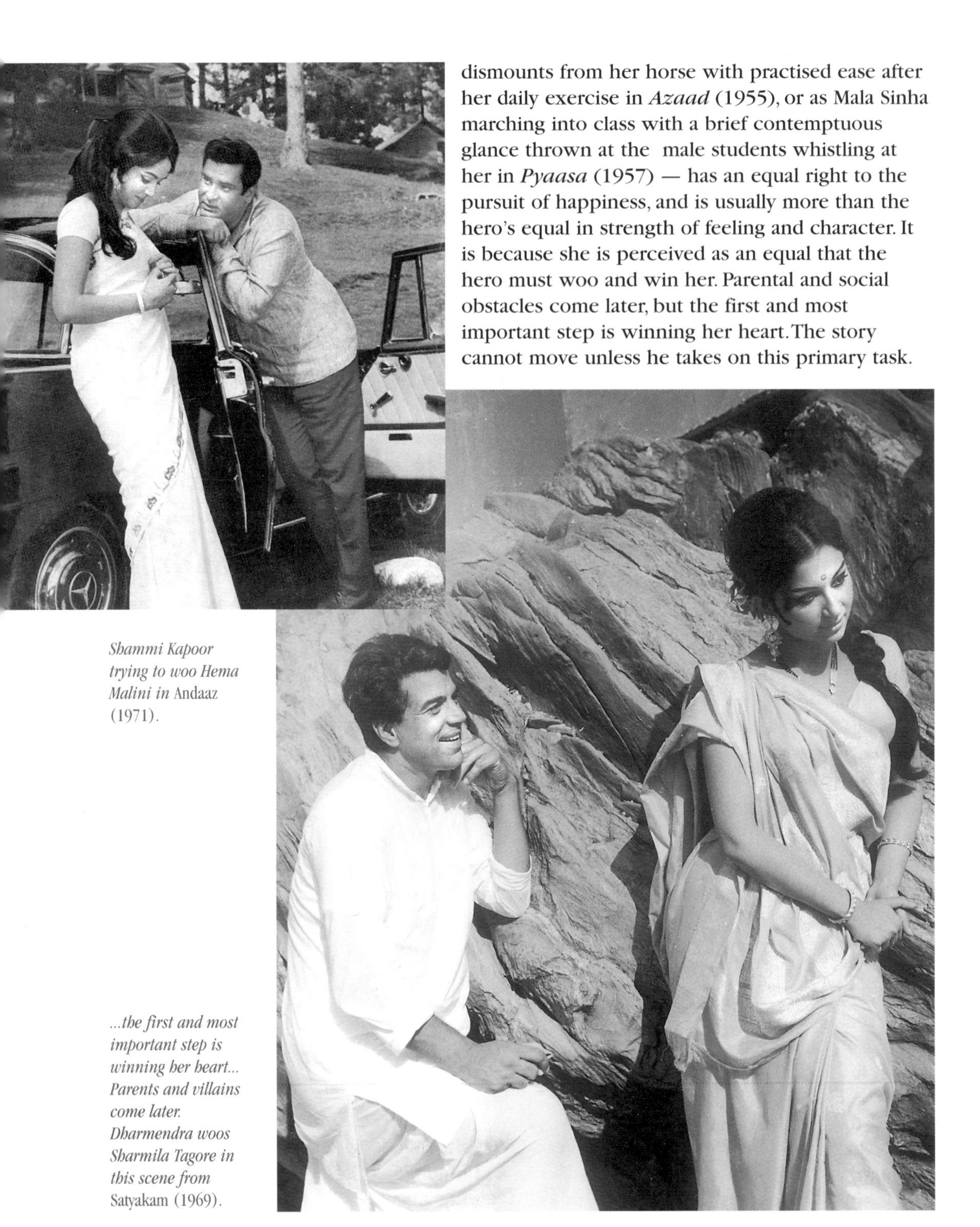

Shammi Kapoor trying to woo Hema Malini in Andaaz (1971).

...the first and most important step is winning her heart... Parents and villains come later. Dharmendra woos Sharmila Tagore in this scene from Satyakam (1969).

In this project, the hero must sometimes change his whole identity, as happens, for instance, in *Kashmir Ki Kali* (1964), where the heroine is a mere flower-seller in Kashmir, while the hero is a big *sahib* from Bombay. But she doesn't care a fig for *sahibs*, so the hero presents himself as the *sahib's* driver, and this charade continues through much of their courtship. In *Asli-Naqli* (1962) again, it is necessary for the hero to hide his upper-class identity, and live in a poor people's chawl in order to win her heart. It also works the other way sometimes: in *Anari* (1959) the rich heroine has to pose as the domestic servant in her own home in order to elicit the jobless hero's interest.

Love on the screen, in short, is the great equaliser.

Even in a medieval romance like *Mughal-e-Azam*, set in 16th century Agra, where Anarkali is a domestic servant in Prince Salim's palace, the power equation between them changes when the prince falls in love with her. Anarkali's friend now enters as a key mediator and messenger between the two lovers. A few days pass and some letters are secretly exchanged, before the prince summons the courage to ask her to meet him at a stipulated place and time. After some hesitation, she obliges him — her master and lover — by keeping the appointment.

As the story unfolds, it is Anarkali who emerges as the stronger character in the conflict with the emperor. At no point, secondly, do we see Anarkali doing any of the chores that other domestic servants are seen to do. She is only shown dancing before the emperor because the queen mother asks her to, on the occasion of Lord Krishna's birthday, Janmashtami.

From their very first meeting, which takes place with Salim shooting an arrow to unveil a figure he thinks is a statue, Anarkali is presented to us as someone very different from the rest of her class. After the unveiling, he and Akbar are astonished to discover that the statue was actually a living woman (Anarkali) standing in as a favour to the sculptor who had failed to complete the work assigned to him. So Anarkali's first appearance on screen is as a woman of exceptional courage, who risks her life just to protect an artist from imperial wrath.

The post-colonial Hindi film, moreover, in taking a stand against casteism and feudal consciousness, endorses the claim that women as much as men have the right to marry for love. Not just marry for love, Asha Parekh in *Dil Deke Dekho* goes a step further by denouncing her would-be husband for having stolen from her 'the right to dream': 'I hate him for that,' she announces to her friends, and then proceeds in the rest of the film to sabotage this arranged marriage. A new idea was proposed and popularised by the movies — reasons of the heart. Those reasons justified the woman's right to choose her life partner.

Happiness, in these films, is arrived at when a couple overcomes social obstacles to their love, and also obstacles between and within themselves (as in *Aawara, Shri 420, Pyaasa, Sujata* and *Sitara*).

The number of Raj Kapoor-like Aawaras and Anaris, Dilip Kumar-like Salims and Sharaabis, Nargis-like Mothers India and Meena Kumari-like Chhoti Bahus quietly walking around the streets of India and cutting across local ethnicities, ran into millions by the end of the '60s. In countless Indian hearts the characters and styles created by these and other major film stars of the 1950s and '60s continue to live in a myriad individual permutations and combinations. Shammi Kapoor was the star who redefined the very meaning of being young in the 1960s, until Rajesh Khanna came along and dominated the 1967-73 period. Change the names of the movies and the stars, and the same can be said of the 1990s generation.

Falling in love with cinema's idea of love

When you say, as I do in these essays, that the movies are an important, living part of your imaginative landscape, you don't really mean movies in general. No, you mean some movies, some scenes, some characters, some songs. We viewers are discriminating, eccentric individuals. While lists of favourite films vary from one viewer to another as a result, variety is only half the story. The other half is shared tastes, which result in some films becoming big box-office hits — because they figure on most viewers' lists. The imaginary towns or villages of these shared 'blockbusters', populated by characters like Radha in *Mother India*, Chhoti Bahu in *Sahib, Bibi Aur Ghulam*, Gabbar Singh and the armless Thakur in *Sholay*, Raju the jobless young man of *Shri 420* and *Anari* etc, are what we hold in common. These characters are us, or part of us at any rate. Love stories in this context are distinctive in that our involvement with their characters is a little more intimate, and a little deeper than with big, emblematic characters like Radha, Raju, or Gabbar Singh.

In *Mughal-e-Azam* for instance, our involvement is greatest with Anarkali, who is visibly nervous about her meetings with Prince Salim, furtive in her desire for him, and mature in her handling of the conflict inherent in desiring someone with the social status of a prince. Salim and Akbar, in contrast, are characters with a capital 'C'. They are admirable, but not figures who invite your involvement, as does the vulnerable Anarkali.

From my list of love stories, here are some which have given me pure, total, viewing pleasure, and also shaped my sensibility — *Barsaat Ki Raat, Taraana, Sujata, Paying Guest, Mughal-e-Azam, Aar Paar, Mr &*

Meena, played by Indrani Mukherji in Dharamputra (1961)*. You can't blame the hero for being smitten by her, especially when she thinks his amateurish poems are worth reading (!)*

Mrs 55, Benazir, Anpadh, Ek Musafir Ek Hasina, Ek Phool Chaar Kaante, Bambai Ka Babu, Shola Aur Shabnam, Teen Devian, Dharamputra, Teesri Kasam, Bluff Master, from the black-and-white era, and *Mere Mehboob, Phir Wohi Dil Laaya Hoon, Teesri Manzil, Kashmir Ki Kali, Ek Duje Ke Liye, Chashme Baddoor, Chhoti Si Baat, Guide, Umrao Jaan, Muqaddar Ka Sikandar*, and *Dilwale Dulhaniyan Le Jaayenge*, from the colour era.

The pleasure in watching the first meeting, for instance, between Dilip (Shashi Kapoor) and Meena (Indrani Mukherji) in Yash Chopra's *Dharamputra* (1961) came from the charming combination of naturalism and fantasy. Dilip, a student leader-cum-poet, is smitten by Meena, a girl in his college, and happens to ask his sister about her. The time and place are 1940s, pre-Partition Delhi. Meena, it turns out, is his sister Rekha's friend. So Rekha (Tabassum) calls Meena over for lunch the next day. Dilip returns from college after searching in vain for Meena in various classrooms, and is shocked to find her — the woman of his dreams — sitting in his room, reading his poems!

At first he is tongue-tied. She, on the other hand, is completely relaxed, for she likes him, his room, his poems. Seeing her interest in his poems, he offers to recite a *ghazal* he wrote just last night — which was written while dreaming of her (though he doesn't tell her that). Inspired by this dream-come-true situation, he renders the *ghazal* in song -'*Bhool sakta nahin tumhaari aankhen, neend se bhaari tumhari aankhen*...(Can't forget your eyes, these eyes which are so heavy and beautiful with sleep...)'

It is a charming, simple song. They end up holding hands by the time he reaches the last stanza. As they do so, we see him on the floor, she on the chair next to him...Their souls having made contact, it seems natural that they should be holding hands towards the end of their very first meeting. They are in love, and you are in love with them.

Unlike most films, Dilip and Meena don't dance around trees, nor do they go to some beautiful locale such as Switzerland or Budapest as has become so common in recent years. They remain in the room, he singing his *ghazal*, she smiling at being adored so poetically by a handsome, creative young man. Just outside the room, Dilip's mother and sister stand smiling indulgently at the lovers. The song ends when they can't hold themselves back anymore and barge in to express their happiness at the event.

Another treeless scene-cum-song that is a personal favourite — though I don't have anything against trees per se, on the contrary in fact — is from Guru Dutt's *Aar Paar* (1954). The scene is the interior of Birju's (Guru Dutt) taxi, where his ex-beloved, Shyama, has come to explain why she did not run away with him as promised some days ago. He refuses to speak to her, despite her best efforts to explain her conduct. Meanwhile, the taxi cruises through Bombay's streets. As a last resort she breaks into song, using words which she knows he wants to hear from her: '*Ye-lo main haari piyaa*...(Okay-okay, I lose, you win, my love...)'

Thus disarmed, Birju slowly, reluctantly, but in the end happily, relents. In thus bringing him around to her point of view, Shyama provides us a lesson in love-play — she alternates between throwing herself at him, and drawing away the next moment. She sweet-talks and flatters him, then plays at being rejected. The net effect of this performance is to boost Birju the taxi driver's ego and reduce the magnitude of her lapse in his eyes. The result?

And this is what disapproving fathers do to young love: Salim and Anarkali soon after Akbar has rejected any possibility of their marriage.

You guessed it — towards song's end, Birju puts his arms around her and draws her close, and she snuggles up even closer. 'Now don't you ever leave me again,' he seems to say, without saying it. Throughout this scene, not a word escapes Birju's lips — he is one of those strong, silent types — but his face speaks volumes. The happiness on Shyama's face at having finally brought him around is more, much more than that of a cat who has licked a bowl of cream.

What appeals to me about this scene is the way her singing turns the lovers' quarrel into a journey into the protagonists' hearts and inner conflicts. They are in love, but he has no place to stay, his income barely enough to support himself. She, the daughter of a garage owner, is almost 'affluent' in contrast. And then the relief, even pleasure at finding them make up and come close again. Finally, all is well with the world...

Endnotes

1. Love never surrenders.

2.The madness of youth.

3. Love has no culturally legitimate place in Indian society, and marriage is viewed essentially as a property alliance between socially compatible families. This is not to imply that love does not exist, it does, but it is a scandal each time. So strong is the family-marriage paradign that we cannot even imagine it happening in our film fictions without Family and Culture coming in the way. The villain in Hindi cinema is often someone who exploits these two forces to his advantage, especially in the films of the 1950s and '60s.

4.The spate of attacks in June 2001 by Muslim fundamentalists on cinema halls screening Sunny Deol's Gadar in Bhopal, Delhi and other cities is the most recent example of the hazards faced by films on historical themes. Perhaps anticipating trouble, the film makers added the sub-title — 'A love story' — to the film. It helped, but only partially.

5. How 'real' is real, is admittedly a question which varies from one viewing culture to another.The degree of credibility — call it 'naturalism' — expected of a Hollywood movie character is greater than what is expected by us in Hindi cinema, but the latter too has its rules of who counts as real and credible, and who doesn't.

References

Ashbery, John. 1989. *Reported Sightings*, A Knopf, New York.

Bhargavi, P. 2000. "Chalo Cinema", *Bombay Times*, 18 October.

Hansen, Kathryn. 1992. *Grounds for Play: The Nautanki Theatre in North India*, University of California Press, Berkeley.

Mehta, Salone. 1999. "Devastating Divas", *Bombay Times, The Times of India*, 27August.

Pritchett, Frances. 1985. *Marvelous Encounters — Folk Romance in Urdu and Hindi*, Manohar Books, Delhi.

Riesman, David. 1955. *The Oral Tradition, the Written Word and the Screen Image*, Antioch Press, U.S..

Reisman, David. 1974. "The Oral and Written Tradition" in *Explorations in Communication: An Anthology*, (eds.), E. Carpenter and M. Mcluhan, Beacon Press, Boston.

Reuben, Bunny. 1993. *Follywood Flashback*, Indus, Delhi.

Valicha, K. 1998. *Kishore Kumar*, Penguin Books, Delhi.

Wenders, Wim. 1986. *Emotion Pictures*, Verlag der Autoren, Frankfurt.

FILM - ROJA,

Lyrics: P K Mishra
Music: A R Rehman

Dil hai chhota sa, chhoti si asha
Masti bhare mann ki bholi si asha
Chaand taaron ko chhoone ki asha
Aasmaanon mein udne ki asha) - 2
Dil hai chhota sa, chhoti si asha

Mahek jaaoon main aaj to aise
Phool bagiya mein mahke hain jaise
Baadalon ki main odhoon chunariya
Jhoom jaaoon main banke baawariya
Apni choti mein baandh loon duniya!
Dil hai chhota sa, chhoti si asha
Masti bhare mann ki bholi si asha

Chaand taaron ko chhoone ki asha
Aasmaanon mein udne ki asha
Dil hai chhota sa, chhoti si asha
Masti bhare mann ki bholi si asha
Swarg si dharti khil rahi jaise
Mera mann bhi to khil raha aise
Koyal ki tarah gaane ka armaan
Machli ki tarah mach loon yeh armaan
Jawaani hai laayi rangeen sapna
Dil hai chhota sa, chhoti si asha
Masti bhare mann ki bholi si asha

Chaand taaron ko chhoone ki asha
Aasmaanon mein udne ki asha
Dil hai chhota sa, chhoti si asha
Masti bhare mann ki bholi si asha

The world about us would be desolate except for the world within us. There is the same interchange between these two worlds that there is between one art and another, migratory passings to and fro...

— Wallace Stevens (1994)

Ishq Aazaad Hai!

LOVE in Hindi cinema, as any fan will tell you, is subject enough for a whole book, maybe several books. In that case, the previous essay can claim to be an appetiser at best, which has touched upon some important issues, all of which are crying out for a more extended treatment. If that is how you feel, then this postscript is for you.

One reason for the seeming inexhaustibility of love as a subject in Hindi cinema is that here *ishq* does not simply translate as 'love'; it means much more. Mere love is for us offscreen mortals, if we are lucky. Cinematic *Ishq* on the other hand, is Love, Life, and everything in between!

Ishq Is Identity

Ishq is that big thing you do in life on becoming an *Aashiq*. On screen, this means being a free, romantic spirit, a rebel against injustice, a closet poet with high singing skills, an expert demolition man, and a good son engaged in reconstituting his whole life around *ishq*.

Ishq is identity: it sets you apart from the herd.

If love was all there was to *ishq*, then a lover was all the hero or heroine need be. But as we see in film after film, the two protagonists are much more than that. They have to be — the whole nation is watching.

Not just watching, but vicariously living another life through them.

Ishq is an omnibus term, open to many interpretations. Sum it up for the moment by calling *ishq* in Indian cinema 'a Liberalism of the Heart' — a liberalism that tolerates no social/cultural barriers of any kind in relationships, especially between the *aashiq* (lover) and his *maashuqa* (beloved).

Guns, fathers and villains are no match for the young daughter empowered by Ishq. Nutan and Raj Kapoor play the threatened lovers in this scene from Dil Hi Tho Hai (1963). *Nazir Husain is the angry gun-toting father, egged on by Pran the villain.*

Bharat Bhushan as Amaan the poet, just before delivering the verbal knockout punch in the qawwali *contest in* Barsaat Ki Raat (1960).

As Amaan Saheb (Bharat Bhushan) the poet-protagonist of Barsaat Ki Raat, one of the big romantic films of the early 1960s, proclaims at a climactic moment: '*Ishq aazaad hai! Hindu na Mussalman hai ishq...!*' (Love is free, a liberation! It is neither Hindu nor Muslim, but something bigger...). Love thus conceived is not a private affair between two people; it is a religion.

In cinematic country, *ishq* can make rivers sing, it can make God weep, it can melt rock, it can move the beloved to finally leave hearth and home (as in *Barsaat Ki Raat*), it can restore speech to the woman who has become mute (as in *Ghazal* 1964), it can render a forbidding father and society powerless. It can even snatch the heroine, our innocent victim, from the jaws of death. There she is, walking in a white sari down the railway track, walking determinedly to her death. Here comes this big, frightening engine with a full train in tow! Will the hero make it? A nano-second before the train actually hits her, our hero, guided by *ishq*, has reached the site and pulled her to safety. Whew! Yama, lord of death, has once again lost to Love and God. (Jingle bells, jingle bells...)

None of us are surprised, really, that he manages to save her. He had to. Nothing is impossible in Hindi cinema. God is a constant presence in our cinematic universe, no matter what happens in the real world.

Ishq is Music

Music is often the vehicle, the critical agent of Love, in making the impossible possible in this country of our imagination. Not in suicide scenes, of course, but in most other situations which require that the separated lovers seek each other out and overcome parents, villains or society.

The power of the musical word (that which makes the impossible possible) lingers for years and years in the rag-and-bone shop of our hearts — on a shelf there called 'utopia'. Treat the average Hindi moviegoer to one of a hundred favourite songs, and no matter where he happens to hear it, he will be transported.

All the world's a stage…And thank god for that

But before love, god and utopia carry us away, it helps to remind ourselves that the Hindi movie screen is the face of love — *and sex*. And special effects. The close-up and the dolly shot (on specially-designed, expertly-lit sets) are its means of communicating to us the smallest gesture and the subtlest of erotic emotions. The unseen wind machines send the heroine's *dupatta* (scarf) flying at crucial moments from her heaving bosom to the hero's face, and the rain machines help accentuate the heroine's voluptuous curves every time. Raj Kapoor, Bimal Roy, Guru Dutt and Yash Chopra were the four masters of camera and lighting who gave us some of the most unforgettable scenes of Hindi cinema in the 1950s, '60s and '70s.

All the world's a stage, even in filmland. Sunil Dutt & Mumtaz play Romeo and Juliet on stage in this scene from Humraaz (1967).

The make-up, those clothes which seem just right for the situation, the special lighting and camera tricks are, in other words, as integral to cinematic *ishq* as the poetry of the lovers' lines.

The synergy between these elements is what constitutes 'show business'. The show must go on, Raj Kapoor, arguably Indian cinema's greatest showman, was often heard saying. He was only repeating a truism. The show must go on because we viewers *want* it to go on. We need it — the artificial, other-reality of this 'tinsel town' — though we have a hard time explaining why.

Entertainment, Art, and Us

Looking back now at romantic films that succeeded at the box-office in the 1950s and '60s, you find that viewers flocked in the millions to pictures which were more than boy-meets-girl fables. In hits like *Aawara, Baiju Baawra, Nau Do Gyarah, Shri 420, Mr & Mrs 55, Chori Chori, Paying Guest, Chaudvin Ka Chand, Barsaat Ki Raat, Mere Mehboob, Dil Deke Dekho, Teen Devian, Junglee* and *Benazir*, to name a few, the romantic encounter was presented as part of a larger, emotionally engaging social/historical story.

To take just two films from the list above, the *nawab's* one-sided longing for a beautiful young woman he barely knows, and its tragic culmination in his suicide in *Chaudvin Ka Chand* (1960), is part of a larger story about the city of Lucknow and its Muslim urban culture. Similarly, *Chori Chori* is both about the encounter between rich girl-poor boy, and about the female protagonist's passage from girlhood to womanhood in what is overwhelmingly a man's world.

Perhaps this selective box-office success of some and not other love stories is 'natural', considering that the popular hunger for cinema is also a hunger for art, for meaning, direction, world-view. Even as I write this, I am aware that 'entertainment' is all we usually own up to when asked why this film appeals so much, and not that one. It is only when you probe the underlying, personal significance of the 'E' word for a cross-section of viewers that its roots in *our need for meaning* and direction tumble out — albeit slowly, reluctantly. A common response in many interviews conducted by this author was: 'Yes, the film has to be entertaining...but it must also have a good story.' And what is a good story, you ask? 'Well, something where...important social issues are taken up, you know, something contemporary, relevant — a situation, let's say, that I can place myself in and ask: what would I do if I were in her/his place?'

Johnny Walker & Helen provide an action image of two desis in a Spanish mood in Miss Coca Cola (1955).

We are generally a bit vague about cinema's place in our inner lives, and even more vague about the contribution of art. Since social science claims to understand human behaviour, of which this kind of reticence is surely a part, let us look for a moment at the science behind art.

> 'In the widest sense,' notes anthropologist M Herskovits, 'art is to be thought of as any embellishment of ordinary living that is achieved with competence and has describable form.' (Herskovits 1971: 203)

Another anthropologist, Roy Sieber, goes on to refine this useful but crude definition:

> ...The arts, as defined above, are symptomatic of cultural values and they are for the most part oriented positively, that is towards man's search for a secure and ordered existence...The arts at any time or place, in reflecting cultural values, evolve what might be called the "value image" that a culture has of itself. That image can become objectified so that it stands as a symbolic reinforcement of the values it reflects. (Sieber, Roy 1971: 205)

'Oriented positively' is a key phrase when describing the message, the *raison d'etre* of popular art, especially cinema. This positive imperative is a deeply-held convention, an unspoken pact between popular cinema and its viewers. The Happy Family with *siblings who are always supportive of each other* is one such value image. Lovers who are *eternally faithful,* and the Mother *as Anchor* in a rapidly-changing world are two other value images in the world of Hindi cinema (a world usually called '*Hindostan hamara*' in films of the 1940s to the 1970s).

Sex bombs are okay in fantasy, but actually getting one in your hands can be more than you bargained for. Jeetendra discovers this in his encounter with Radhika in the ominously titled Mera Pati Sirf Mera Hai (1990).

Saare jahan se achcha, yeh Hindostan hamara…[1]

It is not difficult to see why eternal lovers, happy families and good mothers became value images in the nation's formative years if we look for just a moment to the world outside the cinema hall — more specifically to the South Asian scenario from the 1940s onwards. In this real world, the year 1947 brought us both the end of colonialism, and the Partition of British India into Pakistan and India. The latter was an especially traumatic event that overshadowed the euphoria of freedom, devastated over a million families and scarred the collective psyche of a whole generation. Neighbours and old friends became enemies when the Partition connected religious identity with territory, putting borders and flags where there had been coexistence. Hindus had to suddenly leave behind homes in mixed neighbourhoods they had inhabited for generations simply because that home was now part of 'Muslim' territory, and the Muslims faced the same uprooting from 'Hindu' territory.

Repairing the shattered fabric of The Family as a social institution was a major cultural and social need in the aftermath of Partition. This was especially so at the level of the individual refugees and migrants engaged in reconstructing their lives in towns and cities that were new to them. Popular cinema (of the period 1950-70) answered this need in its own way — by mythicising the resilience of the family, projecting the nation as an extension of the family, and advocating an open, warm-hearted, modern-minded Indian culture. This openness was not just advocated; *it was glorified as the Good Life.*

This gamble worked, and Hindi filmdom reaped huge profits. Among the films which did this specially well are *Hum Log, Jaagriti, Waqt, Elaan, Mother India, Dharamputra, Shri 420, Mere Mehboob, Sujata, Tere Ghar Ke Saamne, Nau Do Gyaarah, Grahasti, Chhoti Bahu, Jis*

Desh Mein Ganga Behti Hai, and in a much lighter vein — *Ek Phool Char Kante*.

A song from *Jaagriti* (1954) comes to mind at this point. It is sung by a schoolteacher to his students with the inspiring portraits of Mahatma Gandhi and Subhash Chandra Bose looking down on the gathering from the school walls. It goes thus: '*Is desh ko rakhna/ Mere bachchon sambhal ke/ Hum laaye hain toofan se kashti nikaal ke...* (Look after this nation/ My children, with great, personal care/ It is a boat we have just rescued from the storm...)'

Two of the recurrent images of the Family restored focus on marital bonding (Balraj Sahni & Nirupa Roy in Aag Aur Pani*), and mother-son love (Lalita Pawar in* Baanwra*).* *[See Pic on facing page].*

The 1940s were the years when India was drawn into the vortex of the Second World War. It was the decade when the urban labour market grew dramatically, thereby intensifying the urban-rural divide, which only widened and deepened in subsequent decades. The Quit India Movement against the British Raj, the coming of Independence and Partition all happened in this decade. At both public and personal levels, then, the 1940s were the most 'happening' years in 20th-century India.

Nutan learns the philosophy of freedom on our behalf in this scene from Bandini (1963).

Bimal Roy (1909-1966)

Looking at the films made after Partition, especially at films which proved most appealing at the box-office like *Barsaat, Aawara, Bandini, Do Aankhen Baara Haath, Taraana, Baiju Baawra, Shri 420, Mother India, Dharamputra, Naya Andaaz, Asli Naqli, Mr & Mrs 55, Taxi Driver, Sujata, Waqt, Jaagriti, Anari* and *Mughal-e-Azam*, you find that they offered maps and stories to guide us through our turmoil and confusion vis-à-vis the post-colonial meaning of Indianness, freedom, industrialisation, the West and modernity.

(*Bandini's* maker, Bimal Roy, was himself a Partition refugee. *He belonged to a generation of gentle, modest people who prized human values.* — Mahasveta Debi)

'Reality' gets a new look, becomes *naya zamana*

People wanted a tangible, down-to-earth sense of the *naya zamana* (new age) that the 20th century was said to represent. The movies gave us the answers we sought - they were simplistic and vulgar, perhaps, but also persuasive to a degree most of us do not openly acknowledge. A whole nation was converted to the movies. Thus these pictures became much more than 'popular'. The movies made 'reality' bearable for most Indians — by making it appear changeable. (The naturalistic power of the camera was a big help in adding realism to this suggestion, in a culture where camera-realism was a new, mesmerising thing.)

Advocating an open, warm-hearted, modern-minded Indian culture, are Motilal and Shyama in Lalten (1956).

The maps and solutions that cinema provided Indians are what Roy Sieber above calls 'value images'. Value images such as Raju the tramp-like figure of *Shri 420* who picks himself up after being thrown out of the rich Seth Dharmanand's car where he was comfortably ensconced a moment ago. He now finds himself on a long, empty road, and his destination — the big city — is as many as 420 miles away from the site of his abandonment. Instead of feeling sorry for himself, Raj sets out on foot, with a smile and a song on his lips. You can't put this man down; his spirit is too strong for that.

The song he sings - '*Mera joota hai Japani, yeh patloon Inglistani, phir bhi dil hai Hindustani*' - was such a spirited number (laced with a pinch of black humour and self-deprecation) that it went on to become the song of the road, in and after 1955 when the film was released, for young Indians searching for a personal identity and a broad national orientation. Decades later, in 1999, this song inspired the title of a film — *Phir Bhi Dil Hai Hindustani* (Yet My Heart is Indian) — directed by Aziz Mirza.

Even a light-hearted comedy like Satyen Bose's *Chalti Ka Naam Gaadi* (1958) — a title which rather awkwardly translates as 'That Which Moves is a Car' — takes off with a song echoing the same attitude: '*Babu samjho ishaare, hawrun pukaare, pum-pum-pum... Chalte rehna, chalte rehna*...(Watch out, the horn calls pum-pum-pum,/...Keep moving, that's the secret of success today...)'

Love in this climate of nation-building could not be a private affair between two individuals. Even individuals could not be mere individuals; they had to be icons...

Love as religion, and energy

> The primary factor in film is the image, the secondary factor is the sound, the dialogue, and the tension between these two creates the third dimension (of cinematic art).
>
> — Ingmar Bergman

Screen love gets us immersed in it by the filmmaker constructing scenes which set our heart racing. Bergman's point that the tension between image and sound constitutes cinema, helps us make better sense of the famous *qawwali* scene in *Barsaat Ki Raat*, for instance. (A *qawwali* is a contest in verse and song between two groups of singers.) The soundtrack follows a fairly linear build-up from low to high. But the image, the action we see onscreen, is anything but linear. A lot happens both onstage *and offstage* while *Barsaat Ki Raat's* song contest is taking place. The two contending teams consist of the hero Amaan's *protégé* Shyama's group on one side, and the city's leading *qawwals*, an all-male group of professionals, on the other. Amaan is in the audience, watching this acid test of his students' presence of mind and singing skills.

Shortly after the first few two-liners about love's pros and cons have been traded between the contestants, Shyama, the lead singer of the

female group (who is also in love with Amaan Saheb), becomes terribly distressed! *It seems to happen all of a sudden*, and is surprising, considering that she had been preparing for this contest weeks in advance.

A moment later the camera reveals the cause of Shyama's distress: she has just seen Shabnam, the Other Woman played by Madhubala (the Venus of the Indian Screen) enter the hall, panting. When you are as naturally beautiful as Ms M, even panting does things to the beholder's heart. ('It's not fair!' you may exclaim with Shyama, and you would be right…) Unaware of the effect she is having on Shyama, Shabnam continues panting as she leans against a pillar at the back of the hall. Amaan's attention is focused only on the contest onstage, not on Shabnam's arrival. He's unaware of Shabnam's presence, and having been recently ordered out of her life by her father, she is the last person he expects here. Meanwhile, the energy of Shabnam's love for Amaan gets to Shyama — silently, devastatingly. We see all this, our heart is now racing, even more because the characters onscreen don't see.

Cut now to Shyama who faints and has to be carried away by her father. Through all this the soundtrack is dominated by the repartee of the impending winners, the male group, which rubs in its victory with a

"So see you tomorrow at the qawwali," Shyama tells Amaan (Bharat Bhushan) in Barsaat Ki Raat (1960).

two-line refrain that pooh-poohs *ishq* as a wasteful pastime.

Enough is enough, says the God of Love! Amaan the poet/singer steps into this crisis situation and gives us (and his opponents) the best *qawwali* performance of his life. He just floors them, and us, with his defence of love — leaving everyone speechless with the strength of his conviction that love is the best thing that can happen to a human being. This is when he sings '*Ishq aazaad hai, Hindu na Mussalman hai ishq...*' It is a long stanza with nearly a dozen lines, which has become famous as Hindi cinema's most powerful *qawwali* performance. His last line is: 'Love puts man in touch with God,/ It is the most divine ecstasy imaginable...'

Amaan's opponent, the master *qawwal*, concedes defeat. He has no answer for this level of poetic sentiment and embraces Amaan in appreciation of his creative mix of rhetoric and song. Shabnam witnesses Amaan's dramatic triumph while still leaning on the pillar, and feels more certain of her love for him now than ever before.

Amaan's impromptu performance says a lot to the viewer at that moment. One, it is a highly dramatic summoning in song of the beloved, to which Shabnam responds, actually leaving behind her parents, home, everything. All that the parents, especially her father, a police officer, can do on learning that she has gone to be with her lover who is a mere poet-cum-radio singer, is to smash the radio (on which they hear the *qawwali*), in frustration, helplessness.

Notice again in this act of smashing the radio, the tension between sound and image. The song continues to play — undisturbed — even after the battered radio has fallen to the floor. This song is special; it *cannot* be silenced. Nothing the parents can do, in other words, can stop Love now.

Dazed by love for Amaan, Shabnam has just arrived at the qawwali, unannounced–in Barsaat Ki Raat (1960).

The camera cuts back to the *qawwali*, away from the furiously impotent father, to Shabnam, his daughter. As we see her entering the hall, Shabnam looks as though some power greater than herself, some energy, has driven her here. On arriving, she looks dazed, exhausted by this mysterious force. The mysterious energy then touches Shyama sitting many yards away onstage, and causes her to lose consciousness. Shyama faints and collapses.

As she is being carried away, you know that Shyama has lost Amaan to Shabnam...

Look for just a moment now at Amaan delivering his big crushing stanza, which leaves his famous opponent speechless. His lines are: '*Ishq aazaad hai,/ Hindu na Mussalman hai ishq, banday ko khuda banaa deta hai ishq./ Ishq na puchche deen dharam noo, ishq na puchche naata* (Love is free./ It is neither Hindu nor Muslim. Love can turn man into god./ Love does not question religion, love does not question relationships, it just is...)' They are delivered with such spontaneous, total conviction that you cannot help but believe them. He certainly believes in what he is saying, and at this moment sound and image fuse to make him your hero.

A liberalism of the heart

Amaan's reference in the stanza above to love being neither Hindu nor Muslim sounds curious at first, for it is not warranted by anything in the story of *Barsaat Ki Raat*, where the dramatis personae are almost all Muslim and there is no Hindu-Muslim conflict in the story.

But the Hindu-Muslim question was in the 1950s, and continues to be today, a major subterranean issue in India — traumatised as it was by the Partition bloodbath in 1947. The cinematic nation is an entertaining counter-reality, but its reference point always remains the reality of its viewing public — especially the reality of its dreams and nightmares.

Three other films that are contemporaries of *Barsaat Ki Raat* — *Dharamputra, Dhool Ka Phool* and *Mujhe Jeene Do* — also echo this inclusive pluralism in the name of *ishq*, what we earlier called a 'liberalism of the heart'. *Dhool Ka Phool* (1959) for instance, deals with the problem faced by the illegitimate school-going child of a single Hindu mother who has been given shelter by a Muslim uncle. She encourages her child to treat the kind uncle as a father figure. Trouble starts, however, when the child enters school and its attendant social

The film's title Mujhe Jeene Do! *translates as Let Me Live! This plea comes not only from the film's dacoit hero, but also from the spirit-of an Indianness which is Hindu, Muslim and much more.*

life. Once it becomes known to his peers and some neighbours that his 'father' is a Muslim, they harangue him with questions like - what will you grow up to be, Hindu or Muslim?

His Muslim foster father responds one day with this song, which became a popular hit at the time of the film's release in 1959, and is still recalled fondly by people over four decades later: '*Tu Hindu banega na Mussalman banega,/ Insaan ki aulaad hai insaan banega* (You will grow up to be neither Hindu nor Muslim, / Born the son of Man, a Man you will grow up to be...)' Brave words, which soothe the child momentarily, but don't help him very much in the long run, even in the movie.

They do open up a small space, however, off the screen — in the world of our speech and imagination, where an identity that is between the polarity of Hindu and Muslim can begin to be expressed. And this film-derived identity, interestingly, is based not on your roots, nor on the religion your parents profess, but on what *you* make of your own life, your future. (Recall the Wallace Stevens quote at the beginning of this essay: 'The world about us would be desolate except for the world within us...')

The three 'I's of Hindi cinema (Or values in popular cinema)

Returning to the two songs above ('*Ishq aazaad hai*', *from Barsaat Ki Raat* and '*Tu Hindu banega na Mussalman banega*', from *Dhool Ka Phool*), and recalling some of the most memorable lines of dialogue from your personal list of films for a moment, you find that an oft-used term in the discourse of Hindi cinema is '*insaaniyat*', which means humanity, liberalism, kindness. It is the key word, a value image that the protagonists of Hindi films of the 1950s-60s live by. It is a value that was offered to viewers as raw material in their own process of identity-building, especially when confronted with the very 'real' pressures of orthodoxy and social prejudice in their individual lives off screen.

In design and aspiration, '*insaaniyat*' is bigger, more expansive in its scope than 'Hindu' or 'Muslim'. You often hear people saying, 'I'm an Indian, not a mere Hindu.' 'Indian' here has quietly become close to, if not synonymous with, *insaaniyat*[2]. In our cinematic world and especially in the personalities of the heroes and heroines who dwell there, *insaaniyat* is one side of the coin, *ishq* is the other.

The palm that holds this coin is *izzat* (honour): it is the third and the biggest of the 'I' words in Hindi cinema. On the Indian screen, *izzat* is as much about self-respect as honour. For the love story's young hero and

Ishq, Insaaniyat *and* Izzat. *These were, and still are, the three key values around which the stories of Indian cinema are woven. You could call it the Master Mantra of popular Indian cinema at its best.*

heroine, *izzat* is mainly about self-respect; for the girl's parents, however, it is about family honour, especially if they happen to be richer than those of the boy, which is often the case. (An extended discussion of *izzat* appears in the essay on the city in cinema.)

Through their distinctive use of camera, sound, and acting styles — which involved adapting the Hollywood paradigm to Indian sensibilities and colouring this adaptation with folk music and some elements from folk theatre — filmmakers like Raj Kapoor, Mehboob Khan, Bimal Roy and Guru Dutt, along with B R Chopra, Manmohan Desai, Yash Chopra and Gulzar, created a national cinema pivoted on *Ishq*, *Insaaniyat* and *Izzat*. These were, and still are, the three key values around which the stories of Indian cinema are woven. You could call it the Master *Mantra* of popular Indian cinema at its best.

Ideas onscreen are never just a string of words; they are embodied in character and scene, in the style and presence of mind with which the hero/heroine handles those big, critical moments of his/her life story. You can then say that the lead pair's capacity to fall madly, totally, in love, and climb every mountain to take that love to its logical, happily-ever-after conclusion, makes *insaaniyat* an appealing idea. After all, the people who embody it in film after film are your world's top stars, with names like Nargis, Madhubala, Meena Kumari, Waheeda Rehman, Nutan, Dilip Kumar, Raj Kapoor, Dev Anand and Shammi Kapoor.

Skating on the thin ice of 'reality': Movie love and the great Hindu-Muslim divide

Meanwhile back in the real world, so deep is the chasm between Hindus and Muslims that marriage between them is the ultimate taboo. It happens occasionally, of course, but you *don't* talk about it in public. Consequently, when it comes to depicting Hindu-Muslim relationships onscreen, there is virtually no film in the entire corpus of popular Hindi cinema that features a Hindu marrying a Muslim. The exception that comes to mind here is Mani Ratnam's *Bombay* (1995).

Ratnam's film goes all the way in breaking the great Indian taboo. It shows a Hindu youth, Shekhar, courting and then actually marrying a Muslim woman, Shailabano. What made this 'unholy' union even more daring was that Shekhar is not a dacoit like Sunil Dutt's Daku Jarnail Singh in *Mujhe Jeene Do*, marrying a Muslim dancing girl, a social

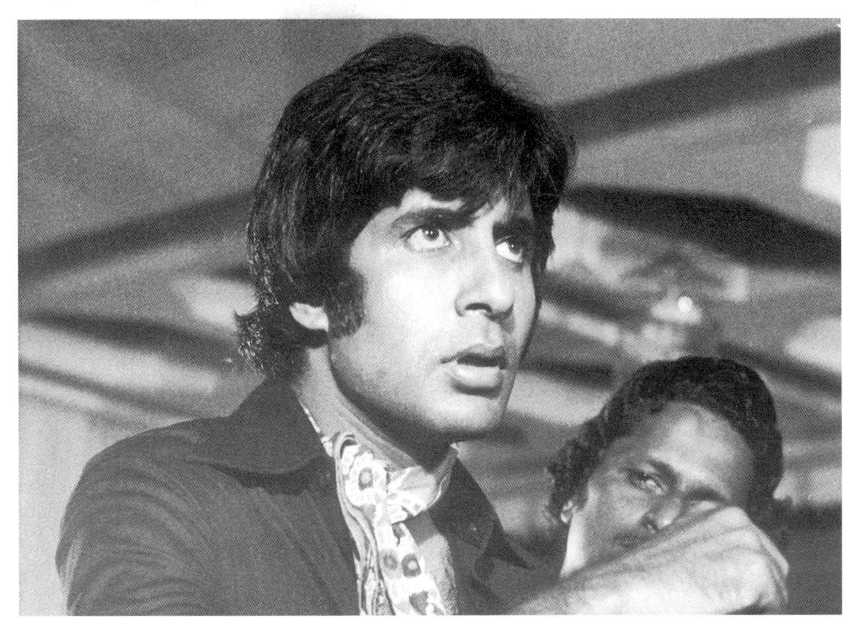

Amitabh Bachchan plays Iqbal the Muslim hero in M. Desai's Coolie *(1981).*

outcast like himself. *Bombay's* Shekhar is a perfectly mainstream fellow, a newspaper journalist, and his wife Shailabano too is a graduate.

Until *Bombay*, you could say that Hindi cinema permitted the Hindu and the Muslim to be brothers-in-arms (*Amar, Akbar, Anthony,* 1977), friends for life (*Zanjeer*, 1973). They could even fight to defend the honour of each other's religion (*Hera Pheri*, 1976). But a certain border would not be crossed. Marriage is that border. The blood will not mingle.

In Mani Ratnam's *Bombay* however, the blood does mingle. Not in the nebulous future as the couple walk into the sunset at film's end, but in the first quarter of the film, when a defiant Shekhar confronts Shailabano's outraged father, slashes his own arm with a kitchen knife, slashes hers likewise, and lets his blood run into hers! Her stunned father is paralysed by Shekhar's act. By the time he recovers a few seconds later, Shekhar has left the scene.

Their marriage later in the film, and their attempt to settle in Bombay in December 1992-January 1993 when the city was torn apart by Hindu-Muslim violence, made this feature film's release in 1995 a 'law-and-order situation'. This story of the Shekhar-Shailabano union was the reason why paramilitary forces marched into Bombay before the film was released. It was also the reason why the film's screening was suspended in Hyderabad, Hubli, Dharwar and Bombay for a while. Movies in the popular mind are clearly not just film fictions; a Hindu-Muslim marriage onscreen is taken even more seriously than one off-screen.

Movies in the popular mind are clearly not just film fictions; a Hindu-Muslim marriage onscreen is taken even more seriously than one off-screen...

As Bombay-based film critic Maithili Rao points out:

> 'There are no Hindu-Muslim romances in Hindi cinema. It has only taken token note of the Muslim as the surrogate sister, the uncle, the courtesan, the good-hearted pathan...'

Scriptwriter and lyricist Javed Akhtar (who also happens to be a Muslim) goes a step further: 'I would never make a film like Bombay because I will not tell a lie, and nor is it possible to speak the truth.'

Filmmaker Gulzar has a different view on this matter, however:

> 'It is possible to show Hindu-Muslim marriages in Hindi cinema, provided you don't make a big fuss about it. Take my film Lekin (1991) — a Muslim marries a Hindu, but does so quietly, without making a song and dance about it. This is also how inter-religious marriages happen in reality. By making a big deal of it onscreen, you invite trouble...Lekin does not hide the duality of their identity, but neither does its plot hinge on this fact alone. (Gulzar 1997)

Another difficult relationship in 'reality' is that between castes, especially those at the very top and those at the lowest rung of the caste ladder — the untouchables. In addition, there are unresolved problems in relations between religious groups, between people bred in different linguistic

cultures like Tamilians ('South Indians') and Hindi-speakers ('North Indians'), etc.This is a broad outline of some of the major divisions and ethnic trenches within Indian society.

All said and done, then, *Hindi cinema caters to a deeply-segmented society*, whose members do not like to look too closely at these divisions — especially in their pursuit of 'entertainment'. In this respect, Indian moviegoers are similar to their counterparts elsewhere. (The white-black divide in American society is similarly handled very gingerly by Hollywood cinema, for instance. Love affairs between white and black protagonists are almost as rare in American films as between Hindus and Muslims in Hindi films.)

In such a social context, Bombay's filmmakers circa 1950 were looking for a key word, a *mantra*, which would ring true, and make money at the box-office.The cinematic *mantra* would have to touch the aspirations of viewers, balancing their pro-change impulses with the fears of an insecure national culture that had yet to reconcile itself with the hedonistic energy of Youth.This new word 'youth' was not only about teenagers of both sexes 'mingling with each other indiscriminately'. It also smacked of the new national elite's tilt towards modernity western style, which conservative nationalists saw as culturally dangerous.

***Ishq* is to Hindi cinema... a central nerve leading directly into the national psyche.**

Ishq was that *mantra*. In Hindi cinema, *ishq* is the meeting point of love, romance, sex, adventure, youthful rebellion, social change and the coming-of-age of man and woman. *Ishq* is to Hindi cinema what the cowboy western as a Hollywood genre has been to Americans — a central nerve leading directly into the national psyche.

Warming conservative hearts

Market-driven cinema cannot afford to takes sides with either conservatives or modernists. In promoting its mantras it has to carry both groups along into its magical kingdom, and make the visit pleasant enough for both to want to return again and again. For the conservatives especially, Bombay's cinema of love occasionally comes up with 'tragic' love stories woven around an Urdu literary metaphor — *shama-parvana*, the moth and the flame.To fall in love is to enter into a relationship that

will *consume* the lover (as the flame does the moth). Two such films are *Julie* (1975), and *Ek Duje Ke Liye* (1980). *Julie* is about the ups and downs of a Hindu-Christian relationship, and *Ek Duje Ke Liye*, a major box-office hit, is about lovers attempting to bridge two different linguistic and geographical worlds — the North and the South, Hindi and Tamil — within the same country. It ends tragically — because Society — as represented by the young lovers' parents — refuses to come to terms with the social transgression their children are bent upon committing. *Qayamat Se Qayamat Tak* (1988) is the other famous love tragedy.

These two are among the few films where love ends in death because of the social chasm separating the lovers' family backgrounds. A much more common cause for tragedy has been 'family honour' and/or the class divide. The two mega-stars of tragic Hindi films in the 1950s-60s were Dilip Kumar and Meena Kumari — who came to be crowned in popular perception and film magazines as the 'king' and 'queen' of tragedy.

When love is not allowed by society, tragedy follows. Rati Agnihotri, moments before what is to be her final and fatal meeting with her lover whose crime is that he is a Tamil Indian - in Ek Duje Ke Liye.

Though they rarely acted together, some of the films that earned them this title were, in the case of Dilip Kumar, *Jogan, Andaaz, Devdas, Deedar* and *Mughal-e-Azam*. And *Baiju Baawra, Benazir, Pakeezah, Bahu Begum, Dil Apna Aur Preet Parayi* and *Sahib Bibi Aur Ghulam* for Meena Kumari. Given the perilous fate of romantic love in patriarchal India — echoing the tragic legends of Laila-Majnu, Heer-Ranjha, Sohni-Mahiwal — cinema's periodic stress on love as a

consuming fire has gone down very favourably with the conservatives. And with the literary-minded modernisers too, to some extent, because Hindi filmdom's song-writers have excelled in the poetry of pain.

To fall in love in Hindi cinema is to knowingly embrace fire — its warmth, its glow, and its propensity to destroy. *Ishq* is the word for this embrace, this act of singular, mind-expanding, do-or-die courage. The tragedy queen or king dies at film's end, but it is a heroic death, a choice that leaves you awe-struck. Here then is a loser who is not a victim; he/she chooses to die by consuming poison, or swallowing a diamond[3]

There is also an exquisite sense of timing to this act: Meena Kumari as *Benazir* (1964) in the film of that name, drinks poison just before coming onstage to present her grandest dance performance to an audience which includes two young people, one of whom she loves. She completes the performance, is supposed to 'die' as per the script, and does, in fact, die.

In so dying, she wins your heart. The young lovers, who can now marry as a result of Benazir's death, are seen laying flowers at her grave at film's end. So death notwithstanding, Benazir lives on — as a superior human being.

Coming now to the modernisers, the big thing about love for them is its gift of self-discovery.

Meena Kumari in Chandni Chowk (1954), *Dilip Kumar in* Devdas (1956).

Self and Other in the Cinema of Love

The basic situation love stories revolve around is the dream (and the anxiety) of two complete strangers starting a new life together. Here the Indian Self meets its Other, and attempts, via love, to come to terms with it.

In addition to being from across the gender divide, this Other in Hindi cinema's best creations is someone who is also from the other side of the rich-poor divide. But all such social complications are revealed much later in any given film. *First they have to fall in love!* And for that to happen they have to bump into each other at a critical moment in their lives.

Chori Chori (1958), for instance, is the story of a headstrong young woman (played by Nargis, the queen of 1950s cinema) who jumps off her rich father's yacht some distance from the Bombay coast in order to go and marry her lover who lives in Bangalore. Her father is opposed to her choice of mate and launches a nation-wide hunt for her. On the run, in the bus to Bangalore, she bumps into Raj, a freelance journalist with a modest income. They come from very different family backgrounds, and almost half the film dwells on the friction between them all through the journey, which turns out to be much longer than expected.

As their mutual attraction-cum-friction gradually turns to love, we see the headstrong young woman's personality slowly transformed. The journey has been traumatic, requiring her to give up the comforts and certainties she took for granted all these years. Even the boy-friend in Bangalore turns out to be untrustworthy, and not exactly pining to meet her.

Renu (Sadhna) the school teacher whose love helped the hero find himself, in Asli Naqli (1962).

At journey's end, she has *found* herself, and the man she loves. The man in Bangalore has been discarded, along with her earlier self. Her wealthy father, happy at this change, has no problem consenting to Raj and Nargis' marriage, despite the fact that Raj the journalist is much poorer.

While *Chori Chori*'s focus is on the young woman's journey, there are a few key scenes which signal that Raj too has changed from a professional journalist interested in her only as raw material for a 'story' ('A Day in the Life of Rich Tycoon's Runaway Daughter'), to Nargis as the woman he would die for.

Similarly, in Hrishikesh Mukherjee's *Asli Naqli* (1962), Dev Anand is a young playboy whose life has no direction until his rich uncle throws him out one day. In the course of learning to survive among the city's poor, he meets and falls in love with Renu, a schoolteacher (played by Sadhana). She responds to his overtures without any regard for his family wealth. It is a meeting of two lost souls in the big bad city, shorn

of all background considerations. Here again the self-discovery and the discovery of love are processes that go hand-in-hand.

So sure is our hero now of his new-found identity that when his uncle asks him to choose between living in the slum or his palatial villa, he does not hesitate to walk out of the villa.

You need the Other to know yourself

If love is about building this very special emotional bridge to the Other who then becomes your personal Other, there may be a good selfish reason for that, suggests the British writer Colin Wilson, in this excerpt from an essay on the subject.

> When the BBC built the first soundproof studios for broadcasting music, they discovered that orchestras played badly in the 'dead' studio. An orchestra likes to hear itself, to hear its sounds bounced back off the walls of the concert hall. A friend of mine was given the amusing job of connecting up a circuit that would pick up the sound of the orchestra, and relay it back to them a fraction of a second later through loudspeakers situated around the studio, thus producing an artificial echo. As soon as they could hear themselves, the orchestra played twice as well.
>
> We all need 'mirrors' to reflect our activity if we are to function at our best. And this is surely the deep significance of the male-female relation...The way in which each of the partners operates as a mirror for the other remains of permanent importance. Freedom cannot operate on a long-term basis without a clear self-image, and the purpose of the marriage partner is to provide this self-image. (Wilson 1985: 70-71)

And this self-image, Wilson adds, has to be something different, something new, for it to support your personal growth. Thanks to love,

> 'Each of the partners is provided with a new self-image, one that differs radically from the reflection thrown back by parents, schoolteachers and work colleagues. Each serves as a magic mirror in which the other sees himself reflected in terms of potentiality.'

The potentiality referred to here is the potential to evolve and grow as a person and as a professional.

Love in the time of achievement

The 1950s were a time when individual achievement was the road to a new kind of identity in urban India. While the process had actually begun some decades earlier under the British Raj and its elitist educational system, Nehru's 'socialist' government in the 1950s opted for mass higher education and the college degree as a ticket to professional careers in the post-colonial, industrialising economy. The college degree sought to erase the inequalities of caste, class and gender. Anyone, went the official discourse, could get a first class in the graduation exam. And having achieved that, anyone could acquire a highly-placed job leading to wealth and power.

The loved one serves as magic mirror. Bina Rai and Prem Nath provide the proof in Hamara Watan (1956).

Popular cinema dealt with this emerging social reality in its own peculiar way – by making achievement 'sexy'. Onscreen, we were given characters whose lives were much more intense than ours, and who had a *Style* that carried *Romance* in every pore of their being. When you combine this Style with the Identity Quest (which is to rewrite one's life in a way that combines desire with professional achievement) you get the Hero of Hindi cinema, circa 1950-2000. As this popular song from the film *Shaan* (1980) sums up: '*Pyar karne wale,/ Pyar karte hain Shaan se,/ Jeete hain Shaan se,/ Marte hain Shaan se*... (Real lovers are those,/ Who love with style,/ Live with style,/ And die with style...)'

India in short was being re-invented – both off-screen and on. Especially onscreen.

In newly-independent India, the middle class urban teenager had a career and a new horizon to look forward to, a career in which his/her parents' identity was secondary, if not irrelevant. Instead of family, caste and *khandaan*, the professional degree now began to count — you were a Doctor, a Lawyer, an Engineer, an Architect, a Journalist, a Plantation Manager, and occasionally even a Poet. Popular cinema echoed this aspiration in films like *Taraana, Aawara, Madhumati, Tere Ghar Ke Samne, Mr & Mrs 55, Sujata, Mere Mehboob*, et al.

It was a democratic *mantra* offered to the nation at large, especially to its younger generation, backed by the establishment of hundreds of new educational institutions across the land in the 1950s and '60s. Hand-in-hand went a substantial boom in job opportunities for graduates; the economic crisis of the 1970s was still far off. The college degree thus became an integral part of urban youth culture from the mid-1950s onwards. The college campus, which brought young people together in a special, secluded space away from the family, was the place where this culture found its home.

In such a time, Love (the harbinger of modernity) in Hindi cinema naturally happened most often on the college campus. This campus where you now spent three to five years of your teens and 20s, *was a radically new kind of social space* in the bosom of Mother India. A country that was still trying to shake off the shadows of the British Raj and walk along the 20th century's urban-industrial road had not quite bargained for the modern college campus and its 'troubles'. While colleges, universities and 'campus affairs' had surfaced in the late-19th century in major colonial cities like Calcutta, Madras, Bombay, Allahabad, Lahore and Karachi, they were elitist little ivory towers until the 1940s.

It was in the post-colonial 1950s and '60s that the country witnessed a major boom in the number of colleges and universities. With this came 'co-education' — the local term for male and female students sitting next to each other in classrooms, and all over the college campus after class!

The college campus, which brought young people together in a special, secluded space away from the family, was ...where the new Youth Culture found its home.

Gradually, hesitantly, the college campus became the place where it was both intellectually stimulating *and fun to be young*! Every glance, every accidental touch between boy and girl was sexually charged — and yet circumscribed — in a setting that was electrifyingly different from family and home. This tension between what was now possible between young men and women engaged in similar career pursuits, and the *denial* of that possibility by Society (and Real Life) is where cinema came in and 'stole our hearts'.

Among the heart-stealers which come to mind here are: *Mere Mehboob, Dhool Ka Phool, Prem Patra, Solvaan Saal, Boy Friend, Pyaasa, Aas Ka Panchchi, Professor* and *Chashme Baddoor*. Two films which deserve special mention in this sub-genre are B R Chopra's *Sadhna (1958)* in which Sunil Dutt plays the college professor who gets involved with a courtesan from the red-light district, and Bimal Roy's *Sujata (1959)* in which Dutt is a Ph.D student who must risk losing his caste status in the cause of love.

Love also of course happened at other sites of middle class achievement, such as the office, the sports club, the nightclub, the picnic spot and holiday resorts like Simla and Kashmir — in films like *Chhoti Si Baat, Mr & Mrs 55, Jab Pyar Kisi Se Hota Hai, Phir Wohi Dil Laya Hoon, Love in Simla*, *Kashmir Ki Kali,* and *Teesri Manzil*.

In this broad scenario of achievement, youth and a new, westernised sense of identity, romantic love came across to us teenagers in the 1960s as another kind of achievement, which we could aspire to, along with that first-class degree.

But alas, *ishq* in conventional/parental wisdom was still 'dangerous,' 'temporary,' 'unattainable in real life', and so on. Society was still not

For young Indians onscreen, love became another kind of basic achievement. Shekhar Suman & Moon Moon Sen in Tera Bina Kya Jeena (1989).

Office romances supplemented those in college, as this one featuring Dharmendra & Saira Banu in International Crook *(1974).*

ready to grant love and romance a legitimate status in modernising 1950s & 60s India. This modern love was just another instance of aping the West, warned the elders.

Popular cinema, thank God, had no such qualms. It went ahead and made the romantic temperament almost the *sine qua non* of Indian modernity.

Here is a small sampler of the way Hindi films were promoted on street posters and in press ads from 1950 onwards: 'Only After A Rain Of Tears/ Comes the Rainbow of Romance!' read an ad for Jagat Pictures' *Raj Rani* (1950).

'*AMBER* — An unforgettable spectacle of chivalry/Draped in the most colourful costumes/ Of an age when Romance was Religion!' read another advertisement. (Filmindia 1950: 48-49)

Stories we live by

At its core, the *ishq* of popular cinema is represented in a few basic themes, which we have outlined above. The imaginary world created for us viewers by Hindi films has come to be populated by leading characters who are free of ethnic moorings, either by accident of birth (being orphans), or by a progressive, cosmopolitan upbringing which makes them living icons of *insaaniyat*.

What we got from the big romance hits of Hindi cinema of the 1950s-'60s was not just love stories, but *psychic mobility* — 'mantras' to enhance the quality of your life as a teenager, images to live your life by. Not all these films had happy endings. What they had instead were endings that made you think, by broadening your mind and your range of experience (vicarious though it may be). My reference here is to films like *Andaaz, Hum Dono, Amar, Chaudvin Ka Chand, Mughal-e-Azam Sangam, Gumraah, Benazir, Guide*, and *Teesri Kasam*.

In the main, of course, the happy ending is paramount.

My list of these includes *Dil Deke Dekho, Paying Guest, Mr & Mrs 55, Taxi Driver, Barsaat Ki Raat, Shri 420, Solvaan Saal, Aar Paar, Naya Daur, Tumsa Nahin Dekha, Shararat, Phir Wohi Dil Laaya Hoon, Junglee, Mere Mehboob, Laatsaheb,* and *Chalti Ka Naam Gadi*. These love stories gave us the happy dream, a dizzy carefree tomorrow wrapped in the close and welcoming arms of Hindustan.

A Hindustan that was shaped by the movies. Mad, generous, brave, culturally vibrant *Hindustan!* The Hindustan of the good life, inhabited by villains, heroes, heart-stopping virgins, vampish sex bombs and everyone in between. Where the villains get their just desserts at the hands of the good, the beautiful, the heroic.

Belonging to this tribe of the good and beautiful are young people with names like Raju the Aawara, Rita the gutsy (but also hedonistic) lawyer, Baiju Baawra, Anarkali, Salim, Gopi, the Anaari, Daku Jarnail Singh (who was a perfect gentleman to his dying day), Junglee, Rocky the one-man band, Bambai Ka Babu, Sujata the irresistible untouchable, Padosan, the Jewel Thief, Mere Mehboob, Rosie and Raju Guide, and last but not least — Gabbar Singh and Umrao Jaan. The last two came much later, in the 1970s and '80s respectively, but have now become fully qualified members of the *enchanted country of our imagination*.

Let Jib Fowles, a historian of Hollywood, have the last word on our subject, while we muse over the similarities between them and us.

> Love affairs are a staple of entertainment because satisfying ones are so elusive and so much desired in the real world. As the 20th century has worn on, the individual's search for sustaining love has become ever more arduous. Into the breach have stepped stars, who through their performances have become the providers of purified romance. A spectator can identify with the star and love as they love, or can fantasise being loved by the leading performer. When the performance is over, the viewer is left with a lingering balm of affection. (Fowles 1992: 27)

Endnotes

1. Our Hindustan is, quite simply, the world's best place...

2. Cinema was not alone in advocating a broad, humanistic liberalism of the heart in 1950s India. Similar advocacies were in the air — from modernist novels, plays, newspaper editorials, and from hundreds of 'progressive-reformist' school- and college-teachers all over the country. The teacher's contribution to civilising society usually goes unacknowledged because it is so quiet and long-term in nature, because she/he opens young minds to grand new ideas as part

of her/his day-to-day teaching work. It is to the credit of films in the 1950s-60s that the teacher often figures in them as an important, positive character. Popular art works best as a civilising force when there is this kind of convergence of impulses and inputs from other 'media'.

3. The irreverent among you might wonder why they never die the way we do — in a car accident, or of a heart attack or cancer. Obviously because that makes for poor cinema. Heroes and heroines are like gods; they can 'die' when they decide to. Yes, car accidents do happen occasionally to these gods, but they always survive. Sometimes they even allow themselves to be crippled by the accident. But that too has a higher purpose — to give the film's story a diffrent twist. As for heart attacks, those are exclusively reserved for their parents onscreen, as we all know.

References

Filmindia. 1950. Vol XVI, No 10, October, Bombay.

Fowles, Jib. 1992. *Starstruck*, Smithsonian Press, New York.

Gulzar. 1997. Personal interview conducted by the author in April.

Herskovits, M. 1971. In *Anthropology and Art,* (ed.) Otten Charlotte, The Natural History Press, New York.

Sieber, Roy. 1971, "The Arts and Their Changing Social Funcion" in *Anthropology and Art* (ed.) Otten Charlotte, The Natural History Press, New York.

Stevens, Wallace. 1994. *The Necessary Angel*, State University of New York Press.

Wilson, Colin. 1985. *The Bicameral Critic*, Ashgrove Press, London.

There is coherence in the main stream of human mimesis: we imitate the things we admire... The direction we take (in our lives) depends on the things we choose to imitate; and the choice depends on the sort of persons we really are...By mimesis we make both ourselves and the world...

Gilbert Murray

Where Do Heroes Come From?
Some Post-Gandhian Answers

INDIA after Independence, Partition and Mahatma Gandhi's assassination, needed a new kind of hero, but did not know it. Mahatma Gandhi had filled the hero's slot so completely for a whole generation before 1947 that his absence left us completely bewildered. On the night of January 30, 1948, after Nathuram Godse had slain the Mahatma, a major human/cultural presence on the national landscape was suddenly, and irreplaceably, gone.

Gandhiji was not, of course, the only hero of that generation; he was only the greatest. Alongside him were people like B R Ambedkar, Bhagat Singh, Subhash Chandra Bose, Rabindranath Tagore, Jyotiba Phule, Gopal Krishna Gokhale, Subramaniam Bharati, and others. But most of them were dead and gone before Gandhi's assassination.

Jawaharlal Nehru did fill the void left by Gandhiji in the 1950s, but only to an extent. Somehow, the nation did not believe that prime ministers and other State functionaries are the stuff heroes are made of. *Heroes* in the popular imagination are beyond jobs and designations. *They are supermen who embody an Idea that captures the imagination*. *Ahimsa, satyagraha,* the courage to defy all forms of State power in the pursuit of freedom and a *swadeshi* lifestyle, were such big ideas.

This was a time when a whole era was coming to an end.The formal dismantling of the British Raj was gathering pace in the years 1948-49, and the process was completed on January 26, 1950, when India adopted its own Constitution as a democratic socialist

Indian wine in Hollywood style bottles. Dev Anand puts on the Gregory Peck look in this shot from C.I.D. (1956).

republic. A new nation, a rather different-looking India (variously called Hindustan, Bharat, and other local names) from the old British colony, stood on the brink of self-realisation. There was one problem, though: ***what was to be the identity,*** in everyday terms, ***of the new Indian?*** More specifically, what should the newly-free, post-colonial, post-Gandhian Indian man and woman look, sound, and dress like?

There were other dilemmas too. How much of the colonial legacy — the schools, colleges, administrative and judicial systems, the monumental buildings — was to be discarded, how much retained? What would the new nation's lingua franca be? Hindi? Which Hindi — the Sanskritised version of Allahabad and Benares, or the Urduised version rooted in cities like Lucknow and Delhi, and popularly known as Hindustani? Why Hindi? Why not Tamil, Bengali, or even English?

It is this post-Independence confusion that popular cinema responded to and reflected, picking up vital cues from Hollywood, ranging from Charlie Chaplin's kind-hearted, but bewildered tramp, to the dangerous Humphrey Bogart or the delectable Gregory Peck. Addressing itself primarily to the urban middle and working classes in the first years after Independence, Hindi cinema managed with an entertaining eclecticism (serving old wine from folk theatre mixed with nationalist mythology in Hollywood-style bottles) to fill this post-Gandhian void — with a degree of success that grew in leaps and bounds between 1951-65. Raj Kapoor's *Aawara* in 1951 was the first of these leaps. A landmark of slick editing and world-class production values, its appeal spread far beyond India's borders to China, the Soviet Union, and north Africa within two years of its release. ***Indian cinema had suddenly 'arrived'.***

By the end of the 1950s, with films like *Aawara, Shri 420, Mother India, Chaudvin Ka Chand, Pyaasa, Naya Daur* etc, the audience for Hindi cinema expanded way beyond its urban constituency to include the new nation's vast hinterland. No one had quite expected box-office cinema to become so popular, not even the filmmakers themselves. Bombay cinema's dramatic popularity in this period was partly because a new generation of filmmakers including Bimal Roy, Chetan Anand, Raj Kapoor, Mehboob Khan, S Mukherji, K Asif and Guru Dutt succeeded in giving the viewing public a brand new pantheon of democratic, free-spirited, good-looking heroes and heroines who began to hold the nation's new middle class, especially their teenaged children, in thrall. Besides, these films were very topical: they addressed feelings and experiences that a teenager could relate to as contemporary, relevant.

The first contemporary-looking hero actually hit the screen in 1944-45, a little before Independence, in Calcutta. Bimal Roy's first film, *Udayer Pathey* (The Awakening), was released in its original Bengali version in 1944, and in the wake of its spectacular box-office success, the Hindi

version, *Humrahi*, followed in 1945. *Humrahi's* protagonist, Calcutta-based Anup Kumar 'Lekhak' makes his living ghostwriting speeches for a millionaire, Rajendranath. He quits this job one day when his sister Sunita (Rekha Mullick) is humiliated by this millionaire.

Anup (played by Radhamohan Bhattacharji) is also a committed, left-wing freelance journalist and a novelist-in-the-making. He gets involved in a major confrontation with his former employer on behalf of the workers in the latter's factory. Evil millionaires in popular Indian cinema often have beautiful daughters who end up siding with the lean, handsome, left-wing hero when the confrontation with the father reaches its climax, and so it goes in *Humrahi* too. In short, the rebel gets to eat his cake and have it too, but only *after* he has been suitably roughed up for his courage by some of the millionaire's hired goons.

What is of interest to us here, however, is not the plot itself but the reception the film was given by Calcutta's young generation in the year following its release. Here are some contemporary accounts, starting with that of the filmmaker Bimal Roy's daughter, Rinki Bhattacharya:

The film which gave us our first contemporary hero: Hamrahi (1945).

Anup's character won the heart of the nation. In this strident, posturing anti-establishment hero, young men ...found a role model. Anup, by the way, refuses to spell out his last name. When summoned for a job, he insists he be called 'Anup Lekhak (writer). To the surprised interviewer Anup retorts: 'Why not Lekhak? When you accept Ghatak or Pathak, why not Lekhak?'

Humrahi's runaway success was due to audacious lines such as this. One record company brought out the entire dialogue track, which became a very popular bestseller. Displaying a confrontationist stance against the British rulers, against caste, class and creed, Anup 'Lekhak' stole the limelight from other heroes of his time. (Bhattacharya,R. 1994: 167-68)

Writes another witness, Tapan Sinha:

Bimal Roy's 'Udayer Pathey' of course revolutionised the cinema of this country. Earlier we did not have such bold lines on everyone's lips. People quoted the film left, right and centre. I don't recall such an impact on our social and cultural life. (Bhattacharya,R. 1994: 125)

This is not to say that the Anup of *Humrahi*, the Raj of *Aawara*, *Mother India*'s Radha or *Naya Daur*'s Shankar filled the void left by Gandhi, Ambedkar et al. No, they created another kind of hero altogether — the Star!

Here was a hero who was far more accessible, even though unreal, a mere figure of cinematic light. But the unreal nature of a Shankar or a Radha was wilfully forgotten or at least pushed into the margins of consciousness by viewers as we proceeded to appropriate them. Cinema's power was life-likeness. It gave us intimate access to the story's protagonist, whose greatness unfolded gradually before the viewer's eyes. The protagonist had ordinary, humble beginnings; his movement up in life was mapped inch by inch by each of the 300-plus viewers in our local cinema hall. We found ourselves disagreeing or disappointed with an unnecessary sacrifice by the protagonist; and agreeing and applauding him/her lustily at the climax as he/she emerged not just the winner, but as our kind of winner, our demigod.

These were my feelings while watching Raj Kapoor in *Anari*, Shankar (Dilip Kumar) in *Naya Daur* (1957), and *Anarkali* (Madhubala) in

Shankar (Dilip Kumar) and Rajni (Vyjanthimala) take a moment's break to pose for the camera during the shooting of Naya Daur *(1957).*

Mughal-e-Azam. Dilip Kumar's Shankar, the horse-cart driver in *Naya Daur*, stands out as a personal favourite from my high school days. Shankar does everything — driving his cart, talking to his horse, wooing the beautiful Rajni who has just arrived in the village, confronting the rich landlord's wicked son on behalf of the aggrieved horse-cart drivers, building a new road all by himself, shedding tears of gratitude when his beloved pitches in to help with the road-building work — with a style which was new, almost unheard-of, and very attractive. Shankar is handsome, strong; Shankar is kind, lovable; Shankar is smart and gutsy, but vulnerable too. That's called living, *that's called being a man*, I said to myself - sometime in the mid-'60s when I first saw *Naya Daur*.

Even more interesting, on second thoughts, are films in which the hero is not a picture of self-confidence but of youthful innocence. One such film is the all-but-forgotten film *Taraana* (1952). As a viewer what appeals to you about Dilip Kumar's Dr Motilal character in *Taraana* is the open mind with which the young, just-graduated doctor takes in the village where his plane has crash-landed. Instead of landing in Bombay where his plane was bringing him from London, he finds himself in a village in the middle of nowhere. Unfazed, this city boy decides to make the most of his first encounter with village India. There is an air of innocence about the young doctor. *He brings no preconceptions to the situation*, just a modern, democratic civility which itself is odd in the feudal world of the village. But our hero seems unaware of this.

He is courteous to the blind old man who has given him shelter; he attends to a co-passenger who has taken ill, as a doctor should. He is surprised at the brusque manner in which his host's beautiful daughter Taraana (played by Madhubala) responds to his demands for help in attending to his patient. Our hero seems unaware of the effect his handsome, dashing presence has on young women.

Similarly in *Anari*, when Raj, a jobless young painter, first visits Nutan's opulent villa, he touches the marble statues scattered on the verandah in wonder. Later, when she tries to get him to demand a high fee for painting the memsahib's portrait, he refuses. Our jobless artist would have you believe that he is totally innocent of the fact that artists tailor their fees to their clients' pockets. It takes much persuasion from her before he finally agrees to use his painterly skills to personal advantage — *but that too for a noble cause*.

Aadmi musafir hai...[1]

Why is this innocence such a recurrent pattern in Hindi films of the 1950s and '60s? One reason is that the hero is making a social statement: you cannot always change society, but you can change yourself. In other words, change, like charity, begins at home. If you would live in a good, non-corrupt society, then you must begin by believing in it yourself, by being innocent and honest in your personal life and in your dealings with others. In short, do unto others as you would have them do unto you. This sounds trite on paper, but as part of a coherent, tightly constructed film narrative, it was appealing. What was appealing was not perhaps the utopian dream brought to life by the character, but the conflict itself, the conflict involved in taking on this innocent persona and then living it.

The hero as a character-in-process. Baiju (Bharat Bhushan) the hero of Baiju Bawra (1952) grows into a great singer.

Another reason for the popularity of noble screen heroes in those decades is the fact that there is something very appealing about the hero as a character-in-process. His whole life unfolds before us as the film proceeds, unlike those deified political heroes who have come down to us ready-made and whole. Sitting in front of the cinema screen, looking at the protagonists groping to find their way, *it is as if we are being offered a chance to live our lives all over again.*

This imaginary journey, which begins soon after the lights go down, ceases to be just a fiction. It strikes a deep chord within.

The men and women who now became engaging characters were those who were re-writing their lives, like Shashi Kapoor & Nanda in this scene from Juari (1968).

At the top of this list of groping, ordinary characters who *stumble* (like us) while finding their way, are the lawyer Amar played by Dilip Kumar in *Amar* (1954), and Raj, the laundry-worker who strikes it rich before realising the Faustian bargain he has made with his benefactor Seth Sonachand in *Shri 420* (1955). Hindi cinema went much more 'ordinary' some years later, in the 1970s and early '80s. I refer here to Amol Palekar's portrayals of the young office clerk in films like *Chhoti Si Baat* (1975) and *Gharonda* (1977), Naseeruddin Shah's timid, straight-and-narrow accountant in Sai Paranjpye's *Katha*, and Farooque Shaikh's college student persona in *Chashme Baddoor*.

True, the characters portrayed by Raj Kapoor, Dilip Kumar, Guru Dutt and Dev Anand in the landmark 1950s films like *Aawara, Naya Daur, Madhumati, Amar, Shri 420, Kaala Pani, Nau Do Gyarah, Pyaasa, Mr & Mrs 55* or *Anari,* were not quite as ordinary as the characters played by Amol Palekar. Nonetheless, each of these 1950s films is the story of a young man's journey, a rite of passage, in the course of which the hero grows and changes. Amar, the supremely self-confident lawyer played by Dilip Kumar in the eponymous 1953 film, is an emotional wreck by the time the film enters its second half, and it ends only with him being totally humbled by a young shepherdess. Raj Kapoor who romanticises the freedom of joblessness in the 1951 film *Aawara* resolves as he enters jail at the film's end, to study to be a lawyer...

The stories that interest us viewers are stories about characters re-writing their lives. And there is good reason for this, says Eric Bentley, the eminent theatre critic and historian:

> 'Would art exist at all if men did not desire to live twice? You have your life; and on the stage you have it again. This is simple, but not on that account less valid....The instinct of imitation is implanted in man from childhood (Aristotle writes), one difference between him and other animals being that he is the most imitative of living creatures...' (Bentley, E. 1964: 9-10) Substitute 'screen' for 'stage' above and it remains equally valid.

Nation-building as *dharma*: The first phase

The air in post-Independence India was filled with optimistic phrases such as *'naya zamana'* (new times), *'naya daur'* (new age), *'insaan jaag utha'* (the awakening of man).

'Nanhe munney bachche teri mutthi mein kya hai? (Little child, what is it that you hold in the palm of your hand?)' asks John Chacha in Raj Kapoor's *Boot Polish* (1954). *'Mutthi mein hai taqdeer hamari!* (We hold our destiny in our hands!)' reply the slum's ill-clad children. Their hopeful, innocent smiles steal your heart — especially because they are in fact wretchedly poor; little blossoms in the dust of a Bombay slum.

In urban India of the 1950s, education, industrialisation and the work ethic were the new Nehruvian mantras for nation-building as well as personal fulfilment. Gandhiji, with his emphasis on the dignity of all kinds of labour, including the labour of the untouchable, had also given the nation a whole new attitude to work.

John Chacha (David) gives Bhola (Ratan Kumar) and Belu (Baby Naaz) a pep talk in Boot Polish *(1954).*

The film *Boot Polish* features two orphans growing up amidst the squalor of a Bombay slum, and the last thing you expect is that they will be your stars, that the whole story will be about them. At film's end, however, you find yourself saying — well, of course it had to be about them, thank god it was about them, and why not, why must all films be about adults...? Eleven-year-old Bhola and his nine-year-old sister Belu find themselves in the care of a cruel, selfish aunt, Kamla Chachi, having lost both their parents. She forces them to become beggars, and beats them at the slightest provocation. She is like the wicked stepmother of our childhood fairytales.

The film focuses on Bhola and Belu's struggle to stop begging and earn their living instead. In their long struggle to achieve self-respect and adulthood, Kamla Chachi is the villain they must free themselves from. Many are the moments when there's no work at hand and hunger tempts them to beg or steal, but they somehow manage to resist that temptation. At stake here is both self-respect for Bhola and Belu, and a chance to rewrite their lives.

In *Boot Polish*, salvation is shown to come not from some mystical source, but from something as ordinary as earning your daily bread and having the courage to go hungry on days when there isn't any.

This message was offered to the nation not in textbooks but as part of a gripping cinematic story, the new art form that had begun capturing the imagination of increasing numbers of Indians from the time of the first 'talkie' *Alam Ara*, in 1931. Not all the films being produced in the '50s were as edifying as *Boot Polish* — far from it — but that too was welcomed by the public in the name of 'variety entertainment'.

Inspired by post-War Hollywood, Indian filmmakers gambled in a big way on star-centred films in the 1950s. Films like *Shri 420, Chori Chori, Madhumati, Naya Daur, Azad, Mr & Mrs 55* and *Mother India* proved them right by becoming major box-office successes. By the end of the 1950s, the film star had firmly arrived on the Indian cultural landscape.

This is how the film star replaced our pantheon of nationalist heroes, by coming in through the window: the window of our hopes, fears and dreams as individuals. Dilip Kumar as the bandit hero in Azad *(1955).*

The names come easily to mind: V Shantaram, Raj Kapoor, Nargis, Dilip Kumar, Madhubala, Guru Dutt, Meena Kumari, Waheeda Rehman, Dev Anand, to mention just a few.

These were heroes and heroines whose screen persona you became intimately acquainted and involved with. You noted your favourite hero's physicality, his voice, his manner of dressing, his hairstyle, the way he carried himself on screen, as well as his private life off-screen.

With a 'national hero' such as Bhagat Singh, Dr B R Ambedkar or Rabindranath Tagore, in contrast, you could not have a personal relationship at all. You related to their ideas, their sacrifice, their vision, or to their poems and stories. Not to their physicality, the way they dressed, or moved, or spoke. Gandhiji was the only exception. His bare chest, his shaven head, his slippers, his walking stick, his watch, his dhoti, all contributed to his unique public persona. The persona began to acquire a surprisingly strong significance for us. You could go so far as to say that the nation came to care much more about these components of his persona than that of any film star. It is difficult to deny, then, that there was something personal in our relationship with Mohandas Karamchand Gandhi; he came to be addressed as Bapu long before he was officially titled the Father of the Nation.

Rekha & Amitabh in Silsila. *Each Amitabh fan has his/her own catalogue of favourite Amitabh moments (or scenes).*

While there is a similarity between our involvement with Gandhiji and with film stars, there is simultaneously an important difference too: we don't identify with him the way we do with the screen's stars. Gandhiji was revered, not identified with.

Amitabh Bachchan is not revered; he is someone you identify with, especially at certain moments in certain films. Each Amitabh fan has his/her own catalogue of favourite moments featuring him. There is a sense in which you could say that each fan 'owns' Amitabh Bachchan — *he is yours to do with as you will.* The viewers' identification is not with the real Amitabh who lives in a Bombay suburb, it is with him as Anthony Gonsalves of *Amar, Akbar, Anthony*, or as Iqbal the *Coolie*, who lives not in Juhu but in the top left-hand corner of your heart.

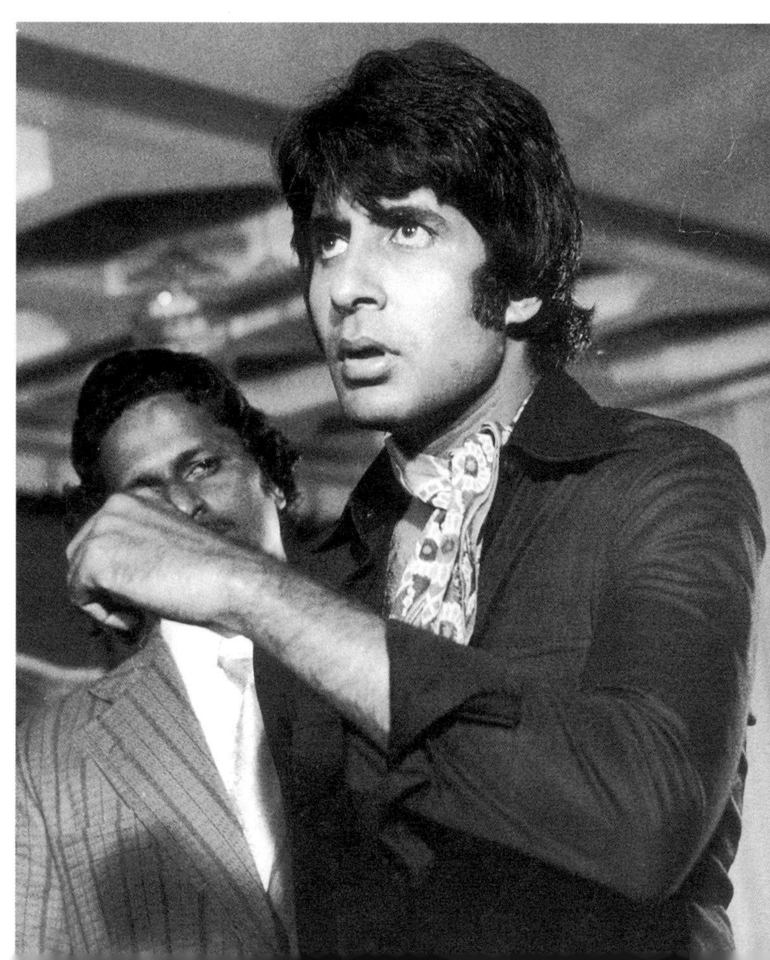

In the case of Rabindranath Tagore or Ambedkar, there is no such divide between the real person and the image; in fact, part of their greatness resides in the consistency between these two domains, a quality we lesser mortals see ourselves lacking.

The old order changeth...

> There is an apocryphal story about an important meeting to be addressed in Delhi by Nehru. The Prime Minister arrived, and remarked to the Mayor that there was an exceptionally good crowd that day. He enquired if there was any particular reason for this. The Mayor hesitantly replied to the Prime Minister (a star in his own right and no mean crowd-puller himself) that among the speakers billed for the evening was a film star. Even the great Panditji had to play a supporting role to the matinee idols of Bombay.
>
> In December (1969) I went to the opening of a discotheque, which was inaugurated by Rajesh Khanna (then the latest movie star). The poor man had hardly arrived, when he was stampeded by mobs of otherwise sane-looking people. Middle-aged Punjabi women produced 100-rupee notes 'for autograph', men in bush-shirts were determined to put their arms round the hero and have themselves photographed...Film stars get mobbed all over the world. In India the intensity of mobbing has to be seen to be believed... (Mehta 1971: 212-13)

So why did our nationalist heroes, who did us proud in the 1920s, '30s and '40s, get sidelined by the 1950s film heroes? Because heroes such as Bhagat Singh had become monuments for 1950s India. As such, they began to be frozen in varying poses of imagined, permanent greatness. When heroes become monuments, they cease to be part of you in a personal sense.

In 1950s India, another process had also begun: that of putting the faceless common man on a democratic pedestal. The upshot of these crosscurrents was that post-colonial India was ready for new heroes who could be related to, heroes who would be people-in-process, like us.

Heroes are men/women of their time. Once that time passes, another pantheon must be created. Calling some of them, like Gandhiji, 'timeless' doesn't help either, except at the level of rhetoric.

More than anything else, for me personally, reading about these great Indians in my schoolbooks is what began their conversion from heroes to monuments. They became chapters to be covered within a syllabus, no more. Nothing about one's teachers or parents seemed to be like Bhagat Singh et al. In the schoolchild's eyes, these great people were names without an address, people the likes of whom were nowhere to be found.

Later in one's life as an adult, these great men are further reduced — to posters on official walls. And if they were really among the top five greats, they became bank holidays, like Gandhi Jayanti.

Heroes, in short, have to be personal, living images if they are not to become lifeless statues, bank holidays, or chapters in textbooks.

Personal in the sense that they must be achievers in contemporary terms, and thereby of use to me in lifting my spirits as an individual — today. In 1950s India achievement itself was being redefined in a society that had opted for industrial modernisation, parliamentary democracy, and cities as the vanguard of a society committed to social change. Achievement in this scenario was to be a great scientist, engineer, doctor — a builder of dams, industries, hospitals and new towns. Martyrdom and personal sacrifice for national liberation had suddenly, quietly, become passé in 1950s India. There was, moreover, an element of continuity with the colonial paradigm here: Prime Minister Nehru and his government had decided to build the new nation on foundations laid over the preceding century by the British Raj.

Farooque Shaikh was the face of contemporary achievement in his role as Siddharth the bright young economist in Chashme Baddoor (1981).

Capital cities like Bombay, Delhi and Calcutta presented a very mixed picture at the social level, however. They were saddled in the early fifties with hordes of traumatised refugees from the Partition, who had fled the newly-created Pakistan leaving behind loved ones, homes, personal savings, and who were now living on government doles while trying to find jobs or start businesses. In addition, there were thousands of migrants, refugees from rural poverty and oppression, who began flooding into Bombay and Calcutta.

The sunny side of this demographic trend was the explosion of urban-centred jobs — in offices, factories, in the construction industry, in educational institutions — during the first decade after Independence. More than ever before, the big city in the 1950s was where the jobs were. But by the mid-'60s there were more people than jobs. With each year after 1965, the gap grew, signalling the beginning of an economic crisis. At the level of individual experience, this crisis was about factories closing down, the shrinking of new job opportunities to such an extent that it hit almost every other person directly or indirectly, resulting in a growing demoralisation at the cultural-psychological level. The new 'system' was ceasing to work, especially for the bottom half of the country's people, barely a quarter-century after the much-hyped dawn of freedom and Indian socialism.

Amitabh Bachchan was the star whose superman-from-the-slums persona was created in the early'70s. Here was a new, very contemporary-looking figure who was not merely strong and self-sufficient; he was also the Great Avenger who ensured that all those who had humiliated him when he was a poor and helpless lad got 'rough Justice' — by fair means or foul. Often enough, he was shot dead in the process, but only *after* 'justice' had been done. As the protagonist of films like *Deewar, Zanjeer, Don, Coolie* and *Laawaris*, Bachchan the lawless avenger captured the public imagination dramatically at the peak of what was both an economic and political crisis in the period 1975-85. Just as Raj Kapoor's Aawara and Dilip Kumar's Shankar had done two decades ago.

The film star - as someone who alternates between Sensitive Poet, Free vagabond, the Great Avenger, and other archetypal selves depending on 'what's up' in the outside world - is a distinctly 20th-century kind of answer for the troubled urban-industrial imagination. As Jib Fowles puts it in his historical analysis of the star phenomenon in the US:

> Previous to the urban explosion (of 1870-1925), Americans had little difficulty in knowing who they were; the very dilemma would have seemed absurd to most of them. Within the confines of cultural heritage, family tradition, church, political persuasion and profession, they were sharply defined. But shorn of these supports and isolated in the new urban milieu, their identities had to derive from the inside, not outside. To establish the self called for establishing one's personality. The stream of humans leaving old modes of life and pouring into a new one needed models of personality — models of worldly, successful, attractive people free of nervousness and self-doubt. Where were such models who could help in defining the individual against the backdrop of urban anonymity? They were...on stage, on screen, and on the playing fields. Stars seemed to exude the perfected confident behaviour that unanchored city-dwellers coveted... (Fowles 1992: 27)

While the American example differs from ours in many respects, it still points to a process that seems familiar in our own experience. The Indian city was supposedly where all the new jobs were, and yet when you actually got there, getting a satisfactory, fulfilling job turned out to be the most difficult thing. Your identity and self-esteem were the first casualties.

Ironically, democracy added to this confusion in newly independent India. Thanks to universal franchise and a parliamentary form of government after January 26, 1950 the common man/woman was suddenly a new political entity being wooed by political parties as 'the voter' with a new, decisive power over political fortunes, but a completely anonymous face in the exploding crowd of the cities.

There was also now a new democracy of the market: the faceless movie-goer determined the fate of films, film studios, and the rise or fall from stardom of each and every actor, every week, simply by choosing to buy tickets for this movie and not that one. While ticket-buying as an act of individual, unpredictable choice had existed ever since movies found a commercial release in the first decade of the 20th century, what was new in the 1950s was the rapidly-growing size of the viewing public, and a quantum increase in its involvement with some movies and some stars, and its rejection of others. The sheer scale of the movie business had now changed: it had grown into a gigantic industry. New, revised myths about the good life today, about how to be (in every sense of that word), were now taking shape in and through the movies.

A hero whose strength of character and work ethic enables him to overcome his lower-class origins. Bharat Bhushan, in Amaanat (1958).

In cities like Calcutta and Bombay meanwhile, there was a lot happening at the cultural level. But the large numbers of new arrivals as well as older residents did not quite know what to make of it.

Enter, an uncommon common man

Popular cinema responded to this uncertainty in the '50s by providing a new kind of hero, a hero whose glory lay not so much in his conquests, his muscle-power, his wealth, his family status, or his leadership qualities, but in his strength of character, which enabled him to overcome the handicap of a humble, lower-class upbringing. Thus the 1950s film hero came not from the nationalist pantheon of the 1920-47 period, but from amidst us, from the aspirations and the loneliness of the post-colonial crowd.

Motilal expresses the loneliness of the post-colonial crowd in Ab Dilli Door Nahin (1956).

For remember, the source of cinema's power is not the filmmaker, but the viewer. It is we who find meaning in protagonists of a certain kind, in their personalities, and in their life-scripts. It is we who make them stars, their films flops or 'super-hits'. Super-hit movies in the 1950s often centred around lost souls, like *Taxi Driver, Humrahi, Aawara, Shri 420, Mr & Mrs 55* and *Anari*, or obsessed singers and poets as in *Pyaasa, Gateway of India* and *Baiju Bawra*. By the '70s, the majority of hit films featured the Angry Young Man (Amitabh-starrers like *Deewar, Sholay,* and *Laawaris*).

An important insight into the special appeal of this new kind of hero is provided by psychologist Carol Pearson in her book Awakening the Heroes Within:

> The paradox of modern life is that at the same time that we are living in ways never done before...our actions often feel rootless and empty. To transcend this state,

> we need to feel rooted simultaneously in history and eternity. This is why the myth of the hero is so important in the contemporary world...It is about fearlessly leaping off the edge of the known to confront the unknown, and trusting that when the time comes, we will have what we need to face our dragons, discover our treasures, and return to transform the kingdom. It is also about learning to be true to ourselves and live in responsible community with one another...When we believe that our journeys are not important and fail to confront our dragons and seek our treasures, we feel empty inside...Psychologists...have a name for (those)...with 'delusions of grandeur', but do not even have a category for the most pervasive sickness, the delusion that we do not matter ...We each have a gift to give — a gift we are incapable of giving if we fail to take our journeys...(You need to) understand your significance and potential heroism. (We must) leave behind a shrunken sense of possibilities and choose to live a big life. Many of us try to achieve a big life by amassing material possessions...but this never works. We can have big lives only if we are willing to become big ourselves and, in the process, give up the illusion of powerlessness... (Pearson 1991: 3-4)

Gandhiji would have agreed with Pearson.

The Hindi screen protagonist, in film after film, undertakes just this journey — from insignificance to heroic significance. And he does it without making a song and dance about it. Understatement was the hallmark of our new hero in the first decade after Independence. Virtually every successful film made in the '50s dwells on his insignificance, his humble origins. Raj Kapoor and Guru Dutt took the lead in this respect. In *Aawara*, the young hero is a petty thief who quietly resolves to study law after completing his two-year jail sentence, in order to become worthy of the woman he loves; in Guru Dutt's *Mr & Mrs 55*, Pritam the hero is a jobless cartoonist who literally lives off his photographer friend's income, but resists encashing cheques which come his way some months later because they compromise his dignity, again quietly, leaving us to discover this only in the film's last moments; in *Naya Daur*, the young horse-cart driver Shankar takes on the seemingly impossible challenge of outpacing the new bus which threatens to deprive all the cart-drivers of his village of their livelihood; in Mehboob's *Mother India*, Radha, a poor farmer's widow, kills her own son to uphold a higher law; in *Mughal-e-Azam*, a lowly dancing girl *dares* to fall in love with Prince Salim, and shames his father, Akbar, before he can punish her.

The message which comes through these films again and again is that ordinary people, including thieves, drifters and dancing girls, can be heroes — if only they are willing to take the risk of being big themselves

Heroes, in brief, perform a useful function, provided they are periodically updated — as happened on the cinema screen in 1950s India. Heroes help you, in the depths of your anxious heart, to gather the resources, the self-confidence, to go back and take on the dislocations and uncertainties of the marketplace. Stars, in short, succeed *for us*. The more plausible their success, the more appealing the star. In most films, leading performers play the role of someone who wins in the end.

Winning, on second thoughts, is not what they all do; some of them lose in the sense of being killed or imprisoned at film's end. Perhaps then it is the way in which you do whatever you do that takes you closer to the core of heroism. As Javed Akhtar remarks in a book-length interview:

> Someone once said, 'A hero is a person who can make a failure look magnificent.' What a wonderful thing to say. When the hero in Deewar failed, it was a magnificent failure. One admired and envied him – 'I wish I could fail like this.'
>
> Devdas is a failure, but what a glamorous failure he was. He drinks himself to death and goes back to the village of his beloved and dies at her gate. What a wonderful death. One would like to die like that. You can hear the audience say to one another in hushed tones, 'Yeh hai hero (This is a hero!)' (Akhtar 1999:73)

Style here consists of an attitude, a quality of being, a personality which speaks both in intimate whispers to individual viewers and in grand gestures which have the whole movie hall clapping — no matter whether he loses or wins. By identifying with noble losers or winners, you begin slowly to acquire the mindset of your heroes and heroines, and along with this a new self-confidence. You may not look as handsome, nor be as tall, nor as poetic, but you now have the star's spirit that compensates for all your other deficiencies. You carry this new self-confidence into your life outside the cinema hall. A crucial part of this self-confidence comes from the filmstar helping you settle the issue of gender persona as an individual style — i.e. what sort of man or woman you will be.

Making failure look magnificent-Sanjeev Kumar in K Asif's 'Love & God' (1971).

Following the example of others, especially that of heroic others, is what we often do. 'Social animals' Aristotle called us long ago. Recall that following Gandhiji, thousands of nationalist movement workers took on parts of his persona, especially the wearing of khadi.

And this was perhaps because Gandhiji brought a whole new glamour to self-denial and austerity — both of which spoke of his inner strength, the strength of his quiet pride in being an Indian. In a colonised nation, he stood out as Mr Self-Confidence!

Such was the popular appeal of Gandhiji's persona in 1930s India that it compelled the nattily-dressed lawyers who comprised the leadership of the Congress to change their whole wardrobe; Mohammad Ali Jinnah was one of the few who resisted, or at least that's what we glean from Richard Attenborough's film *Gandhi*.

Is there really much difference between these freedom fighters and the fans who adapt their wardrobe and their mannerisms in the style of Rajesh Khanna or Amitabh Bachchan? Cyrus, the teenage hero of Ardashir Vakil's recent novel *Beach Boy* puts Khanna 'on' to make himself more interesting to his peers, without giving it a second thought. That, Vakil would have you believe, is what popular cinema is for:

> After seeing *Apna Desh, Kati Patang, Aradhana* and *Namak Haraam* I began to act like Rajesh Khanna. Emerging into the Bombay sunlight, I practised my heavy-lidded glance on strangers. I walked with my shoulders slightly hunched, leant to one side and dragged my feet. I delivered normal speech as if I were handing out an ultimatum. I tried to re-create the rhythms of Rajesh Khanna's speech in English and stroked my cheek as if I were sunk in melancholy thought (Vakil 1998:51)

Similarly, there were hundreds of little Gandhis walking around India in the last decade of the British Raj. Times change; so do role models.

Endnotes

1. Man is an explorer.

References

Akhtar, Javed. 1999. In Kabir, N.M., *Talking Films*. Oxford University Press, Delhi.

Bentley, Eric, 1964. *The Life of Drama*, Athenaeum, New York.

Bhattacharya, Rinki. 1994. (ed.), *Bimal Roy—A Man of Silence*, Indus Publications, Delhi.

Fowles, Jib. 1992. *Starstruck*, Smithsonian Institution Press, Washington.

Mehta, Vinod. 1971. *Bombay: A Private View*, Thacker & Co, Bombay.

Pearson, Carol. 1991. *Awakening the Heroes Within*, Harper Collins, New York,

Vakil, Ardeshir. 1998. *Beach Boy*, Penguin Books, Delhi.

खुदा गवाह

GLAMOUR FILM

خداگواہ

KHUDA GAVAH

DIRECTED BY MUKUL S. ANAND

DUCED BY MANOJ DESAI•NAZIR AHMED MUSIC LAXMIKANT PYARELAL LYRICS ANAND BAKSH

Dreams come true: without that possibility, nature would not incite us to have them.

John Updike

Manliness in Movie-Made India

It was circa 1968–71 when Cyrus, the protagonist of Ardashir Vakil's prize-winning 1998 novel *Beach Boy* (Vakil 1998), was seen learning to walk, talk and hunch his shoulders like Hindi cinema's then leading star, Rajesh Khanna. Cyrus was a member of the third generation of young Indians who sought meaning and personal direction from the stars of popular cinema. Cinematic masculinity, with its larger-than-life quality, has a richness of range: it encompasses the homeless urban vagabond and swashbuckling lover as well as the rural bandit with black handlebar moustache and bullet-proof chest. What makes that armoured chest so peculiarly Indian and lovable is that inside it beats a heart which melts like putty when confronted with '*maa*' (mother) or '*mehbooba*' (sweetheart).

Cinematic masculinity is today and has long been a cultural force. It needs a deeper look because it was, and still is, a key influence on the aspirations of 'real' men — whoever they are…

So who are they? What are real men like?

'Real' men, poor fellows, have come in for a lot of bashing of late — most recently from Shobha De in *Surviving Men* (De 1997), in which she demolishes what little male pride you may have had before opening its pages. Before that too there was some male-bashing from the feminists and indeed, from men themselves.

Self-doubt: Skeleton in the male cupboard

In the good old days, men *did* things — they climbed Mount Everest, they built dams and factories, they held melodramatic wrestling matches between Dara Singh and King Kong for a whole month every year (as used to happen in 1950s Bombay). Giant men would fling each other out of the ring — just for fun. Dara Singh — now there is a *real* man, I thought as a small-town schoolboy. And in Hoshangabad, men alone rode big, noisy Motorbikes, while women did not venture beyond its feminine counterpart - the scooter. Each gender in short, knew its place.

From 1965, however there has grown *a quiet crisis of self-confidence among Indian men*, especially among those of us belonging to the urban 'gentry'. Democracy and the market economy, which were welcomed by us as great levellers of old inequities, have also silently levelled the very basis of male 'superiority' in the public arena. Anyone — we took pride in saying, along with Prime Minister Jawaharlal Nehru in the 1950s — can become the company boss, regardless of gender or class. Anyone could become prime minister too.

In this scene from Hercules (1964), *Dara Singh our wrestling hero gives manliness a muscular clarity.*

In 1962, the Chinese army came and trounced our men who guarded the country's northeast frontier. Shortly after, in 1967, V S Naipaul chose to call us *Mimic* Men, in his famous novel of that name. In Vakil's *Beach Boy*, Cyrus the protagonist muses about one such 'real' young man — himself — growing up in Bombay in the late-'60s:

> It was around this time that there began a realisation that people looked at me as if I were odd, like a turtle amongst antelopes. My hair was too long, my clothes were out of sync, my features were foreign...I wished I could hide these tell-tale signs...The embarrassment of being on display turned into the egotism of showing off, ...of proving myself worthy of recognition, especially by those older than me, while pretending to play the joker. Afterwards there was always the opportunity to tear off this mask and talk to myself...(Vakil 1998:35)

Here now is another view of the depths to which 'real' manliness has sunk — from a poet in Chennai, India's southern metropolis.

SALUTATIONS

Yes! Oh yes!

Indeed I'm blessed!

By God's grace

I have two kids;

Rather strange

Both are

Male.

So?

I am rheumatic,

She consumptive.

The first boy,

Poor chap,

Is quite sickly.

The younger,

To date,

Is quite safe.

But later —

Who knows?

I am a clerk.

Will this do?

Or

Would you like

To have more details?

(Subbiah 1968: 205)

Salman Rushdie, perhaps without intending to, created women characters who are much stronger than the male characters in his Midnight's Children (Rushdie 1981). The scene is Bombay, circa 1960. Strength, stamina and power for Saleem, the novel's 'growing boy' protagonist, are embodied partly in the American comic book hero, Superman, and partly in the figure of his plump housemaid, Padma. Keep the image of Subbiah's rheumatic clerk in front of you as you read this excerpt from Rushdie's novel:

> How I admire the leg muscles of my solicitous Padma! There she squats, a few feet from my table, her sari hitched up in fisherwoman-fashion. Calf muscles show no sign of strain; thigh-muscles rippling through sari-folds, display their commendable stamina. Strong enough to squat forever, simultaneously defying gravity and cramp, my Padma listens unhurriedly to my lengthy tale; O mighty pickle-woman! What reassuring solidity, how comforting an air of permanence, in her biceps and triceps...for my admiration extends also to her arms, which could wrestle mine down in a trice...(Rushdie 1981: 262-63)

Take leave of Padma's mighty muscles, come down the page and you find Saleem's uncle, Hanif, commiting suicide because his wife won't give up her film career (!)

> Deprived of the income he had received from Homi Catrack, my uncle had taken his booming voice and his obsessions with hearts and reality up to the roof of his Marine Drive apartment block; he had stepped out into the evening sea-breeze, frightening the beggars so much (when he fell) that they gave up pretending to be blind and ran away yelling...(Rushdie 1981: 263)

How's that for an image of the Indian Man today? Kader Khan sandwiched between daughters Mandakini and Yasmin Khan in Pyar Mohabbat (1998).

From Indira Gandhi to Amitabh Bachchan

And then there was the way Mrs. Indira Gandhi rose all-too-rapidly to become from 1969 onwards the 'only real man' among Congressmen (and the rest of the Opposition parties for that matter). After the military victory over Pakistan in 1971, she single-handedly symbolised Power. Not just power, also the nation. 'Indira is India,' gushed the Congress President D K Barooah at a public meeting in 1974.

The only counter we men had to her rise, her fall, and her return, was Amitabh Bachchan, the hero of films like *Deewar* (1973), *Zanjeer* (1974), *Sholay* (1975), *Coolie* (1981) etc. Here at last was a *Man* to equal Mrs Gandhi, no matter that this man was only a screen image. The way millions of Bachchan's young male fans carried on in those years, adopting his mannerisms, his famous one-liners from one or other super-hit film and much else, it was as if the Indian male had 'found' himself again, after many a doubt-ridden year. Gabbar Singh, the trigger-happy

A man to equal Mrs. Gandhi at last! Amitabh Bachchan as the towering Coolie (1981) *in the film of that name.*

Two images of cinematic manliness before the demon of self-doubt clouded men's souls. Rajendra Kumar as the day-dreamer in Akeli Mat Jaiyo (1963)*, and Ranjan as Mr. Self-Confidence in* Toofan (1952).

dacoit of the film *Sholay*, added a new variation on the Amitabh theme.

The only problem for us, however, was that this Bachchan-style manliness was quickly appropriated by the urban poor, and especially the criminal elements among them (!)

Given this difficult, confusing world with which the urban gentry had to cope, it is with relief that they turned to films — where their surrogate, the hero, was right on top. And there he stayed, charming the pants off everyone in sight-especially young, beautiful women. There was no doubt at all about his manliness. He may be poor or a middle class clerk, but even so he stood out from the herd as a Man among men.

Self-improvement as the new *mantra*

Let's now turn to another aspect of cinematic manliness. You sometimes hear it said that so-and-so thinks he is Dilip Kumar or Amitabh Bachchan. After Subbiah's poem above, you can hardly blame the poor wretch if he does. Or be surprised that Hrithik Roshan's biceps are the new rage amongst teenagers, who are busy developing their muscles likewise at neighbourhood gyms from Kashmir to Kanyakumari. Or indeed, from Kashmir to Kentucky.

In Bombay, Delhi or Patna of the 1950s you could find many young men modelling themselves on Dev Anand or Dilip Kumar. Consider for instance, this characteristically hyperbolic excerpt from a *Stardust* profile of the latter, and you know why. 'They' in the passage below, refers to us, the viewers:

> The myth called Dilip Kumar. They had conferred on him a Deva (god-like) status. His Apollonian qualities were venerated. He was every woman's dream of an ideal mate; a Devdas, a Salim, a Romeo, a poet, an intellectual, a benevolent patriarch; he came in so many avatars. Perfection personified. Imitated by the young and the old alike. His hairstyle, his attire, his exuberance, even the smile that won the hearts of a million women...(Viju 1994: 262-3)

But for viewers born a generation earlier, in the 1920s-30s, for instance, Dilip Kumar and Dev Anand of the 1950s were young upstarts 'who just didn't have that quality which Motilal, Chandramohan and Saigal had'. The names of screen idols vary with succeeding generations, but not the role they play. The role of providing heart-stopping images *of how to be a better person, a winner*.

Now there's a man for you self-doubters! Dilip Kumar tells Madhubala where she gets off in this scene from Taraana (1951).

Self-improvement has been a key 20th-century *mantra* for as long as one can remember; it seems so much a part of modern city life that hardly anyone talks about it. We tend to take it for granted, just as we do motor cars, how-to books by Zen masters, and the spreading popularity of personal computers. It is in the air today, but it was not always so. Self-improvement, more specifically the attempt to rewrite one's personality, has a special charge in the Indian setting. It is an exercise in breaking away from the worldview of caste-based Hinduism, from 'Tradition'.

interesting way of defining

Amitabh Bachchan in Muqaddar ka Sikander (1978).

Caste, grounded as it is in the idea of a cosmic, pre-ordained, birth-dominated destiny, discourages self-improvement. Result: every self-respecting hero and heroine in our films makes the complete rejection of this caste-based tradition a basic axiom in the development of his/her identity onscreen. Distancing yourself from parental discourse, cutting your umbilical cord, is where identity in our films usually begins, and builds upon.

Take any A-grade film which comes to mind — from *Insaan Jaag Utha, Sujata, Mughal-e-Azam, , Kashmir Ki Kali, Junglee, Pyaasa, Satyakam*, and *Asli-Naqli* from the 1950s-60s, to *Ek Duje Ke Liye* and *Raja Hindustani* in the last decade or so — and you find that the protagonists in each of them make it a point to *reject* 'khandaan' as ideology. Sometimes the very names of our films, like *Naya Andaaz, Muqaddar Ka Sikandar, Dilwale Dulhaniya Le Jayenge (DDLJ* for short*)*, and *Raju Ban Gaya Gentleman* express this faith in the self's power over 'destiny'.

Into the modern muddle of our real-life identities, enter characters who know exactly who they are: like Shankar in *Naya Daur*, Raj in *DDLJ* and Sikander in *Muqaddar Ka Sikander* - each of whom overcomes adversity so spectacularly that he takes our breath away.

Come...Fall in Love
YASHRAJ FILMS
SILVER JUBILEE YEAR
YASH CHOPRA'S
Dilwale Dulhania Le Jayenge
IRECTED BY ADITYA CHOPRA
JSIC JATIN-LALIT LYRICS ANAND BAKSHI

Trying on this or that persona from cinema and literature, or small parts thereof, is all part of one's effort towards self-improvement, which in your late teens is a most important, personal *project*. It is, however, a 'private' project. For you don't want anyone to know that you are concocting an identity cocktail at its natural pace— in your daydreams, in your idle hours of reading and movie-going.

Your deepest transactions with cinema's emotion pictures are specific and very personal, if you think about it. They are often so personal as to be only half-known even to yourself, until 15-20 years later when you are old and grey enough to look back and hum songs like 'Those were the days, my friend,/ We thought they'd never end...'

Exploring our relationship with cinema

Some film stories and characters are a key input into self-making in our teens and twenties. But this 'inner processing' of film is done *half-consciously*. All we are conscious of is the pursuit of Entertainment, which for some reason is an unquenchable thirst. Watching one movie stirs our apetite for the next one, and so endlessly on...

What makes all this interesting is the mystery of it — we don't yet have the concepts, the precise language, with which to map the influence of these emotion pictures. This essay is a freelance sociologist's effort to outline such a map. Firstly, 'influence' is a misleading term because it suggests a one-way traffic from the film screen to our psyche. Perhaps *relationship* — with its evocation of a two-way flow, of reciprocity — is a better way to begin making sense of cinematic masculinity and real masculinity. But let's stay with 'influence' for just a moment.

By the late-'1960s in urban India, the 'strong influence of cinema on impressionable minds' had become a popular cliché. It did not yet alarm too many of society's elders, however. That was to come a few years later with films featuring the bare-chested muscle-and-guns personae of Amitabh Bachchan, Dharmendra and Vinod Khanna pulverising the likes of Amjad Khan and Amrish Puri.

Their rise to stardom coincided with the breakdown of the Nehruvian political consensus of the 1950s-60s and a growing failure on the

Six armed soldiers, or even a dozen are child's play for our screen heroes, especially if you are Vinod Khanna. Scene from Aakhri Daku (1978).

Sunil Dutt confronts his past in Yaadein (1964). *It can also be seen as an image of a nation caught in a cobweb of confusion about its past and future.*

economic front on the streets of 'real' India. After this high noon of sex-and-violence cinema in the 1970s-80s, cable television with its umpteen channels has also come to be labelled a 'baneful influence'.

Why, you wonder, is the middle class intelligentsia, which loses no opportunity to proclaim the resilience of India's 'ancient-yet-modern culture', so anxious about 20th-century media like cinema and television? In the face of 'the powerful influence of the mass media', all we have today is a nation of 'impressionable minds', which must be 'protected'. *How did we become so insecure about our culture, our selves?*

Under the 'mass media juggernaut' lie supine the folk arts as well. But isn't the reason for the eclipse of the folk arts breathtakingly simple? Isn't it just that we the audience do not find them absorbing or entertaining anymore? Something has changed in our mental make-up, irrevocably. And regrettably, perhaps.

For one is not too sure that this change to mass culture is a good thing. Inevitable it may be, but is it good? No clear answer comes up: only lots of seminars, conferences and workshops. Meanwhile, the folk arts for us today have become decorative rituals on annual occasions like Independence Day and Republic Day; rather like Mahatma Gandhi, Rabindranath Tagore and other museum pieces.

Cinema, by contrast, lives and breathes among us *every day*, three times a day. It is not uncommon to come across friends who confide that they watched *Sholay* or *Qayamat Se Qayamat Tak* or some other 'hit' 14 times. M F Husain, the celebrated Bombay painter, says he watched *Hum Aapke Hain Koun* 65 times.

When was the last time you heard anyone say anything similar about a folk performance? The silence at this point is surely not only my own...

What this public anxiety about the influence of cinema points to perhaps is that film heroes/heroines and their responses to the crises in their fictional lives have a very contemporary ring. Cinema's characters make a much stronger impression on us than 'real' characters, who are often a little flawed and incomplete when seen up-close.

Besides, you can't take the real characters home with you and pin them up on your wall as you can with, say, Madhubala as Anarkali in K.Asif's *Mughal-e-Azam*, or Rajendra Kumar as Anwar in H S Rawail's *Mere*

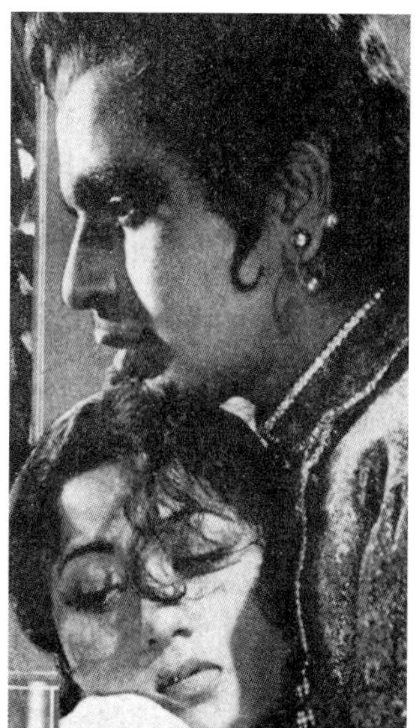

The victory of the cinematic over the real. Immortal images of young love from Baarish (1957) & Mughal-e-Azam (1960).

Mehboob. Characters from real life, like that professor you worshipped back in school, or a childhood sweetheart, keep changing and slipping off any pedestal you may wish to freeze them on. *Cinema's fictional characters, by contrast, are yours forever*. They grow only as you grow.

You can view this victory of the cinematic over the real as a worrying development. Or you can look again, and closely this time, at what these fictional characters really mean to us, deep down, and what makes them so attractive to our dreaming selves. This essay, and this book more generally, is an exploration of the latter view.

Hindi cinema's new masculinity mantra

Having seen in the previous essay where heroes came from in post-Independence India, this one explores post-1950 Hindi cinema's masculinity *mantra*, a mantra that helped us small-town teenagers to define our own sense of masculinity. Dev Anand, Dilip Kumar, Rajendra Kumar, Shammi Kapoor, Shashi Kapoor and Dharmendra joined forces to people our imagination with what it means to be a Man. Pran, K N Singh, Ajit and Prem Chopra showed us what happens to men when they become bad — awful things, some of them unprintable. And Rajendranath, Mehmood and Johnny Walker demonstrated, through their buffoonery and clumsiness, how not to make fools of ourselves. In sum, we are grateful to the movies not only for telling us how to be, but also for telling us how *not* to be.

Dharmendra & Zeenat Aman in Teesri Aankh (1982).

A mass art

Looking back at small-town teenagers now from the perch of the big city where I live, and looking at Cyrus in *Beach Boy*'s Bombay, it is clear that the main difference between the big-city boys and us back then was a time-lag — we in Hoshangabad were always a few months behind. The translation of star dress-styles and mannerisms from the newest hit film into local youth fashion would happen first in big cities like Bombay; we in Hoshangabad followed suit in a second-hand, watered-down version some months later.

The villain shows us how not to be: Prem Chopra & Baby Sonia in Waaris (1969).

These variations aside, by the 1960s, Hindi cinema had begun to electrify and connect people all over the subcontinent in a whole new way. It didn't matter which corner of India you lived in. Calcutta-based film scholar Chidananda Dasgupta recalls his surprise at hearing a tribal woman singing a Hindi film song during a visit to Manali:

> One cold spring morning in Manali (7,000 feet up in the northwestern foothills of the Himalayas), I heard a woman's voice softly singing a Hindi film song outside my window. I went out to investigate and met a family which crosses the 14,000 foot Rohtang Pass every spring, from Lahaul Valley on the Tibet border, to seek work on this side. Every spring they go to Kulu to the cinema there, and the wife was singing a song from a film she had seen the previous year. For her, the experience of a Hindi film once a year was a tiny window on the world beyond the Rohtang Pass. (Dasgupta 1981: 5-6)

Similarly, the January 1967 issue of Picture Post magazine reported:

> Many fishermen reported missing or feared dead in the boat mishaps during the cyclone off the Bombay coast in mid-November might have avoided trouble if they had only listened to weather forecasts instead of film music on their radios. Fishermen plying in the Arabian Sea are known to carry transistor radio sets and are also too fond of light music. A transistor radio was reported to have been found nestling in a raft near one of the sunken boats.

Many fishermen reported missing or feared dead in the boat mishaps during the cyclone off the Bombay coast in mid-November 1967 might have avoided trouble if they had only listened to weather forecasts instead of film music on their radios...

The power of art over life is something we rarely acknowledge in this subcontinent, except as a negative influence. Or is it, you wonder, a power we have forgotten? Or something we have never really been conscious of?

One thing is clear, however. Until cinema came into our lives there was no mass art which cut across this recently-created multi-ethnic nation's folk/linguistic divides in a way which made people in snow-bound Manali sing the same song as was being sung in Bombay. Cinema has helped to create *a new cultural nation* over the last 50 years or so, conjuring up a new idea of a multi-ethnic India where before there had only existed so many indias — kingdoms each with a different name, neighbours who spoke different tongues but had a broadly-shared high culture in common. Call it Brahminical Hinduism, for now.

Cinema is an industrial medium, and it has been quietly knocking down the doors of old culture even as it pays lip service to it. Cinema's allies in this process have been the press, industrial urbanisation and a secular, age-graded, post-casteist system of education.

Suraiya, the singing star of the 1940-50's.

Impressionable minds in the cinematic darkness

As small-town teenagers in Hoshangabad (before television), our relationship with cinema as an art form was a peculiar one: it was the only place you could visit to be alone and commune with yourself without being lonely. Hindi cinema was a friend — a virtual friend in today's idiom — a companion who spoke to you without insisting that you reciprocate, as real friends do. In the cinema hall's darkness you could be completely anti-social, you could whistle, eat peanuts or be shameless in unspeakable ways, and this friend was still there — telling you a story, with some songs, some fist-fights to get your adrenaline pumping, and a hip-swinging *femme fatale*, the vamp as bonus.

Indian masculinity was redefined by the heroes of box-office Hindi cinema from the 1950s onwards, and so successfully was this done that a generation later it was easy to take for granted that film heroes had become the dominant role models for the young. Dilip Kumar and Dev Anand in the 1950s, Shammi Kapoor and Dharmendra in the 1960s, and Amitabh Bachchan in the 1970s and early-'80s are perhaps the greatest redefiners of masculinity thrown up by Hindi cinema after Independence.

In the film *Laat Saheb* (1967) for instance, the hero played by Shammi Kapoor rescues the heroine (Nutan) in distress — but not by slaying the dragon. No, he bends down from a branch where he just happens to be sitting gazing at the landscape and *lifts her off* a runaway horse on which she is riding to her likely death! It takes lightning-quick reflexes, lots of courage and self-confidence (for she is a total stranger to him, and he a poor woodcutter), plus superhuman strength to lift her body in

Vamps come and go, but the hero goes on forever. Dev Anand in Taxi Driver (1954), *and Jayshree T as stereotypical 1970s Vamp (on right).*

motion and hold on to her arms while the horse speeds past below. James Bond couldn't have done it better.

Being a hero, he expects no reward from her (a rich man's daughter), other than a smile and a thank-you. He would have her — and you — believe that he is no more than a rustic gentleman doing his *farz* (duty).

A little later, we see young Ms. Deathwish skiing on a snow-clad mountain, and again speeding towards a 'Danger — Do Not Go Beyond This Point' sign. This being the first time she has come skiing on this hillside, the sign goes unnoticed by her. If she continues moving in that direction, death awaits her in the form of a huge abyss. Our hero happens to be passing by, notices this, trips her up, making her fall on her face, and thereby saves her life again.

What we get in the 1960s and early-'70s Shammi Kapoor persona of films like *Dil Deke Dekho, Raj Kumar, Chinatown, Laat Saheb* and *Teesri Manzil* is a hero whose charm lies not in his innocence, good looks and social conscience a la Raj Kapoor and Dilip Kumar of 1950s films like *Shri 420, Jaagte Raho, Phir Subah Hogi, Naya Daur* and *Madhumati*, but in being a tough, no-nonsense, cynical kind of guy who has both lightning reflexes and physical strength in more than ample measure. (Amitabh Bachchan, reigning superstar between 1975-85, was the culmination of this trend in Hindi cinema.)

Unlike 007 and Dilip Kumar however, Shammi Kapoor can sing, dance and shake his pelvis like no one else — with the sole exception of Elvis Presley who was in another land far away, and being eclipsed at that time by The Beatles. We had no idea that Shammi's dance style was imitative. Elvis the Pelvis was simply unknown in 1960s Hoshangabad;

our hero's wild dancing was, in our eyes, fresh and mind-blowing. Completely scandalous, if you cared to look closely sometimes (which we did). Is it any wonder then that the town's boys went crazy over Shammi Kapoor's wild jungliness? Especially since the girls whom we could barely speak to also loved him, but would never say why.

Ever since his famous *Yaahoo!* song in the 1961 film *Junglee*, the mere appearance of Shammi Kapoor onscreen in subsequent films like *Bluff Master, Professor, Jaanwar, Rajkumar* and *Teesri Manzil*, was greeted with giggles and/or screams of feminine and masculine excitement in cinema halls across the country. From the moment he entered the screen, life for us viewers in the darkness of the cinema hall would instantly shift to a higher gear: every encounter with a woman character became charged with sexual electricity. Shammi Kapoor is credited (or blamed, if you were the parent) with creating a whole generation of wild-haired, hip-swinging *junglees* (savages) in the 1960s.

He did not, of course, invent sex on the screen; but *he gave it a new presence and appeal*. Before Kapoor, sex was hinted at by stars like Raj Kapoor, Dilip Kumar, Dev Anand, but always with some discretion. What Shammi Kapoor did, by borrowing and Indianising Elvis Presley's persona, was to take the clothes off this discretion…

'In the good old days,' writes Partha Chatterjee in his survey of trends in Hindi cinema, 'dancing was not considered a masculine pursuit and the likes of Dilip Kumar, Dev Anand and Motilal, of an earlier generation,

Saira Banu considering Shammi Kapoor's proposal in Junglee (1961).

would have taken exception to the very suggestion that they do more than a few rudimentary steps in their films as an accompaniment to the songs they picturised.' (Chatterjee 1987: 197-98)

This tale of 'good old' masculinity being superceded by the dancing pelvis repeats itself from generation to generation. In the eyes of an earlier generation that came of age watching K L Saigal and Ashok Kumar in 1930s-40s films like *Devdas, Chandidas, Achchut Kanya, Kangan, Kismet* and *Afsana*, Raj Kapoor and Dilip Kumar were 'absolutely scandalous' in their sexuality...

The gender issue

By masculinity here is meant, firstly, what people think men are — the stereotype of masculinity. Among these stereotypes are qualities like physical and emotional toughness, not crying even if you are badly hurt, virility, and a generally superior ability to handle the outside world. Women, by contrast, are imagined to be much less competent in this respect and therefore need protection from the dangerous outside world, which is supposedly peopled by kidnappers, rapists and molesters.

Ajit projects a stereotypical masculinity in this scene from Insaaf (1966).

Stereotypes are usually exaggerations of a grain of truth, and it is easy enough through empirical research to disprove them by citing cases of hundreds of men who are the opposite of tough, etc.

The second aspect of masculinity is what people think men should be — *the gender ideal*. Unlike stereotypes with their claims about what men are, gender ideals posit how men should be. Built into this is the recognition that most if not all men have a long way to go before reaching the ideal. Gender ideals, consequently, are not open to empirical refutation in the same way.

It is this second dimension we will mainly be concerned with here, for that is what popular cinema offers its viewers through the carefully constructed personae of its hero and heroine. My focus here, of course, is only on the male hero, and what follows is a cultural archaeology of the Indian hero, and through him the masculine ideal of the 1950s.

Masculinity on screen is best viewed as a performative

Masculinity is a performative reality; it speaks through what the hero does. Rajesh Khanna, Sanjay Dutt and Dilip Kumar show us how.

reality, in the sense that it is not what one is but what one *does.* It is a condition the hero enacts. In real life too, when you stop to think about it, your gender is created by your actions, in the way that a promise is created by the act of promising. You become a man or a woman by repeated acts, which depend on social conventions and habitual ways of doing manly or womanly things in a culture. Hindi cinema establishes manliness in the way the hero is introduced to us in the first few minutes of his appearance onscreen.

Thus in *Madhumati* (1957), we first see the hero Dilip Kumar surveying from a hilltop the people and landscape of this plantation town where he has just arrived. Conventional wisdom requires the Indian man to prove himself by his confidence and ease in handling the outside world, just as a woman handles the inside world, the home. Wrong or right, these representations of the two sexes have stuck over time.

Confirming this paradigm, Dilip Kumar as the just-arrived plantation manager comes across as lord and master of all he surveys. There is no arrogance in this mastery, just a large-hearted, tall spirit. Here is a person who respects himself, who sees the good side of every situation, and accords the same respect to both his boss and his subordinates. He even has a sense of humour: having been stood up by the peon who was expected to receive him at the railway station, he does not blast the peon when he encounters him a while later, but is satirical instead.

Our hero carries his status as the newly-appointed plantation manager

very lightly – he has the power, of course, but the sword is not flashed needlessly. It rests in its scabbard (where it should), which too is not on display. But we know it is there. He works hard, he is not afraid, he is strong, he confronts his boss as an equal.

Masculinity, circa the 1950s, is also the way Dilip Kumar (the new plantation manager) interacts with Madhumati, a tribal woman (played by Vyjayanthimala). It lies especially in the way he underplays the wound he sustains while saving a poor woman's child from being trampled to death by a horse ridden by an arrogant rich man. In *Mughal-e-Azam*, masculinity is the way Dilip Kumar walks as Salim the prince, the way he embraces his mother. It lies also in the accuracy of his arrow, and in his decision to go to war against his father, the emperor Akbar.

Dilip Kumar's Salim, as much as his plantation manager, is a person who makes his own rules. *In a hierarchical, hide-bound society, he is democratic, open-minded and adventurous*. That he is also good-looking, charming and well-dressed is only a natural consequence of his sterling character. Thus does he become our Star, whom millions of viewers adopt in varied, whimsical ways, and whom subsequent generations of film actors model themselves on. Dilip Kumar epitomised this man of quality, along with Rajendra Kumar, on the Hindi screen in the 1950s and '60s. This was not a man of the people. This was a man who stood out from the herd, and did so with a quiet self-assurance.

On the other hand, following *Barsaat* (1949), in films like *Aawara, Shri 420, Jaagte Raho, Anari* etc, Raj Kapoor took on the mantle of a man of the people, combining Mahatma Gandhi and Charles Chaplin in his unique way.

Dilip Kumar's characters were men who stood out from the herd, and did so with a quite self-assurance.

These were the two main models of masculinity Hindi cinema came up with in its heyday, the 1950s.

The identity crisis of India Britannica

The '1950s in India were the decade of nation-building, a time when people were emerging from the double trauma of Partition and 200 years of colonial subjugation.

But trauma is only half the story; this was a colonialism that had created a new institutional fabric which Geoffrey Moorhouse calls 'India Britannica'. This phrase sums up the British influence on 20th-century India. In India, more than many other colonies, British institutions and values had seeped in and reshaped culture. What resulted from this encounter with westernisation was a new, hybrid amalgam.

A key cultural legacy of India Britannica was that for a whole century before 1947 the white man had served as the Other, against whom the Indian could, and did, define himself as a man, and as a woman.

But when we got rid of the British in '47, Indians underwent an identity crisis. What if you were a Gujarati clerk brought up in a joint family and a small local school in Valsad, or a Bengali of similar background from Birbhum, or a Kannadiga from Bellary, Karnataka? Where in the rich particulars of such biographical backgrounds was *India?* Did it mean Hindu; if not, why not? What did an Indian look and dress like? In short, what exactly did it mean in tangible, everyday terms to be an *Indian*, now that our alter ego, the white Other, had left?

Nation-building never starts with a clean slate; the new Indian government decided to retain many of the key administrative and economic institutions of the British Raj. Prime Minister Jawaharlal Nehru called this 'continuity and change'. Nehru had come of age as a student and lawyer in England. As independent India's most charismatic leader after Gandhiji's assassination in January 1948, Nehru exemplified a specific synthesis of India and the West. As prime minister this translated into policies aimed at building a new, secular India committed to egalitarianism and development.

This did not, of course, solve our identity crisis at the personal level, but it did provide the parameters within which the identity issue came to be addressed by the country's artists, principally its filmmakers.

A military model of manliness

The hero in Hindi cinema before 1947 had been either a legendary figure from one of the two great epics, the *Ramayana* and the *Mahabharata*, or a Robin Hood-like swashbuckling figure (borrowed partly from Hollywood) who rescued damsels in distress while robbing the rich to pay the poor. Gods, queens, kings and bandits loomed large in these films (barring a few exceptions from the late-1930s onwards).

The main thrust of pre-Independence cinema, understandably, was to restore self-esteem in the colonised nation. It was enough for the hero in that context to be patriotic, super-muscular and handsome. Talking of the silent films of the late-1920s, film historian B D Garga writes:

> Films were produced at the rate of one a month...Throwing all norms of taste and technique to the wind, the producer's chief concern was to get a quick return on his outlay. Sagas of chivalry and romance set in exotic princely states and action-packed 'thrillers' featuring musclemen and their molls were turned out in ever-increasing numbers...To match the love goddess and the femme fatale (played by actresses like Ruby Meyers, Ermilene and Zebunnissa), muscular men, tough guys with soft hearts, who did little more than rescue damsels in distress, were created in the image of Douglas Fairbanks and Rudolph Valentino. Master Vithal led the way for Raja Sandow, the Billimoria Brothers and some others... (Garga 1996: 55)

Musclemen and conquerors were equally popular with the more nationalist stream of films. Talking of Baburao Painter's films, Garga adds:

> 'It was in his historical films that Baburao's many-faceted talents came into full play. He chose for his themes the lives of heroic warriors, particularly Shivaji, the man of a thousand legends, whose courage is celebrated in song and story throughout Maharashtra. Sinhagad (1923), Kalyan Khajina (1924)...and Rana Hamir (1925) are films that bear his strong impress...' (Garga 1996: 32)

You could call this *the military model* of manliness, where manhood is directly proportional to the hero's courage and bravado. The military model gave us the conquering hero, the winner of battles and builder of kingdoms. There was also the rebel who took up arms against the coloniser, epitomised in the figure of Bhagat Singh. And there was, of course, a saintly model of manliness, the people's hero modelled on figures like Raja Harishchandra, Gautam Buddha, Kabir, Tukaram, and others.

We need to keep in mind here that *folklore has long served as a key literary reservoir* for popular cinema. But from the mid-1930s onwards, the saint-hero of folk theatre just did not make for gripping cinema; people seemed to prefer watching the hero as superman making mincemeat of his foes, who reminded us subconsciously perhaps, of the young Lord

Kamal Haasan and Rajnikant battle it out in Aakhri Sangram (1984).

Krishna who destroyed demons and evil kings in highly melodramatic ways.

This military model of masculinity (which had been in the making since the 1857 rebellion) preceded the coming of Gandhiji by several generations. It can be understood as a reaction to the effeminate slave mentality that, according to folklore, made it possible for the British to conquer India. The Indian male had been 'castrated' by the British Raj; to overthrow the Raj we needed men with balls. A muscular Indianness was offered as the answer, a manliness composed of robust energy, physical vitality and nationalist courage.

The man who would be free must cultivate the muscle and guts to defy injustice, which was synonymous with the white man's rule. Masculinity in the military mode offered itself to the public gaze. The tall, proud Sikh in a Khalsa warrior's uniform was one such iconic image of military manliness from real life; the Rajput with his handlebar moustache, sword and shield a la Rana Pratap was another, as was the equestrian image of Shivaji.

Military manliness becomes an embarrassment

By August 1947 the coloniser had been shown the door, and Partition had claimed the lives of over a million people in barely three or four

Raj Kapoor's characters treated Gandhiji as their key reference point, as seen in this moment from the film Shriman Satyavadi (1960).

At his most successul, however, Raj combined Gandhi with a dash of Charles Chaplin - in films like Aawara, *and* Shri 420.

months. Manliness as physical prowess had shown its dark side in the mass inter-ethnic killings and rapes which accompanied Partition. What brought an end to the Hindu-Muslim carnage of 1947 was not military-style manliness, but Gandhiji's non-violent, pacifist methods.

It was time to settle down; peace seemed to be at hand. On the morning of January 30, 1948, however, three shots rang out, killing the nation's apostle of peace. So widespread was the public shock and anger that it was almost with relief that we learned that Gandhiji's assassin was not a Muslim but a Hindu extremist, Nathuram Godse. A personification of military manliness, he viewed his act as a patriotic attempt to salvage Hindu pride.

Godse's Hindu-nationalist rhetoric at his trial carried echoes of the violent underside of the independence movement, and of the ethnic divide that had led to the bloodbath following Partition. Meanwhile, the vast majority of people were shocked that one of their own sons had cold-bloodedly murdered the father of the nation.

Post-assassination, the military model of manliness had begun to seem a dubious virtue, though no one actually spoke in those terms. Godse, the 'nationalist' assassin, was clearly no role model for post-British India. The films that were now needed, the stories people wanted to hear at that juncture, had to heal the trauma of Partition and the shock of Gandhiji's assassination. They had to restore trust among the Hindus and Muslims who were trying to settle down.

While doing so, they also had to entertain!

Well, the good news is that the Bombay film industry rose to the occasion and delivered. Not consciously, of course, but it delivered nevertheless. The industry came up with a new kind of hero. And found him in the unlikeliest of places — in the post-colonial *babu*.

Babu is a century-old local slang term for the new middle class of clerks created by the British Raj after the great 1857 rebellion. These were Indians who had been educated in English-language schools and universities with the express aim of assisting their British superiors by acting as middlemen between the Raj and the native populace.

The contempt with which the *babu* was looked upon by the nationalist movement is best captured in this passage from one of our earliest novelists, the Calcutta-based Bankimchandra, writing in the 1880s:

> The word 'babu' will have many meanings. Englishmen will understand by the word a common clerk or superintendent of provisions; to the poor it will mean those wealthier than themselves, to servants the master . . . Like Vishnu, the babu will always lie on an eternal bed. Like Vishnu again, he will have ten incarnations: clerk, teacher, Brahmo, broker, doctor, lawyer, judge, landlord, newspaper editor and idler. Like Vishnu

> in every incarnation, he will destroy fearful demons. In his incarnation as clerk, he will destroy his attendant, as teacher he will destroy the student, as station master the ticketless traveller, as broker the English merchant, as doctor his patient, as lawyer his client . . . as idler the fish in the pond.
>
> He who has one word in his mind, which becomes ten when he speaks, hundred when he writes and thousands when he quarrels is a babu. He whose strength is one-time in his hands, ten-times in his mouth, a hundred times behind the back, and absent at the time of action is a babu. He whose deity is the Englishman, scriptures the newspapers and pilgrimage the national theatre is a babu. He who declares himself a Christian to the missionaries, a Hindu to his father and an atheist to the Brahman beggar is a babu. One who drinks water at home, alcohol at his friend's, receives abuses from the prostitute and kicks from his boss is a babu. . . (Chatterjee 1993: 70)

This self-parody stemmed from Bankim's muscular Hinduism. The *babu*, in short, was what the new Indian was not to be.

Instead he was to be a courageous, honest man-of-action. Mahatma Gandhi's activist-sage persona, which seized the moral high ground in the public arena in the inter-war years, would surely have appeased, if not pleased, Bankim (and the many others whose sentiments he had articulated in his fiction and essays in Bengali).

To be a *babu* or not to be one was not, until Independence, a dilemma. Real nationalists across the country rejected the *babu* image in varying ways. The proud, turbanned Sikh soldier was clearly one such way; the patriotic martyr a la Bhagat Singh was another; Gandhiji's rebel-saint persona was the third variant.

While these variants worked during the days of the British Raj, the problem after August 1947 was that the *babu* was now the new nation's administrative elite, and also its professional class. Yesterday's

Balraj Sahni epitomised post 1947 Hindi cinema's revamped Babu. Seen here with an awe-struck young lady played by Mala Sinha in this scene from Jawahar (1961).

Dev Anand's revamped babu persona had a touch of Gregory Peck in it.

subordinates and clerks (the *babu*, in other words) were today's rulers. India's schools and colleges continued, consequently, to produce aspiring *babus* by the thousands.

It was just not possible, then, for filmmakers to throw the *babu* out with the bathwater.

The metamorphosis of the *babu* in cinema

The only way the *babu* could be hero material for popular cinema in this paradoxical situation was by ridding him of the babu's worst features. In Bankimchandra's diatribe against the babu, the three cardinal sins of the babu were: hypocrisy (as in being a drunken lech outside while playing pious husband at home), spinelessness, and petty tyranny towards those below him in social status.

So Hindi cinema's *revamped* babu was a character who had Gandhiji's honesty and courage, along with Nehru's democratic temper and professionalism. But these two elements still did not make for entertaining cinema. So, following Hollywood's example, they added sex appeal. But sex appeal is not culturally neutral; it is rooted in specific perceptions of beauty, gender identities and conventions of courtship. The Indian hero's sex appeal had to work on his Indian viewers.

In Indianising the Douglas Fairbanks of The *Thief of Baghdad* and the

The good son of the 1950s 1960s is honest, good looking and a big achiever both at work and play. He is also devoted to his mother. Dharmendra embodies all these qualities in Bandini (1963).

Gregory Peck of *Roman Holiday*, our filmmakers had to add elements of the Good Son, because every man in the Indian imagination is either a good son or a bad son.

The good son in Indian folk culture is an *achieved* identity; you are not born with it. And you don't have to be rich either; in fact it helps in most cases to be poor — Surdas is the classic example.

The good son in post-Independence popular cinema is honest, good-looking, and a big achiever — first at school, at university, and then in his career (he goes on to be a doctor, an engineer, a factory or plantation manager). *This is 'aspirational' cinema for an industrialising society.*

The hero as conqueror was becoming an anachronism in industrialising 1950s India. There was an age of conquering heroes in our feudal past — Rajasthan with its heroes like Rana Pratap, Punjab and its warrior saints, Shivaji in the Mughal era.... But in the post-war, post-Gandhian world of 1950s India, the conquering hero was passe.

Even freedom's bomb-throwing martyrs like Bhagat Singh and Rajguru had become anachronisms, thanks to the Mahatma and his new ideas of non-violence and *satyagraha*.

The educated middle class of post-1947 India was being introduced to a whole new pantheon — to the scientist as hero, the artist as hero, the statesman and peace-maker as hero, even doctors, engineers, lawyers and other professionals as heroes. Engineer S Visveswaraiya, for instance, acquired hero status in the south for building the Krishna-Godavari dam. So, instead of kings and conquerors, the Indian public was being asked in the '50s to accept the leader, the statesman, as their new *mai-baap* (lords and masters).

Newton, Einstein, Marie Curie, Bertrand Russell, Rabindranath Tagore, C V Raman with his Nobel Prize — these were the new heroes.

In the 1952 film *Taraana*, the hero is a doctor returning home after getting his medical degree from London; in the 1953 film *Amar*, he is a lawyer; in *Mr & Mrs 55*, he is a sharp-witted cartoonist; in *Madhumati*, a year later, he is a plantation manager, and so on. While caring deeply for his ageing parents, the good son is simultaneously a total romantic. He is an impulsive, courageous man who believes in taking enormous risks, especially once he has spotted the woman of his dreams. Be it night or day, forest or big city, he will not let the opportunity slip out of his fingers.

At play, as much as at work, he is a man of action. And he is a man of action in a society where individual action is socially constrained in a myriad ways. *Therein lies his sex appeal.*

'Action' here does not simply mean brute strength, though he does

Sunil Dutt calmly tells his outraged grandmother (Lalita Pawar) that he will marry the outcaste Sujata, and no one else, in Sujata *(1959).*

display that when the villain leaves him with no alternative. For the most part, however, being a man of action means being decisive, nimble-witted, and having the courage of his convictions. Having decided on a course of action, he does not dither in its pursuit. In Bimal Roy's Sujata (1959), for instance, the hero as played by Sunil Dutt is a Ph. D student from a well-established, upper-caste family in Calcutta. He happens to meet and fall in love with the 'wrong' woman, *Sujata*, who is both an outcaste and an orphan. His family is scandalised at this unexpected development, engaged as they have been in fixing his marriage with another woman who has all the right credentials. Our hero did not know that she was an outcaste orphan when he met her, but when Sujata confronts him with this 'terrible truth', he is surprised but still unwavering in his decision to marry her. Sujata, he says, *is* the woman of his dreams, and her caste status is irrelevant now that he has come to know her as a strong, beautiful, exceptional person.

What follows is the inevitable confrontation with his very orthodox grandmother, his only surviving relative. Unlike us in real life, he does not fight shy of this moment, nor does he seek any family friend or uncle's intervention. He calmly tells his grandmother that he will marry Sujata and no one else. When the outraged old lady threatens to throw him out of hearth and home, he proceeds to oblige her by walking out himself. He eventually returns, after she gives in and agrees to his marital choice.

Interestingly, however, social approval from the community at large is often a key part of the Hindi film hero's sex appeal. He defies his parents in his choice of soulmate or career, but vis-à-vis the larger community he is always and only the good son, the man who is kind to all and sundry. Before we see him zeroing in on the woman in his life and rescuing her from the villain's clutches, he must prove himself saviour-at-large in and around his hometown.

Becoming saviour-at-large is one of the pre-requisites of being the good son. In *Amar*, the lawyer fights a case defending the poor against the village rich; in *Taraana*, the doctor performs an operation on the heroine's blind father, restores his eyesight, and charges not a rupee; in *Madhumati*, he saves a poor woman's baby from being trampled under the speeding horse of his employer, and compels him thereafter to apologise to the lady in front of the whole village.

This good son as saviour-at-large is one of popular cinema's connections with folk culture and epics like the *Ramayana* and the *Mahabharata*, for there too heroes like Ram, Krishna, Yudhishthir and Arjuna play to the gallery, and win the reader's heart before launching on their personal journeys. In the fictional universe of Indian popular culture, then, you have to be a folk hero before you can win the heroine's heart, or even the individual viewer's heart.

Concocting a screen persona that will be commercially successful is always a delicate and complex business, however. While Ram and Krishna were indeed saviours-at-large (especially Krishna), the source of their power was God. The hero persona of the cinema of India Britannica had no such celestial claims. His strength was that he was an educated man, a skilled professional, a *babu* in short. But this was a very unusual babu — he had a Nehruvian commitment to democracy and egalitarianism, laced with a judicious dose of Gandhian asceticism and exceptional moral strength! He was, in short, an Exemplary Man who is seen to both give respect, spontaneously, to the man in the street, and demand respect from the man in the palace.

Egalitarianism was the new *mantra* of our reborn babu. Dilip Kumar epitomised the new hero in the above sense; he created a compelling persona, combining professionalism, egalitarianism and a

Egalitarianism was the new mantra of our reborn babu. Dilip Kumar epitomised this new hero.

Jackie Shroff plays a jobless youngster, the dark side of the revamped babu, in Hero (1983).

gentlemanly British elegance in films like *Taraana, Amar, Madhumati* and, to some extent, in *Naya Daur*. What this combination amounts to in essence is best summed up in these words (quoted in an earlier chapter too) of Carol Pearson:

'(We must) leave behind a shrunken sense of possibilities and choose to live a big life.... We can have big lives only if we are willing to become big ourselves and, in the process, give up the illusion of powerlessness...' (Pearson 1991)

It is not always easy in these films to be big-hearted in Pearson's sense, nor is it always a matter of having the guts to stand up to the boss. Sometimes, as in the film *Amar*, it involves the hero battling his own conscience and risking losing the equilibrium of his well-settled life.

Briefly put, what happens is that the lawyer-hero has committed a sexual indiscretion with Sonia, who comes to him seeking shelter one rainy-stormy night. The next thing you know she's with child, and so much does she love Amar the lawyer that she decides to have his baby out of wedlock, if need be. In the process, she risks becoming an outcaste in her village, but is not deterred. Amar, meanwhile, is engaged to someone else, and preparations for the wedding are already afoot. No one other than Sonia and Amar know who the child's father is. Sonia's continued silence on this matter in the face of mounting social pressure and expulsion from home has its effect on Amar's conscience, who finally confesses that he is the child's father. He must now pay for his indiscretion by breaking off his engagement and marrying Sonia instead. Egalitarianism here means that no one can escape the moral consequences of his actions, not even the hero.

One reason for the growing success of popular cinema in these two decades was that its canvas was broad enough to depict both the sunny side of the good son as the successful professional *and its dark side.* This appealed to those viewers who found that it just wasn't enough to be the good son, and those who had no opportunity to become educated professionals. These were the Indian poor, the unlettered underclass, who far outnumbered the new babus.

This floating population of the dislocated, the marginalised, the victims of industrialisation, found much more to identify with in the characters created by Raj Kapoor in films like *Aawara, Shri 420, Boot Polish* and *Jaagte Raho*. (Three other films in this genre featured Raj Kapoor as the hero though they were not made by him — *Teesri Kasam, Chhalia, and Phir Subah Hogi.*) In Aawara, the good son is thrown out while still in the womb, along with his mother; in *Teesri Kasam*, he is an unschooled bullock cart-driver plying his trade in a rural region, for whom a career as a doctor, lawyer or plantation manager is not even conceivable.

Indianising Chaplin's tramp

Raj Kapoor's *Aawara* concerns a young man who is a victim of his father's misjudgement; a misjudgement highlighting the dark side, the arrogance of the *babu* located in the upper echelons of an unequal society. The father is a prominent judge in Lucknow, who throws his wife out on the street after she is kidnapped by some dacoits and returned a few weeks later. While she had become pregnant before the kidnapping, it only becomes visible after she returns. This leads to the husband's conviction that she's carrying the kidnapper's child, despite her strong denials. Following the terrible tradition set by Lord Ram in the *Ramayana*, he throws her out, to save his reputation as a judge and as a man. (Recall at this point that such judges are explicitly listed in Bankim's *babu* catalogue.)

The child the destitute mother gives birth to some months later grows up among the very poor in a Bombay slum. He becomes a petty thief (played by Raj Kapoor) who later confronts his father the judge in court. In his next film, *Shri 420*, the protagonist finds his college degree of no help in getting a job in the big city. So again we have Raj Kapoor depicting characters who find their futures blocked by Nehruvian India's socio-economic disparities.

The Hollywood persona Raj Kapoor seems to have been most drawn to was not Douglas Fairbanks or Gregory Peck but the Charlie Chaplin of *City Lights* and *Modern Times*. So strong was Kapoor's affinity for the great comedian's characters that he created an Indian version of Chaplin's tramp figure, most strikingly in his film *Shri 420*, but also earlier in *Aawara*.

But again, Raj Kapoor's Chaplinesque tramp in

Aawara is located in the land of the *Ramayana*, in which the tramp confronts not the law nor the system as much as his arrogant, insecure father. This confrontation with the father carries echoes of the one in the *Ramayana* between Ram and his two sons who have had to grow up in a frugal ashram, far from the comfort and luxury of the palace where they rightfully belong.

Similarly, the jobless graduate of *Shri 420*, who enters the screen looking and walking very like Chaplin, is no loner surviving in a cold, bare room à la Chaplin.

On the contrary, within hours of arriving in the city, Raj is informally adopted by an old woman who is poor but kind, and who treats him like her long-lost son. Raj the tramp gets a job in a local laundry within a week of slumming it out in the big city, and this leads him to other jobs that suddenly make him very, very rich.

What ensues thereafter is the dilemma between selling his soul to stay rich and returning to his beloved, a poor schoolteacher who prefers him honest, even if that means returning to poverty. In the end he opts for true love and poverty.

Kumkum plays a woman who believes in the city and in her rights. Seen here giving a piece of her mind to Dev Anand, and to Johnny Walker in CID (1956).

An ambivalent modernity confronts the market

The big city, according to the wisdom of popular cinema and folklore, embodies modernity — which is both liberating and dangerous. One of the all-time hit songs of a 1950s film called *CID* has Bombay city as its theme. The male singer warns listeners to be careful in the city because the city worships only money, because it sanctifies robbery and economic exploitation by calling it 'business'. Interestingly, the female singer — who has the last word — disagrees completely with this view of the city, saying this man is only rationalising his own failure. She adds that more than any other part of Indian society, the city is where you reap what you sow, that it is an economy which is genuinely open to everyone, regardless of caste, gender or class.

Some of this ambivalence towards the market economy and modernity is reflected in the name of one of Raj Kapoor's films, *Anari*, which means a man whose honesty is so extreme that it borders on foolishness. Even when he is not plain foolish, his honesty and generosity make him a character out of sync with the capitalist modernity of India Britannica. Anari, then, is an ironic label when adopted by Raj Kapoor to describe himself, a self-deprecation pointing to another, older conception of good character. It refers to the difficulty of retaining one's humanity in a market economy where money is the supreme value.

He is shown having great difficulty landing a job, and losing his first job as a kitchen manager in a restaurant within hours of getting it because of his insistence on informing the customers about the presence of a cockroach in the *dal*, a very popular dish. Having ruined the eatery's reputation, he is given marching orders.

Knowing that this kind of honesty is a losing proposition, the *Anari* nonetheless stands firm in his honesty. In a society in which, following Marx's prediction about capitalism, all that was solid about Old India was melting into nothingness, the *Anari's* ironic resistance was well-received at the box-office.

Thanks to new communication media, steam engines and mass schooling, Old India had been melting for at least 50 years, but then that was blamed on the British Raj. Not any more. After the British left, the meltdown continued at full speed.

One reason for the film's success was perhaps that this *Anari* character harked back to Gandhiji and his idea of India. Such echoes were gratefully welcomed by a public now beginning to acknowledge that the much-awaited dawn of freedom was a mixed blessing. Numerous inequalities were making the new independence fall far short of the freedom envisaged and promised by the nationalist movement.

Anari was perhaps a response to this widespread disillusionment. Raj Kapoor's simpleton provided one answer: maybe we should scale down our expectations from modernity and the free market, and recover the best, the most humane elements from within our older, home-grown culture.

The big idea Raj Kapoor seemed drawn towards was the Gandhian image of a rural utopia, not Nehru's vision which looked upon egalitarianism, education and electricity as the components of a modern urban utopia. What marks Kapoor's male characters in film after film is their sincerity and guilelessness; they are from another, simpler world; and they'd rather remain there. The theme song of *Anari* expresses just this sense of another India: '*Sab kuch seekha humne, na seekhi hoshiyari,/ Such hai duniya walon, ki hum hai anari/....Duniya ne kitna samjhaya, kaun hai apna, kaun paraya,/ Phir bhi dil ki chot chhupakar, humne aapka dil bahlaaya, khud hee mar-mitne ki zid hai hamari/ ...Dil pe marne waley marenge bhikari, sach hai duniya walon, ki hum hai anari* ...(I've learnt everything, but not cleverness,/ It is true, O worldly people, that I'm a simpleton, a fool/...The world, you have explained to me, is divided between those who are ours and those who are not/ But still I'd rather risk getting hurt, than make such distinctions./ I guess I'm just suicidal/...You're right, those who live by the heart will always be poor/ I guess I'm a simpleton, a fool...)'

These lines conjure up another imagined India, an India of 'dil pe marne wale' (people who live and die for reasons of the heart), a pre-British, pre-industrial India where love, honesty and goodness were the natural currency of social life. Were, but alas, are no more.

Look a little closer at the *Anari*, however, and you find that this simpleton is a very modern kind of man, not someone who smells of custom and ritual at all, nor of old parochialism/provincialism. He paints landscapes as a hobby, he can even do portraits of *memsahibs* for a small fee, he has recently become a hard-working accountant in a pharmaceutical factory, he is having an affair with the factory owner's daughter! So what's the problem? Nothing really, other than his refusal to bend to the growing moral nihilism of the market; he would much rather bend to the call of the heart. (Maybe *Forrest Gump* is late-20th-century America's *Anari* persona.)

For me as a confused young schoolboy watching the film for the first time around 1962-63, Raj Kapoor's *Anari* became a very appealing character, who went straight from the screen into my heart, like water down a parched throat. This appeal was deepened by his theme song: '*Kisi ka dard mil-sakey to lay udhaar,/ Kisi ke waastey ho tere dil mein pyaar,/ Jeena isi ka naam hai*... (Take on the burden of someone's pain, if he gives it to you/ Love someone with all your heart if you can,/ That is what life is all about...)' That song became my guiding spirit.

In a sense, the characters played by Raj Kapoor and Dilip Kumar were the two polar responses to modernity and the market economy in our opening years as a nation. One glamorised the new nation's sunny side, its freedom and its modernism, the other its cost, the losses entailed therein. As you can imagine, both became very popular.

A bridge across the River Fantasy

It needs to be added now that the viewer is also looking at his hero's journey as a limited way out of the social trap, the labyrinth of confusion between old and new lifestyles that post-colonial India was (and perhaps still is). What is absorbing about the hero, what you deeply identify with as you enter his story, is that while he starts from where we are, he always goes *beyond* — into the perilous unknown.

He tempts fate by falling in love with a woman who is an untouchable in the film *Sujata*; by striking a dangerous alliance with a woman who offers him the chance to get rich overnight in *Shri 420*; or by agreeing to marry a rich girl as an arrangement which precludes all marital rights over his 'wife' in *Mr & Mrs 55*. The hero, in short, does not rely on wisdom, cautionary folktales, or even the warnings of friends. *He listens only to his inner voice*; he acts on impulse. The given arrangements — if any — like a job, a family home, then become the social platforms for the beginning of a search for personal truths that will form a practical identity, a working identity. Salim defies his father, the emperor Akbar, in *Mughal-e-Azam* in order to marry Anarkali, to the extent of going to war against him. The city-bred plantation manager in *Madhumati* proceeds to fall in love with an almost illiterate tribal woman, thereby losing his job,

his status, and eventually his life.

> The hero's open-mindedness in the cause of identity building, his willingness to take risks in order to intensify the experience of living, is something we like. It may even be something we desperately want, though the darkness of the cinema hall is often the only place where we admit to this. One of the few who admit to the power of this cinematic darkness is young Cyrus when he says in the novel *Beach Boy*: 'After seeing... *Aradhana* and *Namak Haraam* I began to act like Rajesh Khanna. Emerging into the Bombay sunlight, I practised my heavy-lidded glance on strangers. I walked with my shoulders slightly hunched, leant to one side and dragged my feet. I delivered normal speech as if I were handing out an ultimatum...(Vakil 1998: 51)

The cinema-society relationship is not always so direct. Another dimension emerges if you go back for a minute to Bimal Roy's *Madhumati* and look at it as the narrative of an encounter between urban and tribal civilisations. Being attracted to a tribal beauty (as is the film's plantation manager) is understandable even outside cinema, in reality. But those of us who have felt this attraction have also, typically, held ourselves back, thinking that a serious relationship with such a

Dilip Kumar and Vyjayanthimala in Madhumati (1958). *Desire awakened in 'foreign territory'.*

person would be unsustainable, because of the radical differences in upbringing and temper. But that is reality, whereas what the film is doing is exploring the fantasy of such a relationship.

The box-office success of *Madhumati* suggests that it was perhaps a widely shared fantasy; though these are not issues we ever talk about in the press or even in private. Conversation aimed at identifying and analysing our fantasies is very rare in our society, more so back in the '50s. And yet, daughters of the jungle or of nature abound in films of the 1940s-50s, films like *Barsaat, Amar, Jis Desh Mein Ganga Behti Hai, Taraana*, to name only a few besides *Madhumati*.

The Madhumati kind of fantasy, you could say, arises from the anxiety and excitement of living in a multi-cultural society, where your relationship to the Other alternates between repulsion and desire. This gives rise, firstly, to stereotypes like the stupid Sardar, the aggressive Muslim, the beautiful but unreachable Muslim woman behind the semi-transparent veil, the crooked Sindhi, and so on. Stereotypes are the first level beneath the skin; deeper than them are fantasies thriving on our hopes and fears. All this quiet psychodrama in our mental theatre is not really surprising, given that in India we live amidst so many different 'Others', some defined by class, some by caste, language or religious difference, and then a whole set of Others defined by being part of another mode of existence, another historical cycle, like the tribal.

Film as art plays with these quiet little storms inside the Indian soul...

References

Chatterjee, Partha. 1986. *Nationalist Thought and the Colonial World*, Oxford University Press, Delhi.

Chatterjee, Partha. 1997. "A Bit of Song & Dance", in Vasudev, Aruna (Ed) *Frames of Mind*, UBSPD, Delhi.

Dasgupta, Chidananda. 1981. *Talking About Films*, Orient Longman, Delhi.

De, Shobha. 1997. *Surviving Men*, Penguin, Delhi.

Garga, B.D. 1996. *So Many Cinemas*, Eminence Designs, Bombay.

Dasgupta, Chidananda. 1981. *Talking About Films*, Orient Longman, Delhi.

Pearson, Carol. 1991. *Awakening the Heroes Within*, Harper Collins, New York.

Picture Post. 1967. January.

Subbiah, Shanmuga. 1974. In *New Writing in India*, (ed.), A Jussawalla, Penguin Books, London.

Rushdie, Salman. 1981. *Midnight's Children*, Jonathan Cape, London.

Vakil, Ardeshir. 1998. *Beach Boy*, Penguin Books, Delhi.

Viju, B. 1994. "Frail Humanity", in Savage Tales of Love, *Stardust* Special Issue (May), Magna Publishing, Bombay.

There are so many ways to look at films,
but only a few angles throw new light on the subject... One
angle is to look at the way our films have treated the City ...
It's like a grand mirror with some fantastic scenes, beautiful
grey songs! Some of the greatest moments of Hindi cinema
can be found in those big city stories!? Yes, that is an angle...

H. Mukherjee, filmmaker
(Personal Interview, February, 1997)

The City in Popular Cinema

This essay looks at the way popular cinema of the 1950s and '60s handled the city as a character in confrontation with whom the hero and heroine of the film's story 'find' themselves. Raj Kapoor's *Shri 420* (1955), *Jaagte Raho* (1956) and *Boot Polish* (1954) spring to mind as examples, as do K A Abbas' *Shehar Aur Sapna* (1963), Raj Khosla's *CID* (1956), Om Prakash's *Gateway of India* (1957), Shakti Samanta's *Howrah Bridge* (1958), Guru Dutt's *Pyaasa* (1957) and *Aar Paar* (1954), Hrishikesh Mukherjee's *Anari* (1959), *Asli Naqli* (1962), and Mohan Segal's *Phir Subah Hogi* (1958). Films like these depict a frontal engagement with the big city, which represents a completely new way of life for what was hitherto a predominantly agrarian and small-town society. This makes them very different from films that are merely located in a city, which most of our films are anyway; those are not our concern here.

The city becomes a character in cinema only metaphorically, of course — as an embodiment of the choice between a good, partly-modernised East, and a tempting but basically bad West. At stake, in short, is a choice between honesty and amoral ambition. In this conflicted mental landscape, the city onscreen is embodied in tall office buildings, fancy cars, monumental villas complete with wrought iron gates, turbaned watchmen, marble statues, silk dressing gowns, big black pianos, and broad winding staircases which sweep majestically down to the poor, dishevelled hero, quaking at the foot of it. Why is he all a-tremble? Because he must now, in a few seconds, answer big questions from the silk dressing gown.

Dev Anand is not sure whether to say 'yes' or 'no' to the big question. His feet express 'No', while his face and neck don't want to leave just yet.... Scene from Sazaa (1951).

Questions such as: 'So, young man, where do you want to go? Choose — now! Do what I say, and you can have a villa of your own...(pregnant five-second pause). Or go back into that miserable hut you came from...(ten-second pause). Well...what is your answer!?' On his answer depends not only the story, but also the rest of the hero's life, and our involvement in the movie.

Against the background of a simpler rustic life where your future depended on your caste and the size of your farm, the 20th-century city offered Indians a completely new horizon, a culture of individual achievement and success that had almost nothing to do with caste or family. Success here depended on your education, your intelligence, and your willingness to put personal welfare above the common good. The last of these criteria tends in our city films to be the most important — *the acid test that the protagonist must pass* if he/she is to be our idol, and the film a box-office success. Passing this test means being noble, placing personal welfare last on your list of priorities.

The hero and heroine must rise above the market. And above most other vices typical of the city of silk dressing gowns and opulent villas. The warmest, the sweetest, the most beautifully-lit space in these city films is the interior of the protagonist's hut or room in a poor tenement (as in this scene from *Ek Jhalak*,

...But whoever said that popular cinema had to be true to 'real' life? It has to be true to the city as myth...

1957) Nourished by its human warmth, the self-above-all culture of the city is often condemned as '*beraham duniya*' (merciless world) in film rhetoric and song. Perhaps the strongest instance of such condemnation is Vijay the poet's last song in Guru Dutt's *Pyaasa*:'*Jalaa do, jalaa do yeh duniya,/ Mere saamne se hata lo yeh duniya,/ Yeh duniya agar mil bhi jaaye to kya hai!* (Burn down, burn down this world, / Remove this world from my sight!/ I don't give a damn for this world and its tainted rewards...)'

Of course this is a gross over-simplification of city life as it really is — both today and in the 1950-60s. But whoever said that popular cinema had to be true to 'real' life? It has to be true rather to the city as myth, to the city as an idea in the imagination of a society, which has yet to accept all that the city represents. And what the industrial metropolis represents to Old India (still largely intact in the 1950s) is *social change* — upheavals in the economy, in the polity and in culture. In short, a whole new semi-westernised way of life.

Social change as a theme in the hands of filmmakers is quite different from social change as defined by social scientists, however. While the latter approach the subject armed with theoretical concepts, the filmmaker, like other artists, approaches social change as individual experience, as a felt, sensuous reality. He deals in microcosms, set on an epic canvas. This individual experience of social change is not that of a randomly chosen individual; it is that of an engaging character, a fictional, emblematic individual, who stands for most of us. The films featuring these characters often have emblematic names — *Aawara, Shri 420, Anari, Chhaliya, Pyaasa, Saudagar, Bluff Master*, and more recently, *Amar Akbar Anthony, Deewar, Muqaddar Ka Sikander, Don.*[1] You know, subconsciously at least, even before stepping into the cinema hall, that you will now meet larger-than-life characters with thundering, stop-the-world names, figures *who will conquer the city for us viewers* — the same city which overwhelms us in a dozen ways every day.

It is not enough, in other words, for the fictional character to represent Everyman. The character must also connect with our wounds and most secret aspirations. Successful popular fictions on screen then become exercises in excavating latent aspirations.

"If you keep moping like this , you'll be late again for work. You might then actually lose your job, which is much worse than the fact that some junior is now your senior!" Sanjeev Kumar gets a talking-to from his wife Nivedita, in Jyoti (1969).

In this excavation the filmmaker's archive is the language of mythology and common sense — the popular metaphors people use to express the experience of change. Metaphors like '*ghar*' and '*parivar*' (our home, our family, our ways, our roots) versus '*duniya*' and '*bazaar*' (the public world, the world of commerce). These metaphors in turn derive from a culture's mythology of the Good Life, rooted in ancient epics like the *Ramayana* and the *Mahabharata*. These two epics of a lost utopia are a psychic bedrock, keys to the master archive in the Indian filmmaker's enterprise.

In short, unlike the social scientist, the filmmaker draws from the collective imagination to connect to major contemporary themes. This connection is often not a conscious act. Most filmmakers will deny that they consciously set out to make these connections to contemporary themes. But it is the business of important artistic truths to be unconscious, and of interpreters to dig them out.

Mr. Integrity comes to town

Take for instance a scene like this one in the 1959 film *Anari* (Innocent Fool), where its penniless protagonist, walking the street wondering where his next meal's coming from, chances upon a wallet which accidentally falls out of a rich man's car. He is hungry and desperately needs the money in that wallet, and the rich man can easily do without it. A godsend, you could call it. But what does our protagonist do with it? He embarks, after just a moment's hesitation, on a search for the rich man, on a hungry stomach. After surmounting major obstacles, he finds him and returns the wallet. From that moment, or rather from the moment when he embarks on his search for the rich man, you know that this is no ordinary fellow, that he is one of those larger-than-life characters about whom epics like the *Ramayana* are written.

Films like Anari give us contemporary urban characters... who flatter us by being better than our 'fallen' selves. This sense... of a fall from grace is a key element in our love-hate relationship with cinema.

As distinct from the *Ramayana* and other folk epics, films like *Anari* give us contemporary urban characters who are not just extraordinary, but who flatter us by being better than our 'fallen' selves. This sense, often vague but nonetheless present, of our fall from grace is a central element in the viewer's love-hate relationship with cinema. We like the movies, but we often don't like ourselves for this 'indulgence'. 'Fallen' here is shorthand for this unease, this widespread — even if private and hidden — sense that we are imperfect individuals thwarted by material or social constraints from realising our full potential. We are, as the English poet Rupert Brooke says, 'each in his lonely night, each with a ghost...' The need to escape this burden, even if momentarily, constitutes *the key aspirational element* in our emotional connection with films; it is what makes them popular.

In this scenario, social change on the screen is represented by the adventures, and most importantly the responses, of the hero and heroine to archetypal crises in their urban lives. Crises like homelessness, like losing a job, or being torn between personal desire and family, or having to choose between the devil of monetary temptation and the deep sea of honest poverty. These are crises we can identify with.

The physical setting in which social change as a theme is usually played out on the Hindi screen has been the big city, which is shown to *demand a major re-orientation of the key characters* in the stories.

The city can be both homely and heartless, finds Mala Sinha in Devar Bhabhi (1966).

The films in this genre focus on the protagonists' passage from country yokels to urban sophisticates, or on the trial by fire that makes a Man out of a boy (as in *Aawara, Bluff Master, Bambai Ka Babu* and *Katha*), a Woman out of a girl (as in *Taxi Driver* and *Chori Chori*). Even when the heroes as migrants are shown as coming from towns and not villages (as in *Shri 420*), the emphasis remains on re-orientation, on the ways in which they must adapt to a newer, much bigger world.

Consider how the city was typically 'painted' on the popular, box-office screen in the 1950s and early-'60s. Having brought the protagonist as migrant to the city, the camera proceeds to sketch its buildings and huts, its buses and cars, broad, impersonal roads and small, intimate streets, all of which constitute a new kind of social space. This space is homely familiar and comforting; it is also heartless and hostile.

Interestingly, the very sound of the word 'space' shifts our attention to a special dimension of the city — to parts that are *lived* in. Spaces like a special corner table in a neighbourhood restaurant, or the college campus from which you graduated, an abandoned water pipe converted into a home (most memorably in Raj Kapoor's *Mera Naam Joker* and K A Abbas' *Shehar Aur Sapna*), a neighbourhood park bench (in Guru Dutt's *Pyaasa* and *Mr. & Mrs. 55*),where you first felt the stirrings of love. Spaces stamped with memories, emotional landmarks and relationships.

In these spaces there occur microscopic incidents that highlight individual vulnerabilities and the humanity of key characters. Incidents like the handkerchief Madhubala accidentally drops when escaping from the tennis court in the film *Mr. & Mrs. 55* (1955). That intimate piece of cloth enables our jobless hero Pritam (Guru Dutt), who is smitten by her, to carry a small part of her with him wherever he goes. It transforms the whole experience of the city for him, suddenly making it a place of promise, of the possibility of friendship with this beautiful stranger who now colours his whole existence.

Even...street corners park benches and bus stops come to feel like interiors... thanks to the movie camera.

The city in close-up

Similarly, in *Shri 420*, there is the happenstance of the rain coming down just as Raj and Vidya (Raj Kapoor and Nargis) finish their first cup of tea together at a pavement tea-shop. The umbrella that they share brings them closer, and their feelings for each other crystallise. Even as their hesitant romancing begins, the camera cuts for a moment to the man who served them tea a few minutes ago. We see him sipping from his hot cup, keeping it from the rain, and smiling his approval of their romance. This is like an off-stage expression, which adds extra spice and a touch of reality to what is happening between Raj and Vidya a few yards away.

What we have here is the city in close-up. So close, in fact, that even exteriors like street-corners, park benches, and bus-stops come to feel like interiors—because of what happens in/around them, and because of the power of the movie camera which brings a newly-lit reality to everyday objects. Consider the makeshift school hall in a Bombay chawl in Hrishikesh Mukherjee's film *Asli Naqli*. The hero and heroine (who is a schoolteacher) happen to be there alone after her students have left. It is their first moment alone together after interacting formally in front of the chawl's residents for several days, and hiding their feelings all this while. Dev Anand, playing the hero, seizes the moment to tell Renu the school teacher that he fancies her. It is raining outside, and she can't leave because she hasn't brought her umbrella (!)

The bamboo grille on the verandah just outside the hall becomes their little playground, as she tries to control his advances. In the process the camera offers us the moist, rain-soaked bamboo grille—in close-up, from various angles—as a thing of beauty, and as a frame especially conducive to flirtation. Subconsciously, this bamboo grille reminded me of bamboo trees, of dusty country roads and the smells of a village I had visited long ago. I did not think of all this while watching the love scene onscreen, of course, but it was there, somewhere, at the back of my mind—which is a dark, disorderly little attic of daydreams, whims and childhood memory.

The camera in Asli Naqli ***offers us a rain soaked grille... as a frame especially conducive to flirtation.***

This much is clear, however — after *Asli Naqli*, I can't look at bamboo grilles and verandahs in a casual way ever again; they are now inhabited — by Renu (Sadhna's) shy, irresistible smile.

The filmmaker's city

The whole vocabulary of the city on the movie screen is distinctive; its neighbour in this respect is the city in the novel, the folktale. The social sciences seek to define the city as a social structure, and explain how it came to be that way. The filmmaker's goal is a little less ambitious: it is to provide a tangible, emotional sense of what it feels like to be in this place, in this character's shoes, at this time. The movie camera is star-obsessed: it glories in the way She smiles and swings her hair ('*teri zulfein*', in Hindi film lingo), it lingers on His style, on the way he walks, say, after he has just lost his job or found his lady love. *Movies*, as we said earlier, are emotion pictures - they *are moments in emotional time,* moments of action, moments of choices made.

At the end of *Shri 420, CID, Asli Naqli, Anari* or *Mr. & Mrs. 55*, seen for the first time with teenage eyes, you came away with a vivid sense of how their lead characters handled the challenges and opportunities of Bombay — as young people of modest means and immodest spirits. Yes, *immodest spirits* are the one thing you learnt from cinema: to lead a

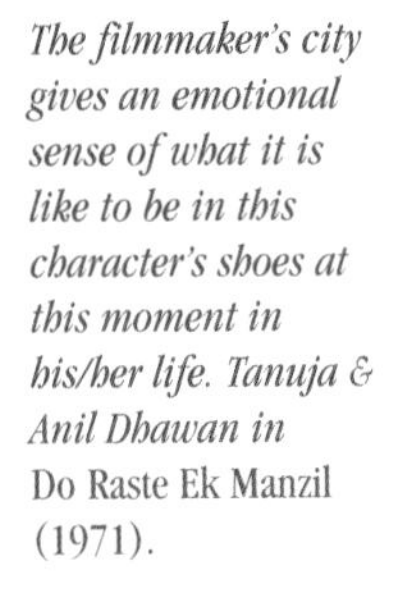

The filmmaker's city gives an emotional sense of what it is like to be in this character's shoes at this moment in his/her life. Tanuja & Anil Dhawan in Do Raste Ek Manzil (1971).

multi-layered existence, where your economic or family status can be one (and low), but the condition of your spirit is another (and high)! In today's idiom this would be called having an attitude. In the 1960s, Rajendra Kumar, playing the student hero of *Aas Ka Panchhi* (1961), phrased it thus: '*Dil mera ek aas ka panchhi, Udta hai oonche gagan par*...(My heart is a bird of desire, which cruises high in the sky.)'

On returning from this flight, however, the same 'bird' must deal with a father who insists that he reduce himself to a junior accountant. In the very office from which Father is soon to retire. The only way to cope with this sad paradox is by living in real and imagined worlds simultaneously, thereby keeping open a window of possibility, from which the bird of change might one day enter. Even if it doesn't, at least your soul has its personal supply of fresh air.

Our new heroes were young people of modest means and immodest spirits. They still are.

In our movies, however, the bird always comes for the hero — by the Interval, if not earlier. The hero and heroine's ways of handling the city are so unreal, even mythical. For us in everyday life they are memorable *because they are so unreal.* The appeal of myths does not depend on factual accuracy; their reach is simultaneously higher and lower.

The factual understanding that viewers of these films got of a city like Bombay was, consequently, limited. And yet, after seeing even one of these films, you found a viewer here and another one there holding forth on 'city life' and other related, lofty topics amidst friends, with an authority and worldliness (acquired only a few hours or days ago from a film) which held the audience in thrall. His success in carrying off this bluff depended, of course, on how well he was able to do an imitation of Raj Kapoor, Guru Dutt or Dev Anand — without seeming to copy. The effectiveness of the visible often depends on the invisible.

The city: A brief history

Popular cinema works on its audience at many different levels: the European-style architecture of the rich man's mansion, for instance, evokes both awe and disapproval: to reside in such a house in post-colonial Indian cinema is to be already tainted. Good people like us will not choose to live in structures that are reminiscent of the British Raj; good people live in modest houses that have an open, come-one-come-all character. The cottage in which Vidya (Nargis) lives with her wheelchair-bound father in the film *Shri 420* is in this sense a 'good' abode.

The city in colonised India was the site where West met East in a much fuller engagement than anywhere else.

The camera makes a number of such quiet statements, which together furnish the viewer's moral universe. Popular cinema is an ongoing exhibition of emotion pictures — a *mela* (carnival) of sorts. Perhaps the French term '*melange*' comes closest. The significance of these emotion pictures derives from the fact that they are updated moral fables. As such, they are also maps for a new nation finding its feet in the aftermath of Partition, Independence, and the cultural upheavals of capitalist urbanisation.

A fuller understanding of the cultural resonance of the city and social change in post-Independence Hindi cinema requires us to briefly take into account the colonial past. The city in colonised India was the site where West met East in a much fuller engagement than anywhere else. And this continues to be the case even today.

Bombay, like other colonial cities, was oriented toward the ocean. Picture shows the Royal Yacht Club on Bombay's eastern sea face.

Bombay, Calcutta and Madras share a common history as major urban centres that evolved during the period of British rule. Established respectively in 1668, 1696 and 1637, they were not indigenous Indian cities, but were built by the British in order to develop their trade routes with India. As a result, the three cities have a common reference system. Neither sacred nor ceremonial cities, they are not oriented towards a sacred place, or the cardinal points of an imperial compass, as an Indian city might be. Their orientation, rather, is toward the ocean; all three began life as port towns. Until the early-19th century, the East India Company's factories were the nuclei of military, commercial and governmental activities in these cities.

From the very beginning, the form of the three cities was designed to meet the Company's trade and commercial needs. Each city contained a fort built to protect European traders and their defending armies from encroachment by competitors and the native population. In both Calcutta and Madras, a large open space surrounds the fort, symbolising physical separation between the native population and the colonial power. With a little variation, a similar physical separation existed in Bombay too. (Dossal 1992: 10-25) Historically, the ethos of these colonial port cities was alien to the Indian. It had no link with sacred values, but was essentially commercial in tone.

The British evolved a new urban form in India after 1750. Writing of Madras, Susan Lewandowski describes the new form as

> intrinsically Western, characterised by the separation of work and residence — related in part to the growth of an industrial mentality, and an ideology of individualism becoming prevalent in the European world. (Lewandowski 1977: 209)

Each of the three cities developed an area recognisable as a central business district, with a concentration of banks, insurance offices, stock exchange, courts of law and public offices. Very few homes were to be found in this central area, in contrast to the native Indian city, where both commercial and residential land uses reached maximum intensity in a central bazaar. To rub in the difference between West and East, the residential areas in these colonial cities were sharply demarcated as European and Indian. The former had large bungalows and gardens

In each colonial city, a large open space surrounds the fort, which has a concentration of offices, courts and banks.

alongside wide boulevards, a pattern reflecting concerns for space and the autonomy of the nuclear family. Indian neighbourhoods continued to be densely populated, with narrow streets and closely packed houses clustered around temples and/or mosques.

These three cities have survived colonialism and are today amongst the metropolises of post-colonial India. Their continued primacy has shaped the nation's conception of a modern, urban lifestyle. None of them are as 'orderly' now as they were under the British. India has taken them over and amended their western urban form in a myriad ways.

An unresolved balance between western culture and post-colonial Indianness prevails in these ex-colonial cities today. This uneasy peace finds its representation, often very crudely, in popular cinema. What is relevant here is that these cities made possible a radically new kind of urbanity and public culture that devalues caste status, and puts a premium on educational achievement and professionalism at work.

Cinema as a medium and as an art form is itself a part of this break in the social fabric and the folk culture of Old India.

Mulk Raj Anand's novel *Coolie* evokes a sense of this new urbanity through the eyes of Munoo, a hill-town boy, on his first glimpse of Bombay:

> Munoo emerged from the Central Station. Before him was Bombay; strange, complex Bombay, in whose streets purple-faced Europeans in immaculate suits, boots and basket hats rubbed shoulders with long-nosed Parsis dressed in frock-coats, white trousers...in which eagle-eyed Muhammadans with baggy trousers, long trunks and boat caps mingled with sleek Hindus clothed in muslin shirts, dhotis and white caps;...in which electric motor-horns phut-phutted, victoria and tram bells tinkled tinga-linga-ling; ...in which was the babble of many tongues which he did not know at all. (Anand 1935: 177)

The modern city was widely seen as a strange place, where the rules of the social order were new, different. So how did Hindi cinema in the two decades following Indian Independence come to terms with the western-style metropolis? It created *another metropolis, an imaginary Bombay*, which was like the real city, but also somewhat like the village in its homeliness, its family-centred culture. And yet, this imaginary city was refreshingly unlike both the real city and the village. Occasionally this imagined city was named—Bambai, Dilli, Kalkatta—but often it was enough to just call it '*shehar*' (city).

Before Munnoo was Bombay, in which cars, buses and trams dominated this strange landscape.

The characters engaged with this imagined city, and took us viewers along with them. This '*shehar*' was miles away, psychologically, from our real houses, streets and traffic. The horse-cart featured in the film *Victoria No 203* (1970), for instance, is a horse-cart all right, but unlike those in real life, this one is driven by a beautiful young woman, played by Saira Banu, to whom all those things happen which are supposed to happen to 'the poor'. One of those things is that she is orphaned and must now survive by plying her late father's *victoria* (the local name for horse-carts in Bombay), and hiding her femininity behind a fake moustache and male attire. Another of those things is that there are diamonds worth a huge fortune hidden in the cart, which she doesn't know about! The imagined city is an exciting place where there is never a dull moment.

Here is an image of the city created by popular cinema, as rendered in this poster painting by an anonymous Bombay artist in the 1950s.

Unlike social scientists or urban planners, Bombay's filmmakers and scriptwriters had to deal with the difficulties and confusions of the metropolis, while simultaneously making places like Bombay and Calcutta come alive *as cities with a tantalising future and endless possibilities at a personal level.*

Take yourself back to 1950s India, which had participated actively, even if unwillingly, in the Second World War. Hundreds of our soldiers had died on the battlefields of Europe, and others had returned to tell tales about that world. London, New York, Berlin, Paris, Moscow were now commonly-known names, and popularly imagined as the places where history was being re-made every other day. Closer home, Calcutta and Bombay were looked upon as the two big engines driving India into the future. The industrial metropolis was, by wide consensus in the 1950s, the future. Filmmakers in their role as storytellers had to take account of the city as India-Modern, more so since Prime Minister Jawaharlal Nehru endorsed modernity as a desirable national goal in his speeches and policies throughout the 1950s.

The Indian soul confronts freedom city

The big city both attracts and repels us. London, New York, San Francisco emerged by the 1950's as the future. And yet, we were not 100 percent sure that this should be so in India too.

Popular cinema, as we have seen, puts a premium on feelings and aspirations. To be concerned with aspirations also requires the filmmaker to be concerned with fears and anxieties about too much change too soon. Folk literature and theatre were, and to some extent still are, filled with contrary attitudes towards the city. So also is Hindi cinema, which can be called folk cinema without too much exaggeration.

This *ambivalence* in the popular arts echoes the fact that we have not yet made our peace with the big city; it was and still is, both attractive and repellent. We have yet to own up to the pleasures and the responsibilities of the metropolis. Since major metropolises like Bombay, Calcutta, Madras, were essentially British creations, the anti-colonial, nationalist response was to reject the big city, and urbanisation more generally, as a lifestyle deeply contaminated by colonial western culture.

Mahatma Gandhi went so far as to

say that every coin earned in the city is marked by sin and slavery, that India lived in its villages, in the labour and the products of its farmers and artisans. It was village life that was truly Indian. In Gandhiji's defence it must be said that his rural utopia was egalitarian and democratic, which meant that he was highly critical of rural inequities, especially the caste system.

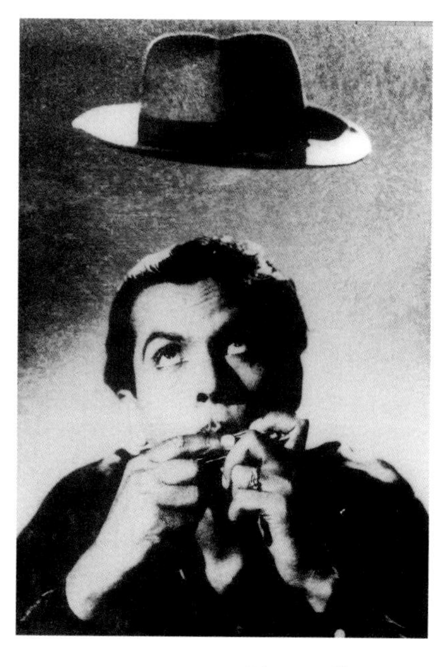

Johnny Walker sings a somewhat unGandhian song in CID (1956).

Gandhiji apart, nationalism has often mobilised its constituency around images of the motherland and the blood of her martyred sons and daughters. At this level, nationalism is deeply agrarian in its inspiration; it is also *deeply anti-urban* in its hostility to pluralism and ethnic heterogeneity.

Given this nationalist legacy of anti-urbanism, it is an interesting paradox that most of the films that were major box-office hits in the first decade after Independence were quintessentially urban films. It is my contention that this has to do with the way cities were described, imagined and inhabited onscreen. As the American poet Wallace Stevens remarks: 'People do not live in places, they live in the descriptions of places.' Embedded in this sense of description is an element of aspiration, and mythology.

A popular song from the 1972 film *Gaon Hamara, Shehar Tumhara* (Our Village, Your City) puts it thus: '*Nai hawa mein udne dekho ban ka mor chala/ Apna gaon sambalo main to shehar chala/ Suntey hain shehar mein jab sawan bhadon aata hai/ Paani ki boondon ke badley harey note barsata hai*...(This village peacock is leaving the forest to fly in a new sky/ You take care of the village, I'm off to the city/ They say when it rains in the city, it rains green bucks instead of raindrops...)'

Romancing the city as myth

I remember numerous evenings spent after school at the Hoshangabad Railway Station with my friends. We went there almost unthinkingly; it was as though the road itself led us there. We hung around sipping tea, watching the trains come and go. It was quietly exhilarating to watch people get on to those trains which stopped at Hoshangabad for just a minute or two, before moving on to *Bombay* or *Delhi*. The railway station in our small-town eyes was where you went in order to move on to bigger, more exciting realities like Bombay. We lived, you might say, in a certain 'description' of Bombay as India's Most Happening City. *The movies had elevated Bombay into a myth.*

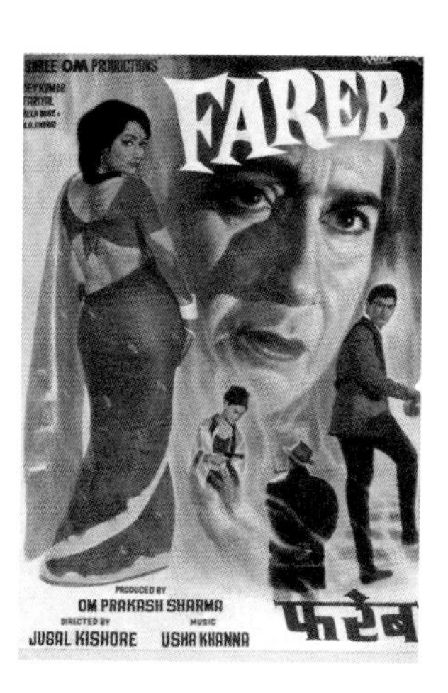

Temptation and Sin—embodied here in the Vamp, played by Faryal— are what the city offers at its best. Those who succumb are doomed to become villains, like the duo played by Ranjit & Sudesh Kumar in this scene from Duniya Ka Mela (1974).

Sudipto Kaviraj writes below what Wallace Stevens would call a very interesting 'description' of the westernised city in 1950s India:

> Democracy in the decades after independence was not merely a political principle; it also had a clearly marked space of residence. It was universally known to live in the city. The city — Calcutta and Bombay par excellence — had that mysterious quality, liberating and contaminating at the same time. It regularly broke hearts and conceptual structures. Well-intentioned young men from the traditional countryside, Bengali novels always showed, never came back with their innocence unimpaired. The city liberated them by corruption, and corrupted them by freedoms denied in the idyllic countryside...(Kaviraj 1999: 149)

Money, marketplace & moral corruption

Prem Chopra, plus a whiskey bottle, make up the archetypal villain image, in this still from Bairaag (1976).

Every story needs a villain, however. He has to be a rock-like obstacle that the protagonists come up against, and in overcoming him, they 'find' themselves. Gandhiji and the nationalist movement had already demonised Money and the Marketplace.

The two 'M's coalesced in the city, providing filmmakers of the '50-'60s a readymade demon, the arch-villain against which to pit the protagonists of

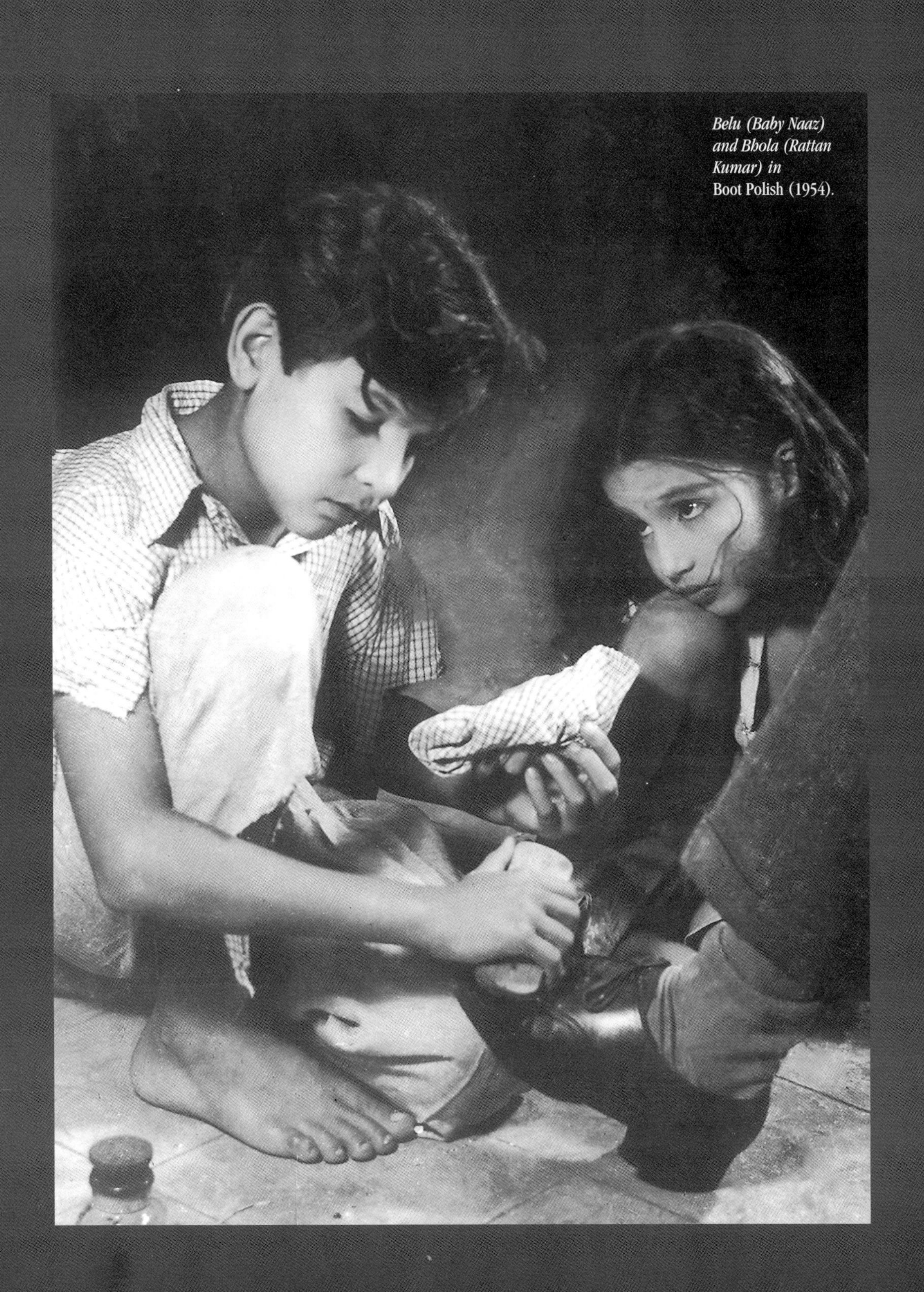

Belu (Baby Naaz) and Bhola (Rattan Kumar) in Boot Polish (1954).

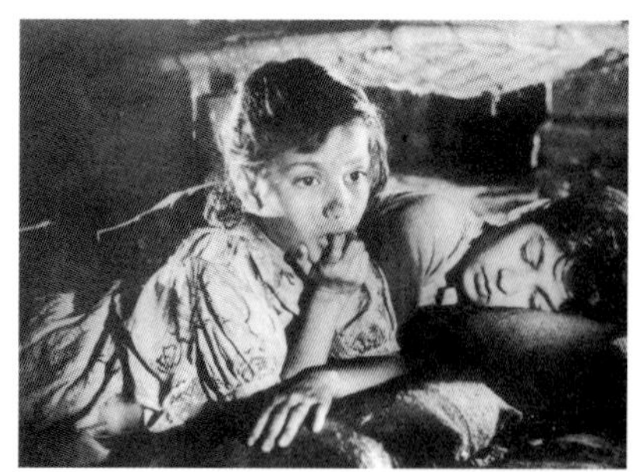

The two orphans of Boot Polish (1954).

their stories. *Izzat* (Honour) and *Pyaar* (Love) were at stake in these city films. These two virtues, these films told us, are a form of personal wealth, which cannot be bought and sold in the marketplace.

Within this broad (and simplistic) ideological framework, the stories and characters of these films have created a powerful place for themselves in the popular imagination.

Look closely at some of the key city stories. The first is Raj Kapoor's *Boot Polish*. It features two orphans growing up in a Bombay slum. Twelve-year-old Bhola and his nine-year-old sister Belu have lost their parents and find themselves in the care of a cruel, selfish aunt, Kamla *Chachi*. She forces them to beg, and beats them at the slightest provocation. She is like the wicked stepmother of our childhood fairytales. The only ray of hope in Bhola and Belu's miserable life is John *Chacha*, a bootlegger with a kindly disposition. (Bootleggers were a common feature of the urban landscape of 1950s India, given the liquor prohibition in this decade.) One day while begging in a train Chitkoo, a shoeshine boy, taunts them for being beggars. Seeing Chitkoo working, Bhola realises that Chitkoo can demand payment for his work while he and his sister must suffer the indignity of being beggars.

From this point on, the film becomes the story of Bhola and Belu's struggle to stop begging and earn their living instead. In their struggle

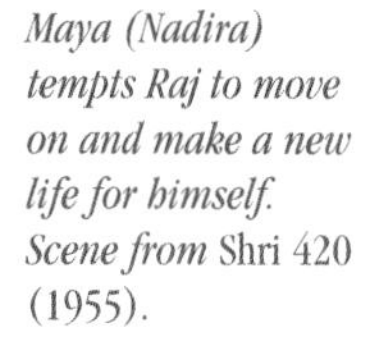

Maya (Nadira) tempts Raj to move on and make a new life for himself. Scene from Shri 420 (1955).

to achieve self-respect, Kamla *Chachi* is the villain they must free themselves from, and John *Chacha* is their mentor. Many are the moments when there's no work at hand and hunger tempts them to beg or steal, but they just about manage to resist that temptation. Honour, one of the two key *mantras* mentioned above, translates for Bhola and Belu into self-respect, which in *Boot Polish* is shown to come from earning your daily bread, and developing the courage to go hungry on days when there isn't any.

The urban classic of Hindi cinema is, however, *Shri 420* (1955), which translates in English as 'The Conman'. It tells of a penniless small-town graduate (Raj Kapoor) who comes job-hunting to the big city where he doesn't know a soul. It is the story of his critical encounters with the big city as a whole new world. The first of these encounters is with the motherly, street-side fruit vendor who gives him his first meal after his long journey and a place to sleep at night. The place to sleep is just a hut on the pavement where she herself resides. The second encounter involves a beautiful but poor young schoolteacher with whom he falls in love. Then suddenly, riches come his way when he finds himself catapulted overnight from a low-paid laundry worker to a cardsharper. This creates a major moral dilemma: he must either forsake all the money he has suddenly earned as a conman, or risk losing these two women — the schoolteacher and the motherly fruit vendor — who constitute his home, metaphorically speaking, in the big bad world of Bombay.

The face of temptation, which is also fashionably western, and a little too modern for Raj (and for most Indian men) in Shri 420! *The temptress is Maya (Nadira).*

The temptation to move on, to leave them behind and make a new life for himself is powerful, and Raj gives in at first. After all, he rationalises, he is robbing the rich to benefit the poor (!). But his beloved, Vidya (Nargis), just does not buy this justification for a career based on fraud and deception. They part ways as a result, until Raj discovers one day that his rich employer has just made him the key player in a massive financial fraud — this time on hundreds of the city's poor. Among the victims is his adopted mother, the poor fruit vendor. This, for Raj, is the last straw. A wrong done to 'Ma' has always been where the Indian hero has drawn the line — in folk theatre for centuries, and in folk cinema ever since it came into existence. In a dramatic climax, Raj throws up this high-profile but shady career for these two women — the one his friend and wife-to-be, the other his adopted mother.

The emotional strain of giving up the pleasure and power of being very rich in the big, modern city in the name of honesty, love and poverty's imagined dignity has, however, been such that Raj packs his bags to leave the city for good: 'It's too much to cope with,' he explains. Besides, he is unemployed again. At the film's climactic moment, however, when he is at the city's outer gate so to speak, we see him being persuaded by Vidya to return to the big city and accept the challenge of that life,

The Courtesan & the Nawab who fall in love, but can never marry. Rekha & Farouque Shaikh play the doomed lovers in Umrao Jaan (1981).

warts and all. To use an American cliché, she makes him realise that he 'can't go home again'...

Shri 420 is perhaps the only film in which this question of leaving the city is explicitly posed, and it is resolved in the city's favour. Having done so, the question seemed settled in Bombay filmdom, and almost no Hindi film of the 1950s or '60s ever posed it again. Instead, they busied themselves coping with city life from the inside, from the viewpoint of those who had come to stay.(Two exceptions do come to mind — *Do Bigha Zameen* (1953) and *Jab Jab Phool Khile* (1965), but neither can really be called city films.)

From this point on, our city films branch off in two directions: *one, to redeem the old, pre-colonial cities* like Lucknow, Old Delhi and Hyderabad which had fallen into disrepute after succumbing to the British colonisers over a hundred years ago; and *two, to romance the chawl*, the neighbourhood of the poor in the industrial metropolis.

The cinematic *chawl* offered viewers a lifestyle and habitat culturally and spiritually superior to the loneliness and corruption of the bungalows and skyscrapers of the rich. In films featuring Lucknow and other pre-colonial cities, the conflict was between old-world cultural

Love, Lucknow style. Tanuja & Shashi Kapoor show us the way they did it back in the old days, in Benazeer (1964).

Letter-writing in the pre-Email era. So who will get this princess's love poem? Nishi has the answer in Sher Afghan (1966).

refinement and modern greed. Money and the Marketplace were, basically, the common enemy that both kinds of films battled against.

To say that the British hijacked us into the industrial metropolis in the first half of the 20th century and left us there is only part of the urban Indian story. For alongside Bombay and Calcutta there existed many older, pre-colonial cities that constituted another kind of urban reality, the reality of old, *nawabi* graces surviving amidst economic decay and the ruins of Mughal architecture. These old graces (which had for generations been part of folklore and miniature art) were brought out of the cultural attic by filmmakers like Guru Dutt, B R Chopra, H S Rawail and their scriptwriters, dusted off and polished into a major fictional resource for building an Indian urbanity on screen.

Thus Guru Dutt's 1960 film, *Chaudvin Ka Chand* (The Full Moon) opens with a song eulogising Lucknow as the capital of Awadhi culture. Lucknow's women, it says, are exquisitely beautiful, their natural demeanour and conversation embodies centuries of grace. Lucknow's men, similarly, are men of their word, who know how to be rich, who are generous to a fault, and who know the meaning of loyalty and friendship. To gladden the heart of ecologists, the song also praises the old trees in the city's congested lanes and streets where there are birds

So who is she? Wife Nigar Sultana questions her famous poet husband played by Bharat Bhushan- in Mirza Ghalib (1954).

on every branch, adding to the music of everyday life.

The Lucknow of *Chaudvin Ka Chand* is a place vibrant with *bonhomie*, fraternity, old-world grace and intense love affairs behind the veil. Through almost the entire first half of the film you are taken from one 'feel good' moment to another. There is the meeting of the three friends at the *nawab's* mansion — a home that epitomises the Good Life. Backslapping, jokes and proclamations of filial love mark the meeting. Though one of the three friends — the host — is a wealthy *nawab* (Rehman), the other is an ordinary store clerk and unpublished poet (played by Guru Dutt), the third the unemployed son (played by comedian Johnny Walker) of a police official. While never letting you forget that the *nawab* is much higher in social status than the other two, their friendship is presented to viewers as one that totally transcends class differences. To call this unrealistic is to miss the point. Aspirations are what popular cinema is about, and what we have here are the social-democratic, modernist aspirations of late-1950s India pasted onto old-world Lucknow.

This introduction is followed in the film by a fateful trip to the *bazaar* where the *nawab's* eyes meet, for less than a minute, with those of a beautiful woman (played by Waheeda Rehman) who will henceforth colour his dreams. Her name is Shaida, but he doesn't know that yet. Before the *nawab* can come back to reality, she is gone, becoming one among dozens of *burkhas* milling around in the crowded *bazaar*. After this comes the episode of Johnny Walker about to be punished by his police officer father for returning home rather late one evening. The angry father has lined up a dozen boots to give his truant son the hiding of his life. Looking at the boots, the son is horror-struck. His mother, pleading his case with her husband, saves him at the last minute! So what you have is a sweet, charming little world where everything is in its place, and there's a place for everything.

In this setting of a refurbished urban utopia is played out the tale of three friends, two of whom unknowingly fall in love with the same woman. When they realise this near the film's end, one steps out of the other's way, by committing suicide! You can't ask for more. Rivalry between men (which is a common experience in our real lives at work and at home) rears its familiar, ugly head for a brief while in *Chaudvin Ka Chand*, and then is resolved forever — by *noblesse oblige*.

This quality of leaving you with the feeling that you can't ask for more is, the film suggests, synonymous with Lucknow, with urbanity Hindustani style — *tehzeeb*, in one Urdu word. The Muslim men of Lucknow as depicted in this film echo the opening song: *they are gentlemen* who will pay with their life in order to uphold their code of honour and generosity. The man who commits suicide is Lucknow's leading aristocrat, who unknowingly gives away the woman he desires to his own friend in marriage. The aristocrat had seen her but once, and that for a moment in a crowded bazaar. And he still does not know her name or family. His friend, who accepts her in marriage, gets to see his bride's face only after the wedding ceremony — on the marital bed, literally. On learning about this terrible mistake a few weeks after the marriage, and realising that he still desires her and none other, the *nawab* ends his life.

That this *nawab* could use his power over his friend, who is indebted to him in a dozen ways, does not even occur to him. The use of power and wealth to gratify personal desire is not something Lucknow's men do. On the contrary, the *nawab*'s dying wish, whispered in his friend's ears, is that his wife (Shaida) must never know that she is indirectly the cause of the suicide. Why? So that she never has to bear the guilt that might follow on learning the cause of this suicide (!)

Consider for a moment now, the relationship between the cinematic, imagined city, and the real city. In the real Lucknow of the 1950s, the vanished past of *zamindari* affluence, and of Urdu as lingua franca weighed upon the Muslim population. Partition in 1947 had also left the section of Muslims who opted to stay back in India haunted by self-doubt — *did they do the right thing by staying on?* Would Hindu-secular India really make place for them in its Partition-bruised heart? Lucknow more than other cities had been hit particularly hard by the Zamindari Abolition Act of 1954: the old order was forced to yield place to the new, leaving the Muslim *zamindars* and their large retinue of dependants traumatised and disoriented. A few lines from Mirza Ghalib come to mind at this point:

> 'O heart, consider even sorrow's song / To be a consolation; / For, one day, this body / Will lie without sensation.' (Varma, P. 1989: 116)

From this background came the 'nawab sahibs' of folk legend and later, of cinema. This excerpt from Qurratulain Hyder's novel, 'River of Fire', set in Lucknow of 1955, evokes the pain of Kamal, the son of one such nawab who has just returned home after graduating from Cambridge University, England:

> Kamal reached Lucknow. He entered the gates of Gulfishan and saw a changed world. The trees in the garden withered. The lawns were choked with weeds. The garage and stables had been turned into godowns. ('All Pakistan-bound relatives dump their extra luggage in here,' his mother had told him.) The out-houses were lying desolate. His eyes searched for Gunga Din. He looked forward to seeing Qadir and Qamrun. He called out the old servants' names — Hussaini's wife and Ram Autar and Ram Daiya. Finally he went to his old room, fell on his bed and began to cry...Was he so disturbed to see his father's destitution? He'd spent his life railing against the feudal order. Now after the abolition of zamindari, they were almost starving in Gulfishan...The Raja of Nanpura is selling his crockery, Raja Mehtab Singh has become penniless. Mummy has sold half her jewellery... (Hyder 1974: 44)

Bombay's leading filmmakers, many of whom (like Guru Dutt, H S Rawail, B R Chopra) were themselves refugees and migrants saw this disorientation and impoverishment of the Muslim in post-Partition India and sensed the need to provide an antidote, a world of fantasy that harked back to a glorious past. Thus *Chaudvin Ka Chand* (released in June 1960) locates itself in a golden age — it could be yesterday, it could be a hundred years ago. What is clear, however, is that the *nawabs* and *zamindars* are still very much on top in this Lucknow, and no Hindu appears anywhere in this story of a happy, fun-loving, gracefully romantic Muslim world. The film was a great box-office success, and helped its producer Guru Dutt overcome the heavy financial losses incurred by the failure of his earlier film *Kaagaz Ke Phool*.

Many other movies playing out variations on this theme followed *Chaudvin Ka Chand, Mere Mehboob* (1963) was one of them. The others included *Bahu Begum, Benazir, Ghazal, Mere Huzoor, Pakeezah, Mehboob Ki Mehndi, Paalki*, and *Nawab Sahib*...

Endnotes

1 *The Vagabond, The Conman, Mr. Native, The Crooked One, The Thirsty One, The Merchant, Bluff Master and ... The Wall, The Alexander of Fate, Don*—all released between 1951 and 1980.

References

Anand, Mulk Raj. 1935. *Coolie*, Delhi, Hind Pocket Books.

Dossal, Mariam. 1992. *Imperial Designs, Indian Realities*, Delhi, Oxford University Press.

Hyder, Qurratulain. 1974. In *River of Fire*, from Jussawalla, Adil (ed.), *New Writing in India*, Penguin Books, London.

Kaviraj, Sudipto. 1999 "The Culture of Representative Democracy", in Chatterjee, Partha (ed.), *Wages of Freedom,* Delhi, Oxford University Press.

Lewandowski, Susan J. 1977 "Changing Form and Function in the Ceremonial and Colonial Port City in India: An Historical Analysis of Madurai and Madras", *Modern Asian Studies*, II, 2.

Varma, Pavan. 1989, from Diwan-i-Ghalib, in his book *Ghalib: The Man, The Times*, Delhi, Penguin Books.

On every street in every city, there is a Nobody who wants to be a Somebody.

-Advertisement for the film Taxi Driver

Enter, The Wandering Migrant

To the impoverished rural migrant and the dispossessed Partition refugee, the big city represented a strange and hostile environment. In the eyes of these variously unsettled newcomers — whose numbers ran into the millions in the first two decades after Independence in 1947 — the industrial metropolis was a huge, anonymous place where no one cared whether you lived or died, and where you had constantly to be on guard lest you lost the few valuables you had. It was also, of course, the place where you hoped to make in a few years (if not months) much more money than you had lost.

> In the big city the twin spirits Romance and Adventure are always abroad seeking worthy wooers. As we roam the streets they slyly peep at us and challenge us in twenty different guises. Without knowing why, we look up suddenly to see in a window a face that seems to belong to our gallery of intimate portraits; in a sleeping thoroughfare we hear a cry of agony and fear, coming from an empty and shuttered house…(A) slip of paper, written upon, flutters down to our feet from the high lattices of Chance; we exchange glances of instantaneous hate, affection, and fear with hurrying strangers in the passing crowds; a sudden souse of rain – and our umbrella may be sheltering the daughter of the Full Moon…; at every corner handkerchiefs drop, fingers beckon, eyes besiege, and the lost, the lonely,… the mysterious, the perilous changing clues of adventure – are slipped into our fingers.
>
> — O Henry, On New York as quoted in Blanefield 1988: 128

The big, fast-moving city was seen as a place where tricksters and conmen wait to ensnare the innocent. In fact, contemporary Bombay's theme song, featured in the film *CID* (1956) echoes this: '*Zara dekh ke chalo, aage bhi aur peeche bhi/ Yeh hai Bumbai meri jaan!* (Watch where you go, look in front of you and look behind/ For this is Bombay, my love!)'

One response to the dangers of city life in some of these urban films was to offer viewers a daredevil, street-smart hero who has mastered the ways of the city — while still being poor. Raj Kapoor created this persona most memorably in his 1951 film *Aawara* (TheVagabond). Another variation of this persona, again by Kapoor some years later, was *Shri 420* (The Conman), who is shown to succeed in the city only when he is transformed from the innocent rustic migrant to a cardsharper and a fictitious *maharaja*.

Take our lost, quietly anxious viewer to the cinema hall and what does

The big, fast-moving city was seen as a place where tricksters thrive. This collage from S. Lateef's film Society (1955) *says it all. Kumkum is the hotel dancer (on the centre), and Iftekhar the Hollywood style plain clothes detective loading his gun.*

he/she find? He encounters interesting characters like the two mentioned above. He also finds that the cinematic city, be it Lucknow or Bombay, is basically a friendly neighbourhood with many comforting, familiar features. The most important of these is that here, in this 'neighbourhood', everyone knows you by name. Everyone. And almost everyone is decent and good. There is the odd but lovable eccentric, but most important, there is one resident who is so attractively female, so worthy of true love... In the Lucknow of *Chaudvin Ka Chand* and *Mere Mehboob*, almost the whole town knows the principal protagonists. In fact, those who don't simply don't exist! They are faceless, a passing crowd of no significance.

This, after all, is your personal city, and it is pleasurably different from the real one outside.

The cinematic city, then, is like the shade-giving *banyan* tree, custom-made for us residents of (and refugees from) the real city. We do in our real lives try and build neighbourhoods wherever possible — even in the loneliest and biggest of skyscrapers — but there is only one problem: real neighbours are ever so difficult, and some of them are really strange! Not at all like those in the movies.

The cinematic city is a friendly neighbourhood, where neighbours compensate for the missing family, as young Shyama finds out in Teen Bhai (1955).

Home-life in the city needs you to co-exist with many eccentrics within your own family. Domestic scene in Ek Phool Char Kaante (1960).

A world out of joint

The inequality of the modern metropolis is itself a central narrative in many Hindi films. The narrative in *Shri 420* centres on the conflict between the 'upper' city, the affluent domain of Seth Sonachand (literally 'Mr Gold') and others of his class, and the 'lower' city, the home of Raj the laundry worker, representing the labouring poor and their unemployed friends who live on the pavement below the rich man's mansion. The movie camera uses this part-real, part-constructed urbanscape to explore and suggest the displacement of people within their own land. A displacement that is economic as well as cultural. The protagonist of Hindi cinema's city films often does not know how to dress, talk or even walk in the upper city: he/she is an awkward, clumsy simpleton. The majority of characters in these films look at big villas and multi-storeyed buildings from the outside — in much the same way you look at sin, with its confusing mix of temptation and damnation.

Represented by voluptuous, foreign-looking mansions with big, imposing iron gates enclosing a world of opulent sofas, chiffon curtains and huge halls hung with chandeliers, these films present a city fraught with ethical ambiguity, if not downright injustice. In *Anari* for instance, the rich man who owns a pharmaceutical factory is not such a bad fellow through the film's first half; he gives our hero a job, is kind-hearted, rewards hard work, and has a beautiful, unmarried daughter (played by Nutan).

Motilal, in this scene from Kushboo, (1954) *as a fully paid-up member of the 'upper' city. The hotel's name, on which the camera dwells, is double-edged: its claim to being 'beautiful' can only be tested (and tasted) by the rich minority.*

But there comes a point when he must risk his company's reputation because bottles of a poisonous drug and a cough syrup have accidentally been exchanged in his factory, making it difficult to distinguish one from the other. People have begun to die because of this mix-up, but owning up to such a deadly mistake could destroy his company's reputation. The owner decides not to come clean, thereby triggering a major ethical conflict with our honest hero, who demands that the whole batch of drugs be recalled from the market.

For our hero, there is no ethical ambiguity — human lives are obviously much more important than a company's reputation. The owner sacks our hero; little realising that this one act will spell his doom in the moral universe of the city in popular cinema. (Heroes, as any Hindi film fan could have told that owner, are not for sacking. You don't sack God.)

Not surprisingly then, within this moral landscape the big houses and gleaming corporate offices are not just physical features of the city's skyline. They speak; they are emotionally loaded. Moreover, they are downright inaccessible (and yet desirable). Combining envy and disapproval, the movie camera dwells on their opulence in a way that mirrors the antagonism of the down-and-out populace, which resides in pavement shacks or cramped tenements.

The clubs and villas of the rich with their sinfully attractive ways. Rehman in this scene from Miss Bombay (1957) *provides a glimpse of life in the 'upper city'.*

Chalte-chalte, kahaan aa gaye hum? [1]

The image of a people displaced within their own borders is a key motif in our city films, but in a symbolic way. The real city teems with refugees, impoverished peasants, and a large floating population of visitors, coolies, traders and construction workers grouped by village of origin. Even those who have apparently stable clerical or executive jobs in offices are not quite free from this pervasive sense of displacement. They live in big, busy neighbourhoods, or more often in tall buildings, sharing walls and lonely corridors with strangers who are different, often difficult, and sometimes even dangerous. Hindi novels, plays and short stories dealing with the city in the 1950s-70s have occasionally articulated this experience, but in a muffled fashion.

Popular cinema has more than made up for this lack, even if crudely — by focusing on the homeless job-seeker who, even if he has a rented room, doesn't know where the next month's rent is coming from. Manmohan Desai's *Bluff Master* (1963) is one of the best examples of this, as is Subodh Mukherji's *Paying Guest* (1957). In Hindi cinema of this period, Old India grapples with the modernity of the industrial metropolis. The hero or heroine are inevitably displaced persons.

An image of the real city on screen. Vinod Khanna: All I want is some sugar and milk. Rekha: Not now. Later, when my brother returns.

There are shades to the hero's displacement. In Guru Dutt's *Pyaasa* (1957), Vijay the simple-living-high-thinking protagonist is an unpublished writer expelled from his joint family by his brothers because he does not yet earn a living. What kindles our interest in the movie is not Vijay's displacement per se, but the events that follow it. Resigned to sleeping on park benches and eating erratically, our emaciated, dishevelled but very sensitive hero embarks on a search for a file of his poems that has been sold off as waste paper by his callous, semi-literate brothers. The merchant who bought it recalls that 'some young woman bought it only yesterday', but he does not know her name or address.

So how then is Vijay to find her? As any Hindi film buff will tell you, there is only one way. And that is to tramp the narrow, dark streets of the city until your ears pick up a song-in-the-making. On getting closer, of course, you discover that one of your own lost poems is being rendered by a beautiful young woman in some hovel — le lotus en swamp! Thus our hero Vijay (Guru Dutt) meets our heroine Gulabo (Waheeda Rehman) one lonely night in a park. Cities, especially the cities of our dreams, have long existed for just such adventures on lonely nights; that is what they are for. All lost beings, if they are important for the hero/heroine, will be found. And when they are, they will take the story in a new direction.

Gulabo is not merely poor, however, but a street-walker who picks up customers from parks and street-corners. But this being a Guru Dutt movie which breaks stereotypes, she is not a hardened, worldly-wise prostitute. No, Gulabo is a bit of this and a bit of that. Like Vijay the displaced intellectual, she too is a misfit in the red-light district. The most unsettled figure in the film, paradoxically, is Mala, who was the most settled of them all until she accidentally encountered Vijay at a college reunion.

Mala (played by Mala Sinha) and Vijay were lovers back in their college days. That was years ago, though we are not told how many. But now she is a happily married, upper-class housewife married to a rich publisher. Our first glimpse of her is of her shopping for saris. From the moment she first encounters a sloppily dressed and impoverished Vijay at the - college reunion, her life is never the same. And when Vijay (recently recruited by her husband at his publishing office) lands up some weeks later as her husband's 'servant' at a party in her home, she is totally shaken. Vijay meanwhile, is in his poetic element at that moment as Spurned Lover No 1!

The artist and his muse: Though this scene featuring Waheeda Rehman and Guru Dutt is from Kaagaj Ke Phool *(1959), here too she plays a successful filmstar who is sensitive to the artistic frustrations of the unemployed film director played by Guru Dutt.*

Since these screen figures are supposed to be our larger-than-life dream-selves, is Guru Dutt the filmmaker suggesting that we are all misfits in the big, bad city?

Displacement is also central to many of Raj Kapoor's classics. Raju, the character Kapoor plays in these films of the 1950s, frequently lands up in situations that shake his very identity. These identity crises happen suddenly, for a few tortuous moments, but they are interspersed with comedy. For example in *Aawara*, he is a thief who, while escaping from the police, seeks shelter in a house which turns out to belong to a judge, who is the guardian of Raju's childhood sweetheart, Rita (Nargis). While waiting for her in the hall, Raju pockets an expensive-looking ashtray lying on the table.

The very next moment Rita, his old flame, enters the room. Recognising him, she says on coming closer, 'Oh...and I thought you were a thief.' He replies, 'That is what I am,' and quietly replaces the ashtray on the table. (She dismisses his confession as a joke.) Similarly in *Jaagte Raho* (1956), a simple country yokel desperately looking for a drink of water in the city is mistaken for a thief and forced to hide in a building where he encounters various forms of lawlessness. Like Charlie Chaplin, Raj Kapoor generates humour from the experience of displacement, and various responses to it.

Bhootnath, the protagonist of Guru Dutt's later film, *Sahib, Bibi Aur Ghulam* (1962), is a country bumpkin who has just come to Calcutta. The day after his arrival he's taken by his host to meet a prospective employer. Bhootnath wears his new shoes for what is probably the first time in his life, and they squeak loudly with each step he takes! The result: his arrival before the employer is preceded by these noisy squeaks, and then we see him entering the room for the interview with a pair of big, shiny shoes in his hand. In this brilliantly comic sequence, Bhootnath the rustic is Displacement personified.

Beyond displacement

Look a little closer at the underlying structure of these films, however, and you find that displacement is only half the story. Consider Raj, the small-town migrant in Shri 420, during the first 30 minutes after reaching Bombay. The same young man who was so confident and upbeat about his resilient Indian heart while tramping the distance to Bombay (singing '*Mera joota hai Japani, yeh patloon Inglistani...phir bhi dil hai Hindustani*') is instantly undone by the big city's frenzied human and vehicular traffic.

After stepping out of traffic's way, the beggar he meets forecasts doom

Raj the newly arrived migrant gets a taste of life on the street with three residents of the 'lower' city, in Shri 420 (1955).

for him because Raj expects to get a job on the strength of his education. The beggar mocks him, remarking that this city, this Bambai, is not for simpletons. Moving away, Raj slips on a banana peel, then has all his money stolen, and is finally thwarted even in his attempt to sleep on the pavement by those who have already occupied it.

But wait, it is not all a tale of displacement. Wanting to buy bananas from a fruit vendor moments after leaving the beggar's cynical company, but being penniless, he gets two bananas from her on credit. When he says he doesn't know when he will have the money to pay her, she replies: 'That's okay, I'll just pretend that my son ate them.' Raj is very grateful for her kindness, and asks, 'So how old is your son?' She smiles, and answers, 'Oh, hmm, about your age, I guess.'

That night, as he struggles to find a place to sleep on the pavement, his fairy godmother — the fruit vendor, of course — materialises again and rescues him. A day or two after this pavement life, Raj gets a job in a laundry. He finds Vidya, the beautiful schoolteacher, soon after that. Displacement is followed by comfort plus romance, which in turn is followed by displacement, and so on. There is a pattern here, a swing down and up. This kind of swinging between displacement and comfort continues throughout the film; you could almost call it its rhythm, its underlying emotional structure.

Dev Anand, in another very popular, very urban film *Kaala Pani* (1958),

Dev Anand the young journalist seeks his father's forgiveness for having come so late to meet him, in Kaala Pani (1958).

plays an intense young journalist working at a Bombay newspaper. One day at home he stumbles upon a piece of paper showing that his father, who he thought was dead, is actually alive. Confronting his mother with this, he learns that his father is serving a life sentence in a jail in another city, Hyderabad, apparently for a murder committed 15 years ago, in 1943. Dev drops everything and leaves for Hyderabad. (Heroes, unlike us, are not people who think ten times, and weigh all the pros and cons before taking such big decisions. No, they act. *They think on their feet, in motion.*) On arrival, he finds a father who has disowned him and his mother, for betraying him. Says the father to his shocked son: 'I was framed. I am not guilty. And your mother — she did not even bother to hear this from me!' (Displacement, here we come!)

The rest of the film is about a son setting out, in a city in which he has no one to turn to for help, to establish his father's innocence by digging up and re-examining the case which has now been closed for 15 years. To do this, however, he must stay in Hyderabad indefinitely, and risk losing his Bombay job in the process. No matter, the film suggests, it is much more important that the son mend broken bridges with his victimised father. (This is another thing about heroes — their priorities are crystal clear, not a muddled mess like ours. They know who they are, where they are going, and what they should do when dilemmas arise. And we don't want them to be otherwise. For they are the doubt-free projections of a doubt-filled public.)

The hero, Dev Anand looking through old newspaper records to reopen his father's case in Kaala Pani (1958).

Barely five minutes of screen-time after he makes this solemn promise to his father, we find him in a local newspaper office, asking to look at the paper's 1943 issues. And who does he meet at this office? A busy but absolutely stunning Madhubala, as the paper's chief reporter who almost makes him forget what he came looking for. They look at each other, sparks fly, music stirs the air for a few seconds, and a love affair, marked by many acts of kindness from her, seems inevitable. (Comfort, once again. Allah be praised!)

The story as it unspools on the screen, however, is not only about them and his research into a closed legal case. Another attractive young woman enters our hero's life shortly after, but the displacement-comfort pattern is at work through it all.

Another attractive woman enters our hero's love life, thereby complicating his relationship with the beautiful chief reporter played by Madhubala.

Love and the housing question

Love, of course, is the mother of all patterns in Hindi cinema. Let us glance briefly at how it cracks, as wild flowers do, the concrete jungle, the forbidding, high walls of the modern, cinematic city. Time and again in most of these films, poor boy falls in love with rich girl, she reciprocates, they overcome monstrous odds, and then get married. But where then do they go to live happily ever after? Where, in other words, does marital love reside?

Not in the poor boy's hut or tenement, no. They go to her mansion, or to his mansion. If it is to be her mansion, her father will have to be jailed or must die. This happens in *Anari*, and in *Bluff Master*. Whose mansion they will reside in, however, is not as big an issue as the fact that the couple must now move up in life. As we all know deep down, huts have no future. They are fine, even ennobling, as launch pads, but by the time you have 'found' yourself, have married the one you love, and are 25, you have to move on. You have to, that's what city life is all about.

The future is in that mansion, yes, that shamefully opulent villa which you and your movie camera have examined every silk-clad nook and cranny of, while crusading for the great purge. The purge which results, near film's end, detoxifies the villa of all the sin and injustice which went into its making. It is now cleansed and ready to receive the new master or mistress. Occasionally, the new master goes to jail instead of the villa at film's end. This happens in Raj Kapoor's *Aawara*. But he goes to jail only after we know for sure that he is the rich man's long-lost son, that he will return after his short prison term, and that a deeply

You better decide, between that woman and me. You can't have it both ways. says Madhubala to Dev Anand in Kaala Pani (1958).

apologetic father and beaming bride-to-be shall both be waiting at the doorstep when he comes.

While this is as it should be, no pattern is foolproof — in art as in life. *Asli Naqli* (1961) is one film where this choice between mansion and hut becomes a major issue, with the hero deciding close to the climactic moment to spurn the mansion in which he was born and grew up. He chooses, when challenged, to go to the *chawl* of huts and cramped quarters where he 'found' himself and his beloved. This gesture is not where the film ends, however. Something else follows, but it will all make better sense after a brief summary of the film's story.

Money can't buy you love!

While the young male hero is a poor and homeless migrant in most city films, there are a few where he is the rich man's son, as in Hrishikesh Mukherjee's *Asli Naqli*, starring Dev Anand and Sadhana. The character he plays, Anand, is a spoilt rich kid whose parents died in a car crash; he now lives with his grandfather, who is very wealthy. Be that as it may, Anand now squanders his time and his grandfather's money on wine, women and song, until he is openly rebuked by the grandfather one day for being a wastrel. The rich but displaced grandson walks out of his mansion, penniless, into the big city's streets, to find himself. He is picked up, exhausted and hungry, from a park bench by Mohan, a textile millworker returning from work at midnight, and given food and shelter — gratis. (Comfort follows displacement, remember.) He has now entered the *asli* world, the kind-hearted world of workers living together in a *chawl*, like one big and squabbling happy family. For much of the rest of the film we see him living there, working as a bus-driver, romancing a beautiful schoolteacher. (Note here that in the world of Hindi cinema, the poor and the displaced have generosity, humanity and beauty on their side. A little unfairly, all the rich are allowed to have in Indian cinema are silk dressing gowns and opulent villas. No redeeming, human virtues for the rich. And even when beauty is born rich, she crosses over to the poor well before the interval!)

It is only near *Asli Naqli's* end that Anand's cover is blown and his *chawl*-mates learn that he is actually the rich man's grandson. They are furious at this betrayal by someone they have come to love as one of their own! That is the moment when Anand is confronted with the big choice — between mansion and hut, between an honest, morally sound if poor lifestyle, and its opposite. Thus the film's title *Asli/Naqli* (True/False). The plot concludes with the rich grandfather's sudden change of heart forced upon him by the grandson's exit from the mansion, despite the threat of disinheritance. The old man's angry face, which was so full of the arrogance of wealth when confronting Anand with the big choice and delivering the disinheritance threat, crumples as he watches the young man (his only grandchild) going off into his new world — the *chawl*. Anand has made his choice. It is now up to the grandfather to realise that wealth by itself brings little solace. This realisation comes soon enough.

In contrasting the emotional authenticity (and moral 'wealth') of the working class with the emotional barrenness of the rich as he does when renouncing his inheritance and the whole lifestyle his grandfather represents, Anand echoes folk wisdom on what makes for 'real' happiness. The cynic in you might well sneer at Anand's rhetoric and say that this brand of 'real' happiness is useful strictly for consoling the poor. The Beatles in Liverpool, several thousand miles away but around the same time, summarised it all with musical aplomb in their song 'Money can't buy you love…'

At another level, however, Anand's move to the *chawl* where the events of *Asli Naqli* take place is about the need to mediate between the 'heart' (of the rich) and the 'hands' (of the working class). He is the rich young man with a heart that is still pure; he is also the rich orphan whose parents' absence had led him astray until Mohan the poor but large-hearted millworker restored his faith in humanity. The essential message of this film for the middle class and the rich in socialist, Nehruvian India of the 1950s and '60s was that they had better change their equation with the poor, else they would end up being out of step with Young India, and with their own children. While asking the rich to be more humane in their transactions with the poor would be a clichéd Sunday sermon, here clichés are side-stepped by ensuring that the poor are also the young and the beautiful, whom we enjoy identifying with. By contrast the rich, as embodied in the figure of Seth Dwarkanath, the grandfather, are old, stuffy and autocratic — which makes them automatically out of sync with post-colonial India's incipient democratic culture. Being a film aimed at the box-office, however, *Asli Naqli's* message is not a threatening one at all, but it is a message of change. The film's concluding scene says it all.

The grandfather Seth Dwarkanath himself comes down to Anand's hut on the day he is marrying Renu the schoolteacher, blesses the couple, and hands over the documents of his entire wealth (including, of course, the mansion's title deed, where as we said before, the young couple must end up residing) to Renu. The crusty old tycoon's hard heart having finally melted, this is his wedding gift to his grand-daughter-in-law. The entire *chawl*, the 'people' in other words, are now, finally, all smiles. One of them comes forward to insist that the just-reformed Dwarkanath cannot leave before partaking of the food they are all eating to celebrate the marriage of their little world's star couple — Anand and Renu. He demurs at first, but gives in a moment later and takes a bite. Slowly his wrinkled old face breaks into a big, warm smile. The film ends.

Playing with an obvious, stereotyped good-versus-evil motif, the film does not indict urbanisation or its inequalities in themselves, but rather, the abuse of urbanisation. Another vision of the metropolis is offered here, one of managed utopia — of Old India made new by a democratised civility, a new kind of mutual respect between the rich and the poor. Hrishikesh Mukherjee's *Asli Naqli* is a film about enabling the heart of the rich to encompass and come to terms with the hands of the working class.

The *chawl* as utopia

Back to real life again, for a moment. The modern, industrial city tends, as it grows and prospers, to become a conglomeration of segmented, isolated lifestyles, in which an integrative centre, a shared culture, becomes more and more a chimera. Each citizen pursues survival and personal advancement in a marketplace that is very harsh on losers. For better or worse, this is 'common sense' for us living in 21st-century urban India, as also for our counterparts in cities ranging from Moscow, Karachi, Singapore and Hong Kong, to Los Angeles, New York and Paris.

An image of the kind-hearted world of workers living together in a chawl, like one big and squabbling happy family..." Yashodhara Katju and Gope flirt in the kitchen while the rest of the family is away, in Rakhi (1949).

What may be surprising to people today — especially to Indians who are 40-plus and look nostalgically back at the good old 1950s — is that this was basically how the big city felt to migrants and refugees entering Bombay, Calcutta or Delhi in the 1950s. As the beggar tells Raj the newcomer in the 1955 film *Shri 420*: 'This is Bambai, young man. Here new buildings come up every day; much wealth is generated, but not jobs for the likes of you and me…Here people have hearts of stone…' In a similar vein, the popular song from the 1961 film *CID* which begins, 'Be careful where you go/ Look ahead, look left and right,/ And don't ever forget to look behind,/ For this is Bombay, my love,' goes on to speak of how it's a dog-eat-dog world out there, how 'business' is a euphemism for inhuman exploitation, and so on.

If the city is experienced thus by the protagonists of our city films, then the *chawl* onscreen is precisely that integrative centre — the humane, caring, pluralist heart, which is absent in the real city.

The presentation of such a centre, part-fiction though it be, helps us viewers handle the city as a novel experience. You can call it a necessary fiction. In reality, in the real Bombay circa 1947-72, *chawls* did exist in large number — especially around the textile mills, the docks and near railway workshops in Bombay; in Calcutta they were called *bustees*. They housed industrial workers and their families. But these 'real' *chawls* were marked (and divided) by ethnicity — families or male groups of workers clustered according to their village of origin, their language, their religion. This makes them quite different from the imagined *chawl* onscreen, which houses people from all castes and creeds living cheek by jowl in a happy, multi-ethnic mosaic.

Again, honour (*izzat* in Hindi film parlance) is a major issue in the real *chawl*. It represents self-respect and identity vis-à-vis the Other (this Other is constituted by social groups that are ethnically different). Honour on screen, however, is a much broader concept: it is the honour of the labouring poor ('*mazdoor*' in Hindi film parlance) as a composite whole, a class that is inclusive of different ethnicities. The Other here is equally broadly defined — the Rich, often depicted as factory-owners.

This universalising impulse came to post-Independence cinema from the nationalist movement, especially the left wing of nationalism. Popular cinema obliterates all barriers between ethnic groups because, of course, it wants to ensure that all ethnic groups buy cinema tickets. But in the process, it does create a symbolic counter to the ethnic, segmented reality of Indian lives off-screen; it does expand the imagination and the mental/emotional horizons of the viewer.

Thus the *chawl*, the multi-ethnic inner city tenement, becomes a utopia in the city films of the 1950s and '60s. What makes the tenement a

The cinematic Chawl, *like this one in* Tanhai (1961), *functioned in the 1950-60's as a cultural symbol for what is good in the big-bad 'mechanical' city for the middle and lower class viewers, especially those contemplating the city as their future.*

utopia is its cosmopolitanism — the fact that it is home to a wide variety of strangers, intermingling across ethnic boundaries without causing any serious friction. In Nasir Husain's *Baharon Ke Sapne* (1962), for instance, in the setting of a poor Bombay hutment, there takes place an extended courtship between the comedian Rajendranath, playing a shop assistant from Punjab, and Jayashree, the attractive young daughter of a *kelewali* (banana-seller), who also sells bananas. Both she and her mother speak only one language — Marathi. Our amorous shop assistant speaks only Punjabi. He knows not a word of Marathi. As a result, his attempts to woo Jayashree, conducted in the mother's presence, are mired in misunderstandings. While he copes with this linguistic hurdle, however, you know that he will eventually succeed, because love is all he's asking for, and love is one thing that is possible in this make-believe world.

Banana-sellers are also a frequent motif in Raj Kapoor's city films, partly perhaps because they were a distinctive presence — a metaphor for the poor person as an independent figure with personality and spirit — on the streets of Bombay until recently. In *Shri 420*, the first person Raj encounters is the Marathi-speaking banana-seller. This is the Hindi-speaking Raj's first encounter with another ethnic group. But their hearts meet as they tussle to reach an understanding about the price of the bananas. For a moving moment of screen time, *Shri 420* offers the penniless newcomer and the banana-seller to us as two complete strangers who, despite their linguistic difficulties, are generous and have no ulterior motive. They look into each other's souls for a brief moment, like what they see there, and end up adopting one another as mother and son. This transition from momentary affinity to a lasting relationship happens a little later in the film, when Raj is about to be ejected from a patch of pavement where he tries to curl up for the night, his first in Bombay. She intervenes to stop his ejection.

Having somehow gained entry into the chawl, the migrant protagonist of our city films has 'arrived': he has found a social-emotional foothold from which to launch forth into the city of strangers. He has found a 'home' that soon grows to be a mother-substitute. This image of the tenement as mother, an underlying psychological motif in many city films from the mid-1950s onwards, offers viewers a picture of slums redeemed by warm, close-knit family ties and multi-ethnic neighbourhoods, harking back to a cosy ideal village with its friendly tea-stalls, street-side markets, safe ethnicity and naughty but nice sex.

The cinematic *chawl*, the good city within the big bad city, is best summed up as an emporium of heart-warming civilities between people of widely differing ethnic stock. Ethnic walls, by contrast, divide the real *chawl*. They are what sociologist Ira Katznelson calls 'city trenches', where the degree of civility is directly proportional to the social distance between groups.

As Katznelson puts it:

> Most people live on the margin of history. They experience its flux, their lives are shaped by inherited and shifting limits, and their daily behaviour testifies to the constraints on their lives. And yet, people are never merely passive agents of structural imperatives. Within lives whose definitions and possibilities are largely created for them, they create families, symbols, solidary ties, beliefs, friendships, institutions, rebellions. In short, people create a culture, which...composes a set of resources for living in society and for affecting the contours of society. (Katznelson 1981: 1)

The fictional, cinematic *chawl*, the big but benign village within the city, is an example of filmmakers creating a cultural symbol which has a profound resonance for middle- and lower-class viewers in Indian cities, and in smaller towns where youth gaze upon and fantasise about the big city as their future.

The Hindi film that provides the most extended and deliciously ironic treatment of our filmi *chawl* was made almost 30 years after the 1950s films created the *chawl* as a cinematic idea. That film is Sai Paranjpye's *Katha* (1983), a story of two young men, friends from the same small-town college, but with sharply contrasting personalities. The friends embody in their personae two opposing ways of coping with the big city. One, played by Naseeruddin Shah, is a rustic simpleton employed as a clerk in a big, anonymous office. He is the good, obedient, hard-working son who dutifully sends part of his monthly salary to his ageing parents back in the village. The other, played by Farooque Shaikh, is a smooth-talking rogue who survives by his wits and makes the most, rather greedily, of any job he gets for as long as it lasts. *Katha* (Story) is about the storms created by him in the cosy, settled world of the chawl, and especially in the humdrum routine of his friend. The film takes off when the rogue comes to stay 'for just a few days' with his friend, our good clerk.

Katha's chawl, resembling those in films like *Taxi Driver, Asli Naqli, Bluff Master, Baharon Ke Sapne* and *Shri 420*, is a place where you are known by name, and where your guests are soon accepted as the *chawl's* guests. Not only do the *chawl's* residents know you, they remark upon your comings and goings. In short, you matter. You are a character in a non-threatening, familial landscape. The *chawl* is a big, sprawling, extended family. Its walls and staircases are alive with uncles, aunts, nephews and nieces.....Far away from the *chawl*, its opposite in a sense, is the cold, arrogant villa, which is the space of wealth whose sources are immoral.

Secondly, the *chawl* is a place where you are accepted unconditionally, where your class identity, your income, are of little significance. You are valued for just being human. No wonder then that it becomes a haven which you can escape to and relax in. In most ways then, the *chawl* is the antithesis of the city; it is everything the big, bad, anonymous, inhuman city is not.

The accumulation of wealth is a dubious achievement in the society of the *chawl*. If you do have it, you keep it under wraps. The *chawl* is a society of thrift and mutual dependence, of giving and taking of spoons of sugar and half-cups of milk. Much is made of these sugary comings and goings by director Sai Paranjpye in her film *Katha* — as an ironic acknowledgement by exaggeration of trend-setting precursors from the 1950s and early-'60s like *Shri 420, Asli Naqli* and *Baharon Ke Sapne*.

Through the *chawl's* assembly of characters, the city becomes an object on view. The *chawl* gives us the modern industrial city as a subject the viewer can begin thinking about, and developing a relationship with. The cinematic *chawl*, in other words, is not just an image of utopia. It is a lens through which to see and grasp the living, unmanageable city in a familiar, manageable idiom.

A close up of a room inside a working class chawl *from* Baharon Ke Sapne. *Rajesh Khanna plays the young factory worker informing his mother(Sulochana) that he may lose his job tomorrow.*

And occasionally, when the hero of these city films does not live in a *chawl*, he is a tenant in a flat whose landlady embodies all the positive qualities of the *chawl* — despite his inability to pay the rent regularly. Examples of such films that come readily to mind are *Anari*, and *Paying Guest*. No children, husbands or neighbours complicate this surrogate mother-son scenario, especially in *Anari*. From this starting point, the handsome young tenant and the kindly old landlady proceed to construct a utopian nest which is totally insulated from the ravages of the city — that *duniya* often condemned in rhetoric and film song, where no relationship is free of the immorality of the marketplace. (Yes, the real city resembles this *duniya*, but here in this movie space we will get the better of it, not just escape from it — just you wait.)

For the most fulsome picture of the landlady as surrogate mother, there is none to equal the Goan widow-landlady, Mrs D'Sa, portrayed brilliantly by Lalita Pawar in *Anari*. Her little acts of kindness towards her jobless tenant, and her deceptions to hide that kindness, are such as to put most real mothers to shame. The young Indian man in Raj Kapoor's films is hungry for maternal love; he thrives on it, even while putting on his tough and self-reliant act.

Even when the landlady is not shown as overtly maternal, she is still a good-hearted person with a sense of humour—as is Pritam's landlady, played by the overweight comedienne Tuntun in Guru Dutt's *Mr. & Mrs. 55*.

Having created a safe little haven inside the heartless city, the protagonists proceed to engage with the contingencies and conflicts of modern life. The main dramatic conflict in this utopia comes from the class difference between rich boy-poor girl, or vice versa. Occasionally, as in *Shri 420*, it happens that both are poor; the drama then centres around how best to get rich quick and get married. The love story can be sustained in film after film because it is also a quest story, and it is this latter dimension that enables it to engage our hearts and minds. The hero's quest in the city films is to find himself a career and an identity. Identity is a serious matter in Hindi cinema, but not in the way it is in Hollywood films such as *The Graduate, Easy Rider, A Streetcar Named Desire, On the Waterfront*, etc. These films make the identity quest a very individualistic, personalised affair.

The identity quest in Hindi movies is different, and yes, somewhat simplistic. It is an archetypal coming-of-age fable, where the hero goes through a major trial by fire. The trial tests his moral fibre, more specifically the strength of his convictions in the face of great temptation and danger. He becomes our hero by succeeding in this trial, and that success gives him his identity. What varies from film to film is the particular existential situation which comes to constitute the hero's trial by fire: this includes biographical details like the job he has or is about to lose, his being rich or poor, his particular mix of familial obligations and the way they threaten his personal desires.

Halfway through *Shri 420*, for instance, we see the suddenly prosperous Raj looking at himself in the mirror just before leaving for a party one evening. He stands before the mirror as the cardsharper clad in a black tuxedo and white scarf, but what he sees mirrored is the old Raj of a few weeks ago — the small-town migrant with a modest daily wage but not a care in the world. The old Raj smiles with just a hint of mockery at the new one, compliments him on his smart new clothes, and urges him to go and have a great evening. But the new Raj can't leave. He wants to go back to that earlier existence, which also included Vidya the schoolteacher, whom he still loves. But when he reaches out to touch and hold that old Raj, the image disappears, and all we see is the man in the tuxedo. Here begins the hero's identity crisis.

Should the new Raj give up all the comforts of this life, or should he leave behind his impoverished past and give his new career a real chance? We see him driving late at night to a hutment after the party, the very same hutment where he had slept on his first night in Bombay, looking at it from afar, wondering whether he should go up and meet his poor, old friends. If we step back a moment from Raj and the movie, this dilemma can be seen as symbolic of the confusions and sense of loss which urban growth and social change throw up for all of us.

Raj's dilemma in *Shri 420* is framed in strongly moral terms. At stake here is not just one individual's choice, but also the new morality of the capitalist marketplace versus the old virtues of honesty and hard work. The number of people Raj meets in Bombay who have become rich by seizing every opportunity that came their way without getting bogged down in moral qualms, is impressively large. The question is, which morality will prevail? The real world is messy and complex. It will not, perhaps, allow for a clear-cut answer. But here in Raj's Bombay we must have a definite answer to that question.

Almost at the film's climax, Raj is offered the opportunity to take all the money he has made and run, along with a woman friend, Maya, who has got them both air tickets to London. 'Please Raj, let's go, now,' urges Maya, 'the plane is waiting. We'll be gone before anybody knows what happened!'

He chooses not to, and thus becomes our hero. The fact that her name happens to be Maya (Illusion, Worldly Temptation), which the Hindu scriptures frequently warn us against, adds a mythic dimension to our hero's spurning of her. A whole, immoral way of life has thus been spurned.

Guru Dutt and the city

But all heroes are not the same, even in formula-bound Hindi cinema. Take for instance Guru Dutt's negotiation with the city in cinema, which conjures up a markedly different scenario. In his *Aar Paar* (1954) made a year before *Shri 420*, we see Dutt in the role of Birju, a taxi-driver who has just returned from jail, who has managed with great difficulty to land a job as a workshop mechanic, with the owner's permission to sleep in the workshop since he has no other place to stay. A scene that follows this settlement shows him in a corner of the workshop, reading. In another corner sits a pretty young woman, sewing. The actress happens to be Shyama. It is an idyllic scene, an evening at home suffused with cosiness and domestic warmth. While maintaining this setting, reminiscent of descriptions of home, family and hearth by 19th-century novelists such as Jane Austen, the director begins unveiling the idyll's dark side through a bit of play and flirtation between the couple.

Birju is learning to read. She, the workshop-owner's daughter, is educated, probably a college graduate. When he mispronounces the word 'girl', she corrects him, and thus begins their relationship, with him embarrassing her a minute later by enquiring about the correct pronunciation and meaning of the word l-o-v-e!

So who is that woman? Shyama asks Kaalu (Guru Dutt) when the two lovers suddenly cross her on the street one evening - in Aar Paar *(1954) 'That Woman' is played by Shakila.*

The next evening Shyama is a little upset that another attractive woman comes to the garage to chat with Kaalu as though they'd known each other for years. Who was that woman, she is dying to know, but can't ask. Even when she does ask, she gets no answer from Kaalu. He makes her even more distraught by saying that many are the women who are interested in him, that this is just an occupational hazard of being a handsome hunk! She is hurt and withdraws into a corner, far away from Kaalu the braggart.

The next thing you know he is trying to make up, teaching her to whistle, and romancing her — with the result that the grimy little garage becomes a room full of love. Instead of dancing around trees and singing, you see them dancing around cars. In two lives that were drifting aimlessly a few days ago, there is now a goal, a little paradise of togetherness, which is taking shape in their imaginations…

The girl's father (played by Jagdish Sethi) who barges in at the young lover's most romantic moment together, and expels Kaalu (Guru Dutt) from his garage - Aar Paar (1954).

Then comes the expulsion of our hero from paradise, moments after this their most lovey-dovey song: the girl's father barges in and finds them at play! This garage, where life had just begun to acquire new meaning and purpose for our hero, suddenly becomes a garage from which he is expelled — for good. As you prepare to deal with the consequences, you find that our expelled, homeless hero's spirit is still intact, as is his faith in himself. It's as if he is immune to such misfortunes; he begins to plan his future afresh, as soon as the past has boomeranged. He will continue to display this indomitable spirit, this sense of self-worth and dignity, throughout the film. He is, after all, the urban survivor created by Guru Dutt in *Aar Paar, Mr. & Mrs. 55* and *Chaudvin Ka Chand*.

Guru Dutt and Raj Kapoor came to represent very distinct ways of coping with the city in India of the 1950s and '60s. Raj Kapoor sought to represent the condition of the common Indian, the 'people'. Raj, the character Kapoor created and played again and again, is all about this mission of representation, and about the burden of this mission, which he depicts explicitly in a sentimental, self-pitying way in his last film 1970 *Mera Naam Joker* (inspired, it seems, by Charlie Chaplin's *Limelight*). This film was 'Raj's' swan song. After its failure at the box-office, Kapoor made several films, but Raj was never seen again. His time, in Kapoor's, and perhaps also the audience's eyes, had passed.

Commenting on the image of the Chaplinesque tramp, which has been described as 'probably the most universally recognised comic character the world has ever known', Chaplin says:

> One of the happy consequences of electing myself to this post of the average man is that the public has unconsciously confirmed me as a kind of unofficial representative. The average man naturally finds great delight in seeing himself on screen. Dashing and romantic heroes may provide him with a momentary thrill, but sooner or later they fill his soul with despair. Their ways are far from his ways. He will never come vaulting tempestuously into romantic situations dressed immaculately in evening clothes, silencing men with a proud glance while fair women almost swoon at the gallant spectacle he makes...then he (the viewer) spots me shuffling along in my baffled and aimless manner, and a spark of hope rekindles in him. He begins to straighten up and take heart. Here is a man like himself, only more pathetic...(Chaplin 1922: 8)

And here is Raj Kapoor's answer to what made him give up his popular romantic image in favour of the unglamorous tramp:

> Because it had a greater identity with the common man. The element of hero worship is totally alien to the kind of sense of belonging I aspire to. Everybody isn't a Don Juan. When they see me in this image, they say: this man is like us. I found that the image helped in my work and thinking. India has a vast population of subjugated common men. In Shri 420 there is an argument over my right to sleep on a footpath. I say this belongs to the sarkar, who is both your guardian and mine. When I tell him my name, he says to the kelewali, 'Listen, I told you the poor man's raj will come some day.'
>
> Sentences like these greatly appealed to the people...These concepts grew within me and made me play the unglamorous roles. People accepted it beautifully. I was one of them. If I was happy, they were happy, if I was unhappy, they were unhappy...it was that kind of a relationship that I established with my audience...(Kapoor 1979: 104-5)

In contrast, Guru Dutt's uncommon man, the urban survivor, travels light. He carries only his spirit and the burden of his personal fantasies and eccentricities. The city in Dutt's films is treacherous: living there is like skating on thin ice — you never know when it will crack and swallow you. It is for this reason that his heroes travel light, and don't get too involved in any relationship, not even with the woman he loves. He is offered to us instead as a private individual too busy finding himself to take on the burden of representing others.

And when his wishes are frustrated, as happens at critical moments in *Aar Paar, Mr. & Mrs. 55* and *Pyaasa*, he still has the spirit to sustain him — a spirit which dwells within. Guru Dutt's city films introduced the loner, the urban survivor, who has no mother to look after him, as Raj does in almost all of his films. Dutt's hero never has a mother, or much of a family. Well, all right, his protagonist Vijay does have a mother in *Pyaasa*, but he does not live with her. We see her only once, and a few

minutes of screen-time later, he gets the news that she has died. Instead of the mother figure, Guru Dutt's heroes have a friend — often played by the comedian Johnny Walker. This friend is his lone support system, though in *Aar Paar* this friend is a homeless young urchin who can at best offer him moral support. It is noteworthy that Guru Dutt's hero retains his distance from familial relations, even when there is a landlady who could be potentially a mother figure, but is not (as in *Mr. & Mrs. 55*).

Kaalu has just got a job as a driver thanks to Shakila. He is grateful, but she wants love. Kaalu doesn't know what to say—a difficult moment for both hero and 'the other woman' in Aar Paar (1954).

A new era begins

By the time we enter the '70s, the figure of the urban survivor has begun to lose its appeal at the box-office, as has the tramp. Out in the real city of the mid-'70s, there is widespread unemployment and a growing cynicism about the government's ability to deliver its promises. The film hero who now rises from this demoralised social landscape is the Great Avenger — epitomised onscreen by the actor Amitabh Bachchan. Unlike the earlier urban heroes, he is not already an orphan who is thus freed from family ties to construct new ones of his choosing. No, the new 1970s hero is orphaned in full, gory technicolour — he is witness to his father's murder by the bad guys while still a young boy. His mission, on attaining adulthood, is to avenge this and other wrongs by taking the law into his own hands. Thus was born and built the character portrayed in films like *Zanjeer* (1973), *Deewar* (1975), *Lawaaris* (1981), *Muqaddar Ka Sikander* and *Don* (both 1978) by Amitabh Bachchan, whose strength, drive and towering physical stature onscreen equals and often surpasses the city's buildings, which have now become much taller and deadlier than they were in the 1950s-60s....

The city is a dangerous place: even its women are dangerous. Helen in Agent Vinod (1977).

The big city's glass and steel configurations now serve to build up the mythic dimensions of the hero/antihero who is equated with the wounded, angry body politic. This use of the movie camera to enlarge one man to such an extent that he becomes the fountainhead of raw, lumpen power was a major departure in the 1970s from the small man, the tramp, and the poetic urban survivor of city films of the 1950s-60s.

Endnotes

1 Where have we come, a-wandering

References

Chaplin, Charles. 1922. '*In Defence of Myself*, Colliers, November 11.

Kapoor, Raj. 1979. In an interview with M Sahai, quoted in Dissanayake W and Sahai M. *Raj Kapoor's Films*, Delhi, Vikas Publishers

Katznelson, Ira. 1981. *City Trenches*, New York, Pantheon Books.

O Henry, in Blanefield, K. 1988. *Cheap Rooms and Restless Hearts*, New York, The Popular Press.

FILM – PAKEEZAH

Lyrics: Kaifi Azmi;
Music : Ghulam Mohammed

Chalte chalte, chalte chalte

Yunhi koi mil gaya tha - 2
Sarey raah chalte chalte - 2
Vahin thamke reh gayi hai - 2
Meri raat dhalte dhalte – 2

Jo kahi gayii na mujhse - 2
Voh zamaana keh raha hai - 2
Ke fasaana
Ke fasaana ban gayii hai - 2
Meri baat chalte chalte - 2

Yunhi koi mil gaya tha - 2
Sarey raah chalte chalte - 2
Yunhi koi mil gaya tha
Sarey raah chalte chalte
Chalte chalte
Sarey raah chalte chalte
Chalte chalte
Chalte chalte, chalte chalte
Yunhi koi mil gaya tha - 2
Shabey intezaar aakhir - 2
Kabhi hogi muqtasar bhi - 2

Yeh chiraag
Yeh chiraag bujh rahe hain - 2
Mere saath jalte jalte - 2
Yeh chiraag bujh rahe hain
Yeh chiraag bujh rahe hain - 5
Mere saath jalte jalte - 2
Yunhi koi mil gaya tha - 2
Sarey raah chalte chalte - 2

"Music has a natural place in our lives. Right from the shloka you recite in your morning puja while the milk-man who comes whistling on his cycle, to the fakir singing as he begs for alms and your mother humming around the kitchen...Music fills our spaces naturally. It will always be dear to us."

Gulzar (filmmaker, poet)

Main Dil Tu Dhadkan
Cinema, Songs and Us

In the beginning, says the Bible, was the Word. The blessed way to begin each of life's important projects, say Hindu scriptures, is to utter the primordial '*OM!*'. The Koran, similarly, enjoins its believers to utter '*Insha-Allah*!' There seems to be a wide consensus that the Word, uttered with faith, has almost divine power.

The word in this sense is much more than something you use in everyday conversation. This is the word as sound, housed in the scriptures, going into your heart, and then emerging as the voice of your soul, reaching out to God. It is a richly-textured human sound system, combining form and content, where the sound of the word, the manner of its utterance, the faith, the intentions and desires of the person who utters it, the place where the utterance occurs, are all simultaneously involved. The various elements of this human sound system synergise and energise each other.

But what of the life of the word outside the temple? For that, perhaps the best place to look is the world of popular music—which in India after Independence has increasingly been film music. Like any art form, film music has had its highs and lows. For every artist like Shailendra, Saigal, Naushad, O P Nayyar and S D Burman, there are a dozen charlatans. At its best and most memorable, however, Hindi film music has been the creative product, a pan-Indian sangam (confluence), of folk, Hindustani classical, and western pop music at the level of form, and of Urdu and Hindi poetry mingled with street-level English, local legends and folk theatre at the level of content. India has an enormous wealth of folk music traditions. These folk traditions offer a vast musical storehouse for film composers, who have consciously drawn from it.

The Word brought to life outside the temple in this dance scene from Utsav (1985). *Rekha in white embodies Hindi cinema's link with Indian classical music and dance traditions.*

Folk music, says music historian Alison Arnold, is an umbrella term that includes all sorts of music — religious and devotional, festival music and dance, seasonal songs and work songs. Their musical characteristics differ widely in India across region, community, and song types. This variety can be a great resource, as the musicmakers of Bombay's film factory found in the 1950s-60s.

In addition, they also drew upon international musical traditions, Arnold tells us.

> As music composers from different parts of India with varied musical backgrounds and knowledge converged in Bombay in the 1940s, the musical sources upon which these song makers drew increased in both number and variety." A favourite source was Western music...Yet their musical influences were far from limited to Western compositions. Bombay's music directors drew upon Latin American, Chinese, Middle Eastern and other foreign musical styles, as well as upon many native forms and styles. Since this eclectic nature was proving immensely popular with Indian audiences, the infusion of musical styles became a common feature of Hindi film song." (Arnold 1998: 148, 157)

Historical roots apart, the continuing appeal of film songs for the Indian public has been so great that the songs have often rescued poor films from complete financial disaster, and lifted successful films to the status of 'mega-hits'.

You can go so far as to say that no Hindi film can be a mega-hit (i.e. celebrate a silver or golden jubilee at Indian cinema halls), without the presence of 'golden jubilee songs' (as they say in the film trade). Yes, B R Chopra's crime thriller *Kanoon* (1960) was a hit sans songs, but it is the proverbial exception that proves the rule. Chopra himself never risked another movie without songs.

Consider now this observation by Swami Agehananda Bharati, in a magazine article:

> Taj Mahal, the annoyingly washed-down and garbled story of Shah Jahan and his spouse, became a success in the early-'60s, not so much because of its 'historical message' as because of its main theme song, released well before the movie opened in Bombay. 'Jo vaada kiya wo nibhana padega' had been whistled and tearfully crooned by pedestrians and cyclists in India and East Africa about six months before the film's opening. Even quite unsophisticated people said that the movie was bad and that a beautiful and important story like that could have been put to better cinematic use — but this was said with a shrug: the songs were there, and they were good. (Bharati 1977:)

This, as they say in the Bombay film factory, is a matter of the heart: songs are *dil ki baat*; they are reminiscent of the power of the Word. While a fuller discussion of this theme follows below, suffice it to note at this moment that these songs have helped moviegoers (and even many non-moviegoers) discover the sound and rhythm that make our hearts 'Indian'. This discovery has been especially intense for Indians who have left the motherland and settled abroad. The eclectic fusion quality of Hindi film music has greatly facilitated this identification.

These songs have helped moviegoers discover the sound and rhythm that make our hearts 'Indian'.

A very popular song from the mega-hit film of 1955, *Shri 420*, says it all: '*Mera joota hai Japani/ Yeh patloon Inglistani/ Sar pe lal topi Russi/ Phir bhi dil hai Hindustani* (Oh, my shoes are Japanese/ These trousers English, if you please/ On my head, a red Russian hat/ My heart's Indian for all that)'.

This 45-year-old song is still such an anthem that novelist Salman Rushdie gives it pride of place when talking about his love affair with Bombay and how a trip to the city after many years in London provided him with the raw material for his famous novel, Midnight's Children:'

> Old songs came back to me from nowhere: a street entertainer's version of Good Night, Ladies, and, from the film Mr 420 (a very appropriate source for my narrator to have used), the hit number Mera Joota Hai Japani, which could almost be Saleem's theme song (Rushdie 1991: 1)

The Word outside the temple, then, has thrived in India, by enabling a new kind of cultural traffic between the cinema screen and the nation's heart, between culture and the private self. The popularity of film music, which has only grown each year over the last 50 years, may be because it now occupies the place in the Indian heart earlier occupied by folk music.

But film music is a whole new kind of folk music: it does not mark off one subculture from another as folk music does. Instead, film songs cut across linguistic/regional borders within India's federal mosaic and unite various folk cultures into a 'national' culture. So well has this recipe of unification worked in both expressing and shaping popular tastes that it has made film music a growth industry almost without interruption for the last five decades — both in India and among Indians abroad.

If unification is a little too lofty in describing our

SONGS INSTEAD OF SEX: As soon as the scene leads up to the inevitable kiss disallowed by the censor, the song provides a release from the tension into a kind of musical ejaculation. Govinda and Kimi Katkar show us how this trick works in Jaisi Karni Waisi Bharni (1989).

relationship with film songs, another telling dimension of our response to film music comes from Chidananda Dasgupta:

> The song, not only heard but 'seen' in its place at the climactic moment of drama and accompanied by...movements, many of them substituting for the climax to the sexual foreplay of the preceding scene, has become a 'must' to the popular audience. As soon as the preliminaries of love-making lead up to the inevitable kiss and the sexual congress disallowed by the censor, the song provides a release from the tension into a kind of musical ejaculation. Music is both lofty and vulgar. (Dasgupta 1981: 34)

A parallel that comes to mind here is the mass appeal of pop music groups among young people in the West. The popularity of Elvis Presley, The Beatles, Bob Dylan, Simon & Garfunkel et al since the 1960s gradually created a new nation and 'youth' lifestyle which made linguistic and national borders between Finland, Italy, France, Britain, Russia and the US seem odd, anachronistic. Hindi film songs have performed a similar border-crossing role in the South Asian subcontinent.

As in the West, there are good personal reasons for this. Music always seems to work by being very personal before being anything else. Music's subterranean quality has a lot to do with transforming moving pictures (films) into emotion pictures. We may not be able to define how the music works upon us, but we can feel its effects at key moments in a film narrative.

Dil ki baat[1]

The song on film, songs like those in films like *Love In Simla, Mere Mehboob, Professor, Barsaat Ki Raat* and *Junglee*, awakened us irreligious, middle class teenagers of 1960s Hoshangabad to the elemental power of the secular, poetic word. Elemental in the sense of making things happen — onscreen and off-screen. Important things like getting members of the opposite sex to take notice of us, or making a students' picnic a whole lot more fun, or giving us the courage, and the language, with which to voice and thereby discover our inner confusion and yearning.

This was a completely new dimension that film songs brought into our lives. The radio, especially Radio Ceylon's Binaca Geetmala, thrived on

Film songs are the matter of the heart, as is evident from the way Jagdeep summons a song from deep inside. His friend, played by Paintal strums the guitar while trying to make sense of the song. A musical moment from the film Saa Re Ga Ma Pa (1972).

Unseen by the world, but alive to its melodies.

this aural aspect of cinema. It enabled us to take these songs home, into the privacy of our dreams. The radio in the average urban Indian home in the 1950s and '60s occupied a special little corner, which often rivalled God's corner. (The television set occupies that corner today.) A memorable, sensuous image of the radio as a personal dream machine was provided by Madhubala in the film *Barsaat Ki Raat*, as she listens to the film's title song by switching on the radio as soon as she enters her bedroom and discovers that it is being sung by someone whom she bumped into just a few hours ago! The radio, which she is shown caressing while listening to this song, is her personal connection to the world beyond the four walls of home.

The film song often echoed, and gave poetic form to, the emotional ups and downs of each listener's life. Until then, until the easy and frequent access to film music and fantasy made possible by the radio, the idea that the word has power when uttered in a certain way was largely absent from our teenage consciousness, our sense of reality.

Language in action

One song from *Mere Mehboob* (1963), the film's title song in fact, dramatically transformed our small-town sense of reality. It mesmerised us; it took over many of our lonely, day-dreaming hours. Why? Looking back now, the answer lies not so much in the song's music or lyrics, as in its magical effect on us, and on the heroine to whom it was addressed. It demonstrated two things — how the word can move you, the listener-viewer, and how it can simultaneously move the object of the singer's desire: Sadhana. She is moved to tears, and then moved to actually come looking for him — something she hasn't done for the whole year since they accidentally met and felt drawn to each other. Another thing: that is when we first see the film's heroine. That song literally brings the person to life, as though in response to the word.... *'Mere mehboob tujhe, meri mohabbat ki kasam!* (Sweetheart, today in the name of love, come and meet me, for it's now or never!)'

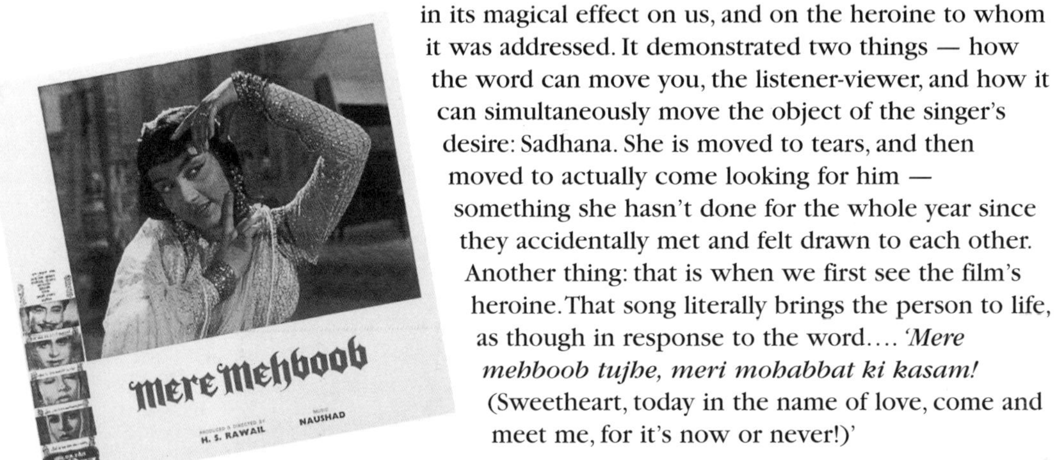

Until that song went forth into the world, into the college hall,

and thence into your heart, she did not exist. This is literally true, for none of us viewers had seen her until then. But now that the word had been uttered, expressed, she appeared before our eyes, her beauty and sensitivity confirming the expectations the word had conjured up. There she was, and the camera which cannot lie caught her crying, the tears rolling big and wet but silent down her cheeks. So she too feels intensely for him, though your hero Anwar can't see that, only you the viewer can.

This simultaneity — between the effect the song and its picturisation had on you, and the effect it was having on her — was too much. It was what literary parlance terms 'an epiphany' — enhanced by the fact that Anwar still doesn't know that she desires him as much. From this point the film took hold of us, and we went with it wherever it led us. There is usually a point at which a successful, romantic film grabs you by the heart, and the libido. Once it does, you will go anywhere with it. So in *Mere Mehboob*, we would have gone to Timbuctoo with those two lovers; all they did, however, was take us from Aligarh to Lucknow.

Music is power

The film song doesn't always have to take you from one town to another; it can sometimes bring your dream object closer to you. Take the film *Professor* (1962), for instance. The film's story really takes off with the heroine and her friend singing a song of expectation and desire: '*Oh koi aayega, aayegaa-aayegaa, humre gaanv koi aayega,/ Pyaar ki dor se bandh jaayega, oh koi aayega!* (Oh, someone will surely come to our village one of these days,/ We'll tie him up with threads of love. Yes, someone will come!)' And sure enough, a handsome young adventurer (Shammi Kapoor) appears on the horizon the very next moment — again as though answering that call, that voice of longing. In the film *Raj Kumar* (1968), we see Sadhana playing a beautiful young tribal princess standing on a river boat singing to no one in particular - '*Aaa jaa, aaa mere rajkumar, aaja aayi bahaar,/ Oh mere rajkumar, tere bin raha na jaaye* (Come, come today my prince, wherever you are,/ For it is spring, and I cannot live without you anymore...)' And lo! We see Shammi Kapoor rising from the water a few yards behind her! He just happens to be hiding in the river from some of the villain's soldiers, but when he hears her song, he surfaces (naturally). This country called 'cinema' is an enchanted world, where everything happens as it should...

The musical word has a strange, compelling sort of power, like the power of prayer, on prayer's condition — that it come from the heart, straight, unmediated, naked into the world. If the song fulfils this condition, anything can happen, including the seemingly impossible.

In the film *Baiju Baawra*, which proved to be the biggest box-office hit of 1952, the musical word's mystical, god-like power receives dramatic confirmation. Unlike *Professor* and *Mere Mehboob*, this film is based on a popular 16th-century north Indian legend about a young man whose singing genius was supernatural in its power. The ability to sing exceptionally well was his main claim to fame, which finds its final expression in his victory over the other 16th-century singing genius, Tansen, in a famous contest in Akbar's court. Here then is a modernist tale of a young upstart outplaying the kingdom's established senior star, with a love affair providing additional spice on the side. The film became very popular, reinforcing the Baiju legend as only cinema can.

Baiju's singing, as it builds up to a crescendo, reduces a solid block of marble to tears! This is the inexorable climax to other demonstrations of music's power, like Tansen's power to summon birds and animals with his music. Some sense of the place of music in the popular Indian imagination can be got from this and other musical legends involving saint poets like Kabir, Meerabai, Tukaram, etc.

Music, in short, has continued to move mountains on the Indian screen,

Music makes for deep communication, apart from melting blocks of marbles. Meena Kumari and Bharat Bhushan as Gowri and Baiju in Baiju Bawra (1952).

subconsciously reflecting the underlying continuity between box-office cinema and folk mythology, where mountains have long existed only to be moved.

Music is self-confidence

Cut now to a film released 25 years after *Baiju Baawra* — to *Amar, Akbar, Anthony* (1977), and you find the young lover combining the passion of *Mere Mehboob's* Anwar with a talent akin to Baiju's. What you get in Manmohan Desai's *Amar, Akbar, Anthony* is a robust young qawwal, Akbar, brimming with self-confidence, drunk, almost arrogant with his knowledge of the power of the musical word.

It is the big night of his performance, the tickets all sold out, but the young woman Akbar loves has had to bring her father as chaperone, and the father aims to keep a strict eye on her. Akbar is onstage, his beloved a world apart, out there in the audience, and therefore inaccessible, except through the performance. And so, Akbar sings to the girl he loves and to her father:

'Purdah hai purdah, haan purdah hai purdah,/ Pardey ke peechche

purdah-nasheen hai,/ Parda nasheen ko main bepurdah na kar doon to, to, to! Akbar mera naam nahin hai! (A veil divides my love from me at this moment, yes it does./ But if I don't tear apart that veil tonight, my name is not Akbar.)' This challenge is couched in song, and the only weapon he aims to use is the power of the word. It is Akbar's use of an intangible weapon that leaves the father almost defenceless.

Gone is the yearning, the tears, the shot-in-the-dark quality of Anwar the graduating student of the 1960s, pleading with his weeping beloved, Sadhana, to identify herself now or never in *Mere Mehboob*. In contrast, Akbar the late-1970s *qawwal*, who is not even a graduate, a mere tailor's son in fact, has the gumption to challenge his beloved's father. The song scorns the father's orthodoxy and backwardness in matters of love, and celebrates her beauty and desirability. The boldness with which he both damns him and praises her is scandalous. But he does this with such style and musical gusto that the audience in the hall, with the sole exception of the old man, is with him all the way.

Yes, we are a conservative, puritanical nation. Fortunately, however, we are also open to ideas, we also seek out and cherish freedom and boundless love.

Rising to the occasion at the song's climax, the beautiful young woman (played by Neetu Singh) defies all convention and joins Akbar on stage! Watching the rebellion of the *burkha*-clad Neetu Singh, we hailed the power of young love! It was another victory for the word, especially the musical word. Down with fathers-in-law-to-be who can only be reactionary in the face of this heart-warming, breath-quickening spectacle.

In 1964, Neetu Singh's counterpart Sadhana summons with great trepidation the courage to finally meet Anwar at the end of the programme. For a moment the two stand facing each other, but her veil has yet to come off. Just as she is about to lift it and speak to him, however, a stranger comes over to compliment Anwar on his performance. Seeing him advancing towards them, she turns and runs away — *duniya kya kahegi* (what will people say)? The long-awaited meeting between the two lovers is thus aborted even before they can exchange names.

And yet, it is this very nervousness, this fear of *duniya kya kahegi* that we in the 1960s identified with. It made the moment when the lovers come face-to-face much later in the film so emotionally charged — for us, as much as for them. Yes, we are a conservative, puritanical nation. Fortunately, however, we are also open to ideas, we also seek out and cherish freedom and boundless love. We are a semi-feudal nation, but we are also a democratic nation. We are a bundle of contradictions and inconsistencies.

The box-office accepts these inconsistencies and uses them as raw material, but cannot afford to be too judgemental about them. After all,

Likeable fictions offer images for a desirable imaginary world, as depicted here by Sohrab Modi and Naseem in Nausherwan-e-Adil (1957).

its success depends on our approval. It has to get us to buy theatre tickets in millions, every day. But approval, mercifully, is only half the story of the cinema-public relationship.

A good, successful film is more than an emotional and cultural mirror. It creates a utopia, a vision of life coloured both by our contradictions as well as our desires and aspirations. What we get then is 'a likeable fiction' which mirrors and extends our imaginative horizon. This extension of the viewer's imagination is where the art of popular cinema lies; that is its core, its appeal, and ultimately its power over us.

The idea that you can be poor and homeless and yet happy, the romanticising of unemployment as a special kind of freedom, was first presented to us in Raj Kapoor's 1951 film *Aawara*. The idea was conveyed most effectively in the film's title song, '*Aawara hoon*...(A vagabond am I...)' Here is a poor young man who does not feel sorry for himself. Instead he comes across as someone who is homeless but also free, poor but also young, vibrant, romantic!

The popularity of bestselling novels is very similar. As literary critic Regina James puts it:

> Likeable fictions the reader takes easily, even eagerly, in. They offer opportunities for identification and for self-reconstruction; they present an Other in which we recognise ourselves already formed, or an Other on which we may aspire to re-form ourselves; they constitute a desirable imaginary world through which we continue the life-work of symbolising ourselves through others and others through ourselves. When texts take us beyond liking, to wonder and desire and delight, they take us over. Yielding to the power of the text, we take the tumble, lose our wretched little selves for a bit... (James 1997: 103-4)

Likeable fictions also present an Other on which we may aspire to reform ourselves. Sunil Dutt and Shyama in Duniya Jhukti Hai (1960).

So thoroughly and interestingly entwined is the relationship between

cinema and us that the key characters of some films themselves provide us appealing images of this business of taking the tumble, and losing our wretched little selves for a bit. As the young wife who has just run away from her uncaring, self-absorbed husband, Waheeda Rehman sings it for us in the film *Guide* (1965): '*Kaanton se kheenchke yeh aanchal, chhod ke bandhan baandhe paayal,/ Aaj phir jeene ki tamanna hai!/ Aaj phir marnay ka irada hai!/ Dil woh chala — aah ha aaa!* (Having freed myself from thorns, and replaced society's chains with dancing anklets,/ I now feel like living for the first time!/ And like dying, for today I'm free/ And there goes my heart, flying skywards...)'

Once again, it seemed that a song had taken the words out of our mouths. It was 1970 when we got to see *Guide*. At the time, we were in college, and this particular song was being sung again and again at student get-togethers and picnics. It was especially popular with the girls. None of them were married, let alone separated from their husbands as the heroine onscreen is. Yet they all identified with it.

Songs which we make our own — as these young women did — are rarely, if ever, mirrors of our lives. They go deeper — they connect with hopes, fears and subconscious desires. With these, we 'continue the life-work of symbolising ourselves through others and others through ourselves', to recall a key line from Regina James' passage quoted earlier.

Oscar Wilde makes a similar observation in his usual oblique style: 'One's real life,' he observes, 'is often the life one does not lead.'

Even when the experience the film song explores and depicts is not part of the raw data of your being, what you often do is project your own needs onto the story, the character. So one found, for instance, that a neighbour's teenage daughter Asha in Hoshangabad identified strongly with Shashi Kapoor who plays a Kashmiri boatman totally lost in the big city of Bombay in the film *Jab Jab Phool Khile* (1965). As an expression of his alienation in the big city he sings, '*Yahaan main ajnabi hoon,/ Main jo hoon bas wahi hoon*... (I feel a total stranger here, / Just let me be, whatever I am...)'

It may seem strange to find that a 16-year-old middle class student in Hoshangabad can find so much meaning in this song without ever having travelled to the city herself. Look a little closer, however, and it begins to make sense. What was happening here was that Asha projected onto the boatman her own feelings of displacement, whatever their actual source and character may have been. Her feelings of displacement needed an outlet, and that was what this Kashmiri boatman's song provided. Art often performs this function — it gives us a metaphor, an image, a song, a persona that is open and

Occasionally, film songs evoke some memorable event in your own life. Such songs and scenes, like this one featuring Meena Kumari and Rajendra Kumar in Zindagi Aur Khwab (1961), *take you into a journey inside yourself.....*

universal enough to be adopted and put to various uses by each of us. It is thus that a work of art comes to acquire meaning.

How a song comes along

Another feature of film songs is that they confront you as part of a full-fledged performance; the best and most popular of them are expressions of key moments in the lives of characters you watch with rapt attention. Having seen (and felt) the song take you inside the character onscreen — as the title song of *Barsaat Ki Raat* or *Mere Mehboob* had done, for instance — it became what we students often called 'an experience'. Why it felt like an experience (pronounced with a special stress we all understood), how it became a memory that stayed on for weeks after the film show — these were questions that frankly did not even come up in our young minds.

Occasionally, these songs are not just part of a screen performance but also of some memorable event in your own life off-screen. Such songs then have a double charge, something real and very personal, plus something seen onscreen. Hearing one of those double-charged songs wafting down purely by chance from a flat overhead, as happened while I waited at a bus-stop in Bombay recently, was an electrifying experience all over again.

Suddenly I was back in Hoshangabad, and the irritation at the bus' delay was replaced by a mood of reverie. For a brief while it did not matter when the bus came; I had already embarked on another journey where that song had put me in fleeting but intense contact for just a few days with a beautiful, older girl from Lucknow who happened to be visiting our little town. I had sat next to her while watching a film with her and her family. After the show, the two of us differed on which song was the film's best. An argument ensued for almost half-an-hour. It ended with her singing 'her' song. So well did she sing it that I almost changed my mind.

What song was it, you will ask? It was Saira Banu singing '*Ja-ja jaa, mere bachpan!/ Kahin jaa, ke chhup naadan,/ Yeh safar hai ab mushkil, aaney ko hai toofaan*... (Go-go-go, my childhood,/ Go somewhere and hide, you innocent fool/ This journey is now difficult, a storm is on its way...)' It was from the 1961 film *Junglee*.

A year or so later, I heard that she had got married and moved far away. Very far away. End of story...

With some film scenes and songs we continue the life-work of symbolising ourselves through others, and others through ourselves. Vyjayanthimala shows us how, in this solo dance sequence from Patrani (1956).

Love is often experienced most intensely at the moment of separation, discovers Shakila in this scene from Taxi 555 (1958).

Memory, meaning, experience

Continuing to explore these recollections of movie-going in my schooldays, I realise that there are multiple layers of emotion hidden inside that word 'experience', the only limited term we could find to register the fact that a song, a scene, or a whole film had made a strong impression on us. A good performance can itself be an essential part of what we call 'experience'. Consider this remark of the late Walter Benjamin, one of Germany's most interesting cultural historians:

'Every feeling is attached to an a priori object, and the presentation of the latter is the phenomenology of the former.' (Benjamin, W. 1973:160-61)

Feelings, he is saying, do not exist in a vacuum; they are attached to specific objects and moments in our lives. Watching great performances, like that of Prithviraj Kapoor as Akbar in the film *Mughal-e-Azam*, or Nargis in *Mother India*, are moments of this kind. Performances, characters, your late grandmother's rocking chair, your favourite doll from childhood, as much as that chance meeting with the girl from Lucknow who came into your life for two-three days and then went away forever, could all be included in Walter Benjamin's sense of 'a priori objects' to which our feelings can become deeply attached.

Our focus just now, however, is on performances as such 'objects'. Through a powerful performance, of which the passionately rendered love song is one instance, what is normally sealed in the heart (the *dil ka taala*, as many a Hindi song calls it) and inaccessible to everyday observation and reasoning, is drawn forth. Our inner feelings, in other words, sometimes have outer origins. The sociologist Wilhelm Dilthey says:

> Meaning is squeezed out of an event which has either been directly experienced by the dramatist or poet, or which cries out for penetrative, imaginative understanding (verstehen). (Dilthey as quoted by Turner, V. 1991)

An experience, notes American anthropologist Victor Turner, 'is itself a process which "presses out" to an "expression" which completes it.' So experience, he is suggesting, is that which is brought to consciousness by expression, by a performance which engages us. Turner again:

> Here the etymology of performance may give us a helpful clue, for it has nothing to do with "form", but derives from the Old French

"parfournir", "to complete" or "to carry out thoroughly". A performance, then, is the proper finale of an experience. (Turner 1991: 13)

Aldous Huxley adds another dimension:

> ...Experience is not a matter of having actually swum the Hellespont, or danced with the dervishes, or slept in a doll's house. It is a matter of sensibility and intuition, of seeing and hearing the significant things, of paying attention at the right moments, of understanding and co-ordinating. Experience is not what happens to a man; it is what man does with what happens to him. It is a gift for dealing with the accidents of existence, not the accidents themselves. (Huxley 1986: 12)

When song meets feeling: *Kuch kuch hota hai*

Songs, then, are a gift from cinema to us for dealing with the accidents of existence. They give a poetic expression and body to, your experience of pain or desire, and in the process help you deal with those feelings better. The chemistry of song and our emotions begins really at the level of instinct — the level of rhythmic sound acting upon our gut feelings. The simple act of humming along with a song you like affects your feelings. It may seem strange, but most of us have seen it happen. All that is required is that you allow the song to work on you — spontaneously, unthinkingly.

Allow it entry, let it roam in and around your heart; the rest will happen of its own accord. The song listened to is a musical order being brought to bear on the chaos of your feelings. Insofar as you the listener make this musical order your own, it subtly changes your whole experience of pain, happiness, and desire. It makes the pain, the desire, more manageable — by providing a certain distance, a detachment from the turmoil and immediacy of your feelings. Music can even be therapeutic, and it does not have to be the classical variety; for many people, the film songs of their favourite composer or singer are even more effective.

If the day at the office had been stressful, my father would play some songs of K.L. Saigal in his room, and emerge with a serene smile a half-hour later.

A memorable image from the summer holidays in those high school days is that of my mother's younger sister (who was then a college-going woman in her early-20s) standing in front of the family radio, which sat atop a cupboard at shoulder-level. She would sneak into the sitting room whenever it was vacant, put on the radio, lean on the cupboard and hum softly along with some of the songs. She did this while standing, and she did it for a

The radio brought film songs home, into the privacy of our dreams. Sharmila Tagore shows us how in this ad in the Filmfare issue of 28 May (1965).

whole hour, sometimes two. At such moments, you felt it had become the radio room, her room, and no one should enter or even pass by lest her listening 'work' be disturbed. The adults seemed to know that something important was happening here, and we children were told not to disturb her in any way. After she had had her day's quota of those film songs, she would laugh and play with us as though re-charged by a powerful tonic.

I can recall vividly a moment when a song came to my rescue. It was a difficult moment in my life as a 19-year-old college student in London. I was lonely, and not coping too well with the pressures of my engineering degree course. One day, while idly humming along with this song from the film *Hum Dono*, '*Main zindagi ka saath nibhata chala gaya/ Har fikr ko dhuen mein udata chala gaya, har fikr ko dhuen mein udaaa*...(I went along with life, accepting all its twists and turns,/ Blowing each worry up in smoke, blowing each worry out of my life...)' I discovered that just voicing one's anxieties in this way helped me emerge from the despondency I had fallen into.

Some years later, what helped me cope with a crushing rejection by a girl I loved was humming this song from the film *Saheli* (1965) — '*Jis dil mein basa tha pyar tera, us dil ko kabhika tod diya*... (The heart which loved you, that heart I have broken and long discarded...)' The better you sang it, and recalled its lines and their tonal flow, the better you felt. Oh sure, the relief was just 20 per cent, but it was that vital 20 per cent. Gradually, over the next two weeks or so, the rejection ceased

Music and dance can also sometimes make for comedy, as Johnny Walker and Helen show us in this scene from Naach Ghar (1959).

to feel devastating, and you began to look at the future with an open mind. Another song, specially designed to look to the future, also helped in the recovery process: '*Badal jaaye agar maali, chaman hota nahin khaali,/ Bahaarein phir bhi aati hain, bahaarein phir bhi aayengi* (A garden does not die because its gardener has changed,/ Many springs have come till now, many springs will come hereafter)'

The point, in brief, is that songs, musical structures and our feelings seem to be related in strangely powerful ways. But our relationship with music has still more dimensions.

From our instinctive relationship with sound, melody and rhythm

Music and dance can also sometimes make for comedy, as in these scenes from Pati Patni (1966). *These are the moments when actors like Mehmood and Mumtaz show us the perils of taking love songs (and themselves). too seriously.*

If listening to a song can make you feel better, then actually singing it will make you dance, and the two together is pure music.

sketched above, it is but a small step to realising that these melodies are also part of an audio-visual package that causes a cognitive, learning dialectic to come into play in our transactions with cinema. Thus it happened that film songs and certain key dialogues furnished us teenagers with the language of courtship and adulthood. Cinema was, after all, the main medium, almost the only cognitive 'place' where we went to get contemporary stories, images, representations of adolescence, of growing up, of gender identity, and of 'love' in its various *avatars*. It was a visual-emotional language which provided instant entertainment and stayed with us long after the show. Is it any wonder then that hearing those songs today is still a moving moment for many of us — 20, 30, even 40 years after the event of our adolescence?

Discovering love through song

'Find expression for a sorrow, and it will become dear to you. Find expression for a joy, and you will intensify its ecstasy,' said Oscar Wilde.

Observe how this finding of expression actually occurs onscreen before going on to do its work on the viewer. It is never just a matter of language, a few new words. It is language in action, language as it emerges spontaneously, wrapped in an absorbing performance which makes the motion picture an emotion picture, and the film song your heart's song. The protagonists draw us into their lives, and having thus entered into a vicarious relationship, we experience situations with them. Intensification of our lives is what we seek, and intensification is what we get — through them, for a short while.

Memorable film songs often attain that status by playing a revealing role in our films, reminding us of popular cinema's links with folk theatre. In folk theatre, sometimes even in modern theatre, the device of the narrator, or the *sutradhar*, is used to clue us in to what is going on inside the actors' minds. But popular cinema's conventions don't allow for that. A film story has to be presented as a story without a narrator, a story that tells itself, and is therefore compellingly real.

With this rejection of the voice-over to spell out 'inner thoughts', and given popular realist cinema's stress on surface reality, filmmakers have used music to give us direct, 'intimate' access to the emotions of the characters. As such, music is a way of anchoring meaning, and eliminating the ambiguities of response. No wonder then that songs are often what you remember most about films — they are the wheels on which you journey into the mind and heart of the character.

The poetry of those film songs gave us teenagers a new, refined way of understanding our emotions and innermost feelings. They did this by giving a linguistic form and body to feelings that we earlier knew only as vague passions and storms. What they did for us, in other words, was to bring an experience into being by providing the language for it. Here for instance is Pramod Shukla, a Delhi-based chartered accountant, reminiscing about film songs and schooldays in the course of an informal interview in January 2000. He did his schooling in Hoshangabad around the time I did: 'Take a 15-year-old who is drowning in self-pity because he has no real friend among the boys in his school, and whom the girls don't find attractive enough for a second glance either. Yes, he has won a few medals in sundry elocution and other competitions, but that hasn't made any real difference. No, he remains the faceless one — in school, and out of it.

What they did for us, in other words, was to bring an experience into being by providing the language for it.

'But one day – oh, how I remember that day! — he happens to hear a song on the radio that seems to have been written just for him. The song is *"Akelaa hoon main, koi saathi hai to mera saaya, akelaa hoon main…*(All alone am I, my only friend is my shadow…)" A few days later he gets to see the film in which that song appears (*Baat Ek Raat Ki,* 1967), and suddenly a whole new phrase, a whole new idea, enters his personal dictionary — akela hoon main, I am alone! *"Jaise kabhi pyaare, jheel ke kinarey, hans akelaa nikley!* (Rather like a solitary swan, cruising along a river bank.)" So, instead of being lonely and miserable, I was now this solitary swan cruising down the river while the world watched. It was so much more glorious and romantic than being just a lonely kid. That's how this kid quietly turned into a "swan".

'That one song gave me a whole perspective on myself, my misery. It came at a time when I needed it. And suddenly people started coming up to me, with the result that I made two new friends. This was a coincidence of course, but it didn't seem like that then…Anyway, once akela became my favourite word, I kept finding other songs with that word, and they made me feel even better…There was that song by the poet Pradeep – *"Chal akela, chal akelaaa, chal akelaaa, / Tera mela peechhe chhoota raahi, chal akela…*(Walk alone, walk alone, / Your world, your people have been left behind now, oh traveller, walk on, alone…)" — which I find myself humming at tense, stressful moments. During exams in college my friends and I used to hum this song in the late-night coffee break, when we were tired of studying. It helped, I don't know how, but it did. All I'm waiting for now is to hear a beautiful woman sing this song to me one day, preferably after work – *"Akele, akele kahaan jaa rahe ho,/ Hamein saath laylo jahaan jaa rahay ho!* (Where, stranger, are you going all alone? Please take me along, wherever you're going…)" Mmmm, no one's ever said that to me yet, but you never know…'

At this point Pramod breaks into laughter, but suppresses it for a moment to go check whether his wife has overheard these fantasies of his.

From artifice to revelation

The way our hero dressed, walked and spoke, the way he went about winning the heroine's hand or getting a job, the way the heroine handled critical moments at work, at home, at play, while handling the hero's advances, the tone of her voice, her flirtation within the shackles of prescribed womanhood — all these cinematic moments were inputs into our individual image banks. And this audio-visual image bank, which varies from one viewer to another, becomes in a way what distinguishes each individual viewer from the other. We used these images subconsciously, as the raw material for identity-building.

My identity cocktail in the last year of school, for instance, was a mix of two parts Dilip Kumar (as seen in *Madhumati*), one part Shammi Kapoor (in *Teesri Manzil*), one part Guru Dutt (as Pritam in *Mr. & Mrs. 55*), and one part Dev Anand (of *Nau Do Gyarah*). A few aspects of your father's persona were also part of this identity kit, but they were deeper

The protagonists draw us into their lives as Agha and Rehana do in this sequence from Hazaar-Raatein, *Having entered this relationship, we live, laugh and cry with them.*

You are the contemplative village beauty played by Sadhana in Parakh (1960) *or Prince Salim in* Mughal-e-Azam (1960) *or Pritam the jobless cartoonist in* Mr & Mrs 55 (1955). *And out of these make-believe selves, you learn to invent a better you...*

down, below the level of conscious identity-building. Others similarly made up their individual cocktails from films that had specially appealed to them. The precise ingredients of each cocktail were a personal secret which each of us guarded (and perhaps still guard) jealously. You have to be 'different', after all.

These identity cocktails do not remain static. We change them as we grow older. Thus Dev Anand may be discarded in your 30s in favour of a bit of the Humphrey Bogart persona in *Casablanca*, or Amitabh Bachchan, and so on. While cinema was not the only source for key inputs into our image banks and evolving identity-kits, its importance as a source was second only to family and school. It was our main story bank.

And stories matter. They matter a great deal, because they are probably the best way to save our lives. You, like Pramod the Delhi-based accountant above, are the hero of your own life-story. The kind of story you want to tell about yourself has a lot to do with the kind of person you are, and can become. You listen to (or watch in films) stories about other people, and the appetite seems to have no end. Perhaps that is because you know, at some subconscious level, that you are — or could be — the hero of those stories too.

You are Anarkali or Prince Salim in *Mughal-e-Azam*, you are Raju in *Aawara*, you are Pritam the jobless cartoonist in *Mr. & Mrs. 55*, or the Chaplinesque tramp in *City Lights*. And out of these make-believe selves, all of them versions of your own self-in-the-making, you learn, if you are lucky and smart enough, to invent a better you than you could have been before the story was told.

Frank McConnell sums it up:

> 'After more than a century of handbooks on the subject, (stories are) still the best version of "self-help" our civilisation has invented. After an even longer spell of literary criticism and philosophising, it is perhaps the best reason for taking stories seriously.' (McConnell 1979: 1)

Film songs — thanks to radio broadcasting and later the small audio tape — are so much more portable than film scenes, and therefore have come to be a very special, endlessly malleable part of our audio-visual image bank. This banking activity is, moreover, double-edged: the appeal of these films songs (like that of films themselves) is both very personal and widely shared: so much so that it creates communities of taste. Thus Fan A reveals that the playback singer Mukesh is 'the voice of my soul', while Fan B is convinced that after Saigal and Pankaj Mullick (the singing stars of the 1940s), film music has only gone downhill, and so on. Individual playback singers' fan clubs express these differences of musical taste.

Such fan clubs do not usually have a formal membership or physical premises, however. They are there, somewhat like groundwater — present as an important resource, but existing like an undercurrent. It needs an occasion like the death or birth anniversary of one such singer for the 'club' to momentarily come into existence. The news, for instance, that a book-length compilation of the late Mohammed Rafi's songs was to be released in Bombay on a particular day in December 1998 made a huge crowd turn out for the book-release function. The numbers far exceeded the organisers' expectations and the number of seats available.

And now for some love songs

The love song in Hindi cinema is often dismissed — unfairly, I think — as a couple dancing around a tree. All love songs are not the same: there are breaking-the-ice songs, songs which cement the couple's relationship, erotic songs, and heartbreak songs, to name just a few types. Occasionally, the love song is a song of self-discovery.

An instance of the latter is a popular 1960s number from the film *Aayi Milan Ki Bela* (1964): '*Oh sanam — terey ho gaye hum,/ Mil gaya mujhko hai sanam, zindagi kaa bahanaa,/ Oh sanam...*' At first sight it seems a typical filmi duet between Saira Banu and Rajendra Kumar, but nothing, you find when you look closely at any scene, is ever exactly the same. In this duet for instance, there is a small twist. Unknown to the two lovers, Saira Banu's fiance, played by an angry Dharmendra, stands in the background with a gun in his hand! It is evening, and they are unaware of his presence. And no, he doesn't use the gun, even at the end of the song. Yes, there is probably something slightly illicit about the meeting between the two, plus elements of daring and danger, but to know more about all that would take us into the details of the film's

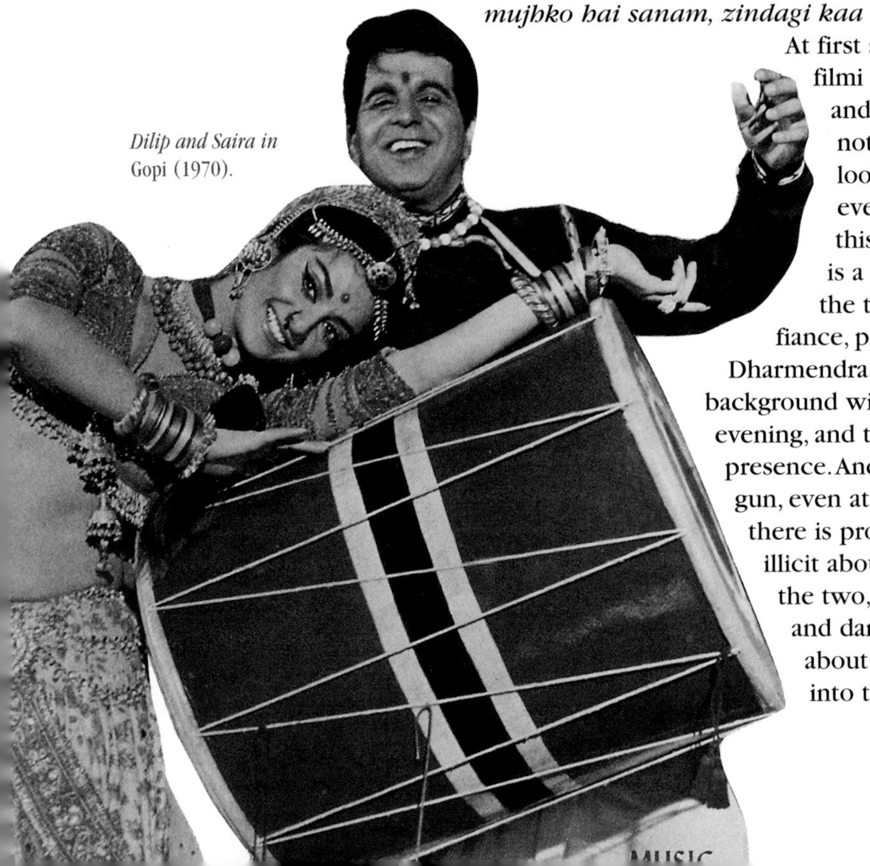

Dilip and Saira in Gopi (1970).

plot.

Let us just focus for now on the song as performance. 'Oh sanam...' turns out to be a case of the love song as self-discovery, a discovery through expression, through getting to know oneself by learning to play with the other. This learning to play — sometimes by just being childish for a few moments, by dancing with feeling and style moments later — is a way of loosening up, of shedding the protective shell of your public mask and entering into a new engagement with the other, which is indirectly an engagement with oneself too. The dancing — presented here as a way of finding your feet, and an expression of happiness at being alone together — serves as 'play' in this sense. While the heroine is the one who is usually the prime carrier of inhibitions in most of our films and love songs, in this song it is the hero.

It is he who is clumsy by comparison: he fumbles, he can't move as fluidly as her. Inhibitions about dancing, inhibitions about expressing his desire, inhibitions about letting go — our hero here is a bagful of inhibitions. Indian cinema's psycho-gurus will probably say that the underlying reason why this male figure can't dance fluidly is that he is carrying this weight of inhibitions on behalf of his male viewers who have even bigger problems with their body language. But for the song to progress to its romantic conclusion, our hero can't continue to mirror our clumsiness; his inhibitions have to go, and they do. Being cinema, moreover, this cultural baggage of inhibitions must be seen to be discarded, and so it is. Without that discarding — done with dramatic flourish — the figure on the screen cannot become our larger-than-life hero. This is an unwritten rule of the entertainment game.

Here is what we see on screen: in the song's opening stanza (called its *mukhda* in Hindi), she dances easily, gracefully. Her movements are in tune with the song, while he follows her, but not too successfully. A moment's pause ensues. Looking unhappy with himself, he takes hold of her hand, pulls her very close, and then pushes her, sending her into a small spin! At that moment of pushing her away, he also begins singing — '*Sooneypan mein achaanak, ek panchchi bola, raat ki rani ka kisne ghunghat khola*...(Suddenly in this dark solitude, a bird spoke, drawing attention to you the exquisite flower, who unveiled this queen of darkness?)' These loving words seem to compensate for what he has just done, rather like a long warm kiss following a show of force. Having sent her into a little spin, he looks happy, and begins dancing with her — in step and in style. It is as though he has both been assertive, and found himself, finally. Our heroine goes along without protest at this bullying, for she is being simultaneously assured that she is his love. That's the good Indian woman for you. *Shabaash*.

Am I reading too much into this momentary lack of sync between the hero and heroine dancing? Let us for a moment turn to what you consider your favourite love song, and explore what makes that work. Picture yourself immersed in, say, one of those Dilip Kumar-Madhubala, or Shammi Kapoor-Asha Parekh films like *Taraana*, or *Teesri Manzil*, when the hero and heroine (before they have become lovers), slip on a stone and fall on wet grass, laugh at the accident while looking at each other, and break into song. At that moment you realise that speech can be nudged into music, that our way of walking (or falling) can be edged into dance; and the things in the surrounding landscape (trees, yes, trees especially) are all possible props for an impromptu *desi* ballet. And it all

adds up to a declaration of confidence.

Two people tap-dancing (or some *desi* improvisation thereof) in perfect time are two people who are flawlessly together. Fantasies are being offered here, but they are not being offered as fantasies, rather as promises, chances, opportunities, indications. And they suggest not so much how to succeed as how it feels to be succeeding.

Love songs, in other words, are not only songs of love — they are concentrated moments of cinema replete with ideas and images of desire, which in turn are culture-specific. Desire and sexuality in Indian cinema have a very different sound and look from desire in Japanese or

Young tribal women are required by our imagination to be innocent of all adult sexual feelings even when they have reached adulthood.

Hollywood cinema. Side by side with the culture-desire connection is the culture-identity connection — aspirations about what kind of man or woman you would like to be also differ depending on whether you are born and bred in Los Angeles or in Calcutta or Hoshangabad. All these things go into a love song, sometimes with fascinating results.

Take this hit sung by the heroine in the film *Shagird* (1966), which throws up some powerful images of Indian-style sexuality and gender identity. Saira Banu plays a quasi-tribal young woman from Kashmir who has come down to Bombay, the big city, for the first time. She is drawn to the young man played by a tall, strapping Joy Mukherji, who is her host's *shagird* (student) and takes time out to show her the city. Gratitude at his kindness and charm slowly turns to love. But being the embodiment of tribal innocence — as our non-tribal filmmakers imagine tribal people to be, on our behalf — she is not supposed to know anything about this feeling called love. She is supposed to be a child-adult, and young tribal women even more than those village belles with dangling pigtails and colourful *ghagra-cholis* are required by our imagination to be innocent of all adult sexual feelings even when they have reached adulthood. So she sings: '*Dil-wil, pyaar-vyaar, main kya janoon re, janoon to janoon bus itna ki main tujhe apna manoon re*! (What do I know of hearts and love, all I know is that I consider you my own!)'

While Bombay cinema's tribal women have been given a near-monopoly on perpetual innocence, this is only the first half of the story. The plot thickens in the second half. Innocence in one form or another, it turns out, is a key attribute when it comes to being the good, desirable Indian woman on screen — both non-tribal and tribal. The non-tribal woman

Bombay meets Kashmir, up close. Joy Mukherji and Saira Banu play city slicker and tribal innocent in Shagird (1967).

differs a little in the way she is depicted as someone who knows only too well what men are after and is therefore on her guard against male advances, including those of the hero — at least for the first half-hour of their encounter. After that, having satisfied herself that he really loves her and will not 'use' her, she slowly gives in. The key word for the desirable non-tribal woman then is chastity, not innocence. She can be cynical, smart, even dangerously 'modern', but underneath it all she has to be a virgin.

Underneath her smart modernity the city woman has to be a virgin. Madhuri Dixit shows us how, in this scene from Ilaaka (1989).

And what of the hero, what kind of man is going to be able to win her? Well, trustworthiness and decency are qualities the hero must have underneath that exterior of a rake on the make. Additional requirements are good looks, and a Lord Krishna-like combination of poetry and muscle: he must be able to sing his heart out when he finds himself alone with her in a garden or on a moonlit terrace, and he must be able to single-handedly bash up all the hoodlums who would violate or kidnap her. In brief, he has to be an irresistible one-woman man.

Consider again the same song, this time through the one-track minds of Hoshangabad's schoolboys and girls: '*Dil-wil, pyaar-vyaar main kya janoon re! Janoon tho janoon... bus itna ki main tujhe apna manoon re!*' Saira Banu is very emphatic in announcing her feelings for the hero. The song both confirmed our tribal belle's innocence, and provided us teenagers obsessed with the meaning of 'love' a definition. This definition had the advantage of spelling out love's content — someone you consider your own, someone you can trust totally and let your hair down with. He is, she tells us, a special friend whom she enjoys being with. Having announced her presumably platonic attachment thus in the song's opening stanza, she resumes playing the innocent child who is blissfully unaware of the sexual effect her tomfoolery is having on him.

This denial of sexuality while yielding to its pleasures was something that appealed deeply to us small-town teenagers of the 1960s, without really knowing why. It somehow rang true with the sexual etiquette around us, which decreed by the 1960s that you can — if you must — occasionally make an exhibition of your desire, as long as you purge it of its overt sexual content. This purging was an absolute must. It was the very essence of 'culture' — Indian culture.

Another song, sung in the film *Teen Deviyan* (1965) by a vivacious-looking Kalpana paired opposite a Dev Anand who looks a little jaded

Kalpana plays the sexually uninhibited woman in Teen Deviyan (1965). *Her exuberance stuns her Don Juan-like lover, played by Dev Anand.*

and anxious compared to her, makes this widespread cultural (and essentially male) sexual discomfort explicit. It is not often that Hindi cinema spills the beans in the matter of sex, but here is one song that does.

Kalpana in this scene is a young, exuberant village lass, he the city slicker, and they have fallen in love with each other barely the day before. Here is what Dev says, in song, in response to the flamboyant way she begins dancing to celebrate her new-found love:'*Arrey yaar meri, tum bhi ho gazab,/ Ghunghat to zara odho,/ Arrey maano kaha, ab tum ho jawaan,/ Meri jaan ladakpan chhodo*! (Oh love, you are too open about everything,/ At least cover your face with a veil,/ Men can't take their eyes off you, don't you understand,/ Please grow up and stop being so uninhibited!)' She dismisses his anxiety thus:'*Jab meri chunariya malmal ki, phir kyun na chaloon main jhalki-jhalki!*...(When my scarf is such a beautiful piece of muslin, why shouldn't I show it off!)' In this scene he's a *shehari babu* (man from the city) bewitched by this buxom rustic belle, and now that he has won her heart he wants to keep her under wraps. The only problem is that the young lady is full of play, *joie de vivre*, and really cannot understand why he resists enjoying the moment.

In contrast, he appears very modern but is in reality unable to cope with the emergence of feminine sexuality. His only response to her zest for life, her expressiveness, is to be scandalised. He can't *bear* to see her fulsome legs as she bares them while dancing; he covers his eyes.

She ignores his pleas to restrain herself — simply because she is happy, and wants the world to share this moment with her! (Recall here our earlier observation that rustic belles, like Hindi cinema's tribal belles, are supposed to be innocent of the effect of their sexuality on men.) Towards the end of the song, our hero throws up his hands and sits down in a corner in the open field while she continues dancing.

So why does her dancing bother Dev so much? Simply put, she breaks one of the cardinal rules of our sexual culture. That rule is: sexuality is never to be overt, not even with your wife. In the privacy of your bedroom as a married couple (preferably with the lights switched off) you can take the wraps off your sexuality, but not anywhere else. It's indecent! It is also decadent and 'western'.

The only people who break this screen taboo on overt sexuality are the villain and the vamp, and they are bad people who always come to a bad end.

Before coming to a bad end however, they must fulfil a key function - to give us viewers a few titillating, close-up images of how much fun taboo breaking can be. And this brings us to the Vamp, who was until recently,

the embodiment of Sex on the Indian screen. She took us, via her kind of song and dance, to hidden but delicious depths of degradation.

Helen, as Kamlesh Pandey a well-known film scriptwriter recalls, was the most vampish of them all:

> "In the private screening room of my mind, whenever I play back the movies of my adolescence, I quickly edit out all the scenes of Helen to savour them later. Just like the projectionist edits out all the kissing scenes and gifts them to the teenaged movie buff (in the film Cinema Paradiso).

The post-independence Indian was an idealist in a socialist nation, thriving on suffering and sacrifice. Death embodied by Dilip Kumar in Devdas was charismatic; so was poverty. Raj Kapoor's *Aawara* and *Shri 420* sang the glories of owning nothing, sleeping on bare earth under the stars, covered only in self-respect! It was consolation perfected into an art form. Rich girls falling in love with poor boys massaged the ego of the impoverished masses; tragedy was king and queen. Only villains smoked, drank and wore suits, echoing the just-departed British. And anything in skirts was forbidden fruit.

Helen, of course, was the most delicious one...

Today, from Madhuri Dixit and Aishwarya Rai to Juhi Chawla and Sushmita Sen, every star... considers it her privilege to flaunt her cleavage. In fact, in post-liberalization India, cleavage-flaunting has become so common-place that it hardly draws weak whistles from the front stalls. But there was a time not long ago when Helen had the sole proprietorship of cleavage, and when she appeared on screen, pimples turned from red to purple.

In an age when every young man wanted a sister-in-law like Nirupa Roy, a wife like Nargis or Meena Kumari, a girlfriend like Madhubala and a sweetheart like Nimmi, Helen was sleepless nights of desire and guilt.

While the faces of Meena Kumari and Madhubala were the favourite book-marks in Algebra and Trignometry texts, sizzling Helen was simply too hot for paper. She belonged to our blood, bones and tissue.

Without any intention of offending the so-called self-appointed guardians of our traditional values, morals and ideals, it is my humble submission that almost single-handedly, and without realizing it, Helen embodied a rebellion against centuries of sexual suppression and poverty-driven socialist economy."

So if you ask: *Indian culture ki puritanical choli ke peechhe kya hai*, one answer would be that there is a voyeur in each of us which mass-market cinema realises must be catered to. A voyeur who wants to see what he is missing, and to vicariously consume what he is being good and cultured enough to deny himself in 'reality'.

What we get then are a few erotic scenes involving the hero and heroine, often in the form of a dream sequence, a rain-dance or sometimes a wedding night. This is in addition to the vamp doing her seduction bit on the hero — often as a cabaret dancer in a sleazy-swanky restaurant, sometimes in a bedroom or a cave, or even occasionally a shower, if nothing else is handy. Again, the hero does not succumb — he is a one-woman man, remember. That one woman has already entered his life, or he is in quest of her; in either case the vamp does not qualify. Meanwhile, the male viewer gets his cheap thrills by ogling at the vamp's attempted seduction. So the puritanical viewer's good deeds are rewarded, but only in the darkness of the cinema hall — away from the prying eyes of culture, society, *duniya*.....

Endnotes

1 Matters of the heart.

References

Arnold, Alison. 1998. *Hindi Film Geet: On the History of Commercial Indian Popular Music*, UMI Dissertation Services Michigan, USA.

Benjamin, Walter. (a). 1971. *Illuminations*, London, Fontana Books

(b). 1979. *One-Way Street and Other Writtings*, London, New Left Books.

Bharati, Swami Agehananda. 1977, "Anthropology of Hindi Films", in *The Illustrated Weekly of India*, Bombay, January 30.

Dasgupta, Chidananda. 1981. *Talking About Films*, New Delhi, Orient Longman

Huxley, Aldous. 1986. *Texts & Pretexts*, Triad Grafton Books, London.

James, Regina. 1997 'Writing Without Authority' article in *Salmagundi* no 114-14, New York.

McConnell, Frank. 1979. *Storytelling and Mythmaking*, New York Oxford University Press.

Turner, Victor. 1991. From *Ritual to Theatre: The Human Seriousness of Play*, New York, P A J Publications.

FILM - NAU DO GYAARAH

Lyrics - Majrooh Sultanpuri

Music - S D Burman

Hum Hain Raahi Pyar Ke, Humse Kuchh Na Boliye
Jo Bhi Pyar Se Mila, Hum Usi Ke Ho Liye
Hum Usi Ke Ho Liye
Jo Bhi Pyar Se Mila, Hum Usi Ke Ho Liye...

Dard Bhi Humein Qubool, Chain Bhi Humein Qubool
Humnein Har Tarah Ke Phool, Haar Mein Piro Liye,
Jo Bhi Pyar Se Mila ...

Dhoop Thi Naseeb Mein, Tho Dhoop Mein Liya Hai Dum
Chandni Mili Tho Hum, Chandni Mein So Liye
Jo Bhi Pyar Se Mila ...

Dil Pe Aasra Kiye, Hum Tho Bas Yoonhin Jiye
Ek Kadam Pe Hans Liye, Ek Kadam Pe Ro Liye
Jo Bhi Pyar Se Mila ...

Raah Mein Pade Hain Hum, Kabse Aap Ki Kasam
Dekhiye Tho Kam Se Kam, Boliye Na Boliye
Jo Bhi Pyar Se Mila ...

Glossary

Aashiq	Lover
Ahimsa	Non-violence
Apsara	Celestial beauty
Ashram	Hermitage
Asli	Real, true
Avatars	Incarnations
Awadhi	Belonging to the region of Awadh, in Uttar Pradesh
Bahu	Daughter-in-law
Bapu	Father, Gandhi
Bazaar	Marketplace
Brahmo	Follower of a Hindu reformist movement initiated by Rammohun Roy
Burkhas	Veils worn by Muslim women
Bustees	Slum dwellings
Chacha	Father's younger brother, uncle
Chachi	Father's younger brother's wife, aunt
Chawl	Working-class tenements
Chhoti bahu	Younger daughter-in-law
Dakoos	Dacoits
Dal	Lentils
Desi	Native
Dharma	Religion, Righteousness
Dhoti	Loose unstitched lower garment traditionally worn by Indian men
Duniya	World
Duniyadari	Worldliness
Dupatta	Scarf worn by north Indian women to cover their heads
Fakir	Mendicant
Filmy	Of the films (adj.)
Ghagra-cholis	Traditional long skirts and blouses worn by Indian women
Ghazal	Poem/Song in Urdu
Goan	From Goa, a state on the western coast of India
Guru	Teacher, spiritual guide
Houri	Ethereal being
..Choli ke peechhe kya hai	What is behind the puritanical blouse of Indian culture
Insha-allah	By the grace of God
Ishq	Love
Izzat	Honour
Jayanti	Birthday, anniversary,
Khadi	Hand spun cotton popularised by Gandhi
Khalsa	Militant Sikh Order
Khandaan	Family, Clan,
Ma	Mother
Maharaja	King
Mantra	Catch-phrase, magical invocation
Masala	Spices or spicy
Mazdoor	Worker
Memsahib	Wife/daughter of a *Sahib*, term usually used for white foreigners. Also used for urbanised upper class women
Mujra	Music and dance usually associated with courtesans
Nawab	Muslim king or landlord, noble
Nawab sahib	Honorific term of address referring to *Nawab*
Nawabi	Adjective deriving from nawab

Om	A term, referring to a sound derived from Hindu philosophy which expresses the universal divinity
Pathan	A tribe/ethnic group from Afghanistan and North-west Frontier Province
Qawwal	Singer of *Qawwali*
Rajput	A martial caste from Rajasthan, Western India
Sadhu	A Hindu mendicant
Sahib	Lord, Master
Sardar	Chief, Leader
Sari	Unstitched garment worn by Indian women
Sarkar	Government, also used to refer to a government official
Satyagraha	Struggle for the Truth, by non-violent means
Seth	Refers to a merchant or person in authority
Shabaash	Urdu word meaning "Well done"
Sindhi	Belonging to the region of Sindh (now in Pakistan) or ethnic identity of Sindh
Sitar	Stringed musical instrument
Sutradhar	Commentator
Swadeshi	National
Teekas	The ritual mark worn on the forehead generally by Hindu women and on occasions also by men
Tehzeeb	Urdu word referring to cultural and social etiquette
Thakur	Person of the landlord caste in northern India
Urdu	Urdu refers to the composite language that evolved as a result of the interaction of Muslim rule in India
Vishnu	Preserver, one of the Gods of the Hindu Trinity
Zamindari	A system of land tenure that the British introduced in the 18th.c in eastern India

Index of Names

A

B

C

D

E

Index of Names

Index of Names

N

O

P

Q

R

Index of Names

S

Index of Key Terms

A

B

C

D

E

F

G

H

I

J

K

Index of Key Terms

L

M

N

O

P

Q

R

S

Index of Key Terms